Betty Crocker's

NEW CHRISTMAS COOKBOOK

Betty Crocker's

NEW CHRISTMAS COOKBOOK

PRENTICE HALL

NEW YORK   LONDON   TORONTO   SYDNEY   TOKYO   SINGAPORE

PRENTICE HALL
15 Columbus Circle
New York, New York 10023

PRENTICE HALL and colophon are
registered trademarks of Simon & Schuster Inc.

BETTY CROCKER and BISQUICK are registered trademarks of General Mills, Inc.

Library of Congress Cataloging-in-Publication Data

Crocker, Betty.
    Betty Crocker's new Christmas cookbook.
       p.   cm.
    Includes index.
    ISBN 0-671-79927-4
    1. Christmas cookery.   I. Title.   II. Title: New Christmas
cookbook.
    TX739.2.C45C73   1993
    641.5′68—dc20   92-35119
                                      CIP

Designed by Levavi & Levavi
Manufactured in the United States of America

First Edition
10 9 8 7 6 5 4 3 2 1

Front cover: Gingerbread Village (page 277)
Back cover: Roast Goose (page 161)
Frontis: Della Robia Apple Pie (page 87)

Introduction

Christmas is a magical, wonderful season, with special, tempting aromas from the kitchen, and presents in the midst of being wrapped, hidden or given. It's a time when we want favorite, traditional recipes—sugar cookies, popcorn balls, fudge, Plum Pudding, Hot Buttered Rum, roast beef, Yorkshire Pudding—as well as new, inventive recipes for parties and dinners. Recipes such as Stained Glass Tart, Easy Angel Cookies, Reindeer Snack and Peachy Cornish Game Hens, are new treats that will spark your holiday cooking. Christmas is also a time of giving and sharing, when we want to remember people and their kindnesses with "a little something."

Because Christmas is celebrated in so many different ways, we wanted to bring together the many elements of the season in one delightful, easy-to-use book. *Betty Crocker's New Christmas Cookbook* is full of creative new ideas, as well as treasured favorites that may very well become part of your Christmas tradition.

At Christmas, the kitchen is very much the heart of the home, so you'll love the first section, "Fabulous Food from the Christmas Kitchen," featuring cookies, candies, desserts, breads, and beverages. From office parties to cookie exchanges to holiday get-togethers, you'll find the scrumptious recipes in this section a pleasure to prepare and share.

Next, "Holiday Menus for Family and Friends" provides twenty-one complete menus and recipes for meals of all kinds during this busy season. Christmas dinners, open houses, casual meals, meals for a crowd or just for two are temptingly collected here. We've also included planning guides with each meal, to help you make the most of your time in the kitchen.

And "In the Spirit of Giving" there are wonderful recipes to make as presents, as well as terrific ideas for packaging your homemade food items into memorable gifts. You'll delight in the charming decorations you can create, from a fanciful gingerbread village, to the elegant Fruitful Bowl, perfect as a centerpiece for your holiday entertaining.

Throughout the book, we have added time-saving tips at the end of recipes to speed preparation, so you can enjoy Christmas to its fullest. And we've added suggestions on entertaining, gifts to fix fast, wrapping ideas, and more.

So, pour yourself a glass of cider, and settle down to browse through the tempting recipes and photographs that follow. We hope many of the wonderful recipes, ideas, tips and suggestions turn into traditions, and make your Christmas the most enjoyable, the most manageable, and the most delicious ever!

The Betty Crocker Editors

Contents

Festive Foods from Your Kitchen

*Spritz (page 10); Merry Christmas Molasses Cookies
(page 5); Truffles (page 49); Stained Glass Tart
(page 92)*

A Collection of Cookies

When it comes to Christmas baking, cookies are usually top of the list! Whether shared warm from the oven, served at open houses or office parties, or given as gifts, we can never have too many cookie recipes. From traditional favorites to exciting new ideas, these recipes will keep your holiday cookie jar full of tempting treats.

Santa Claus Cookies

1 cup granulated sugar

¹/₂ cup shortening

2 tablespoons milk

1 teaspoon grated lemon peel

1 egg

2 cups all-purpose flour

1 teaspoon baking powder

¹/₂ teaspoon baking soda

¹/₂ teaspoon salt

Creamy Frosting (right) or Chocolate Frosting (page 20)

Red sugar

Miniature marshmallows

Currants or semisweet chocolate chips

Red cinnamon candies

Shredded coconut

Heat oven to 400°. Mix granulated sugar, shortening, milk, lemon peel and egg in large bowl. Stir in flour, baking powder, baking soda and salt. Shape dough into 1¹/₄-inch balls. Place about 2 inches apart on ungreased cookie sheet. Flatten to about 2¹/₂ inches in diameter with greased bottom of glass dipped into granulated sugar. Bake 8 to 10 minutes or until edges are light brown. Remove from cookie sheet. Cool on wire rack.

Spread 1 cookie with small amount of Creamy Frosting. (Frost and decorate cookies one at a time.) Sprinkle top third of cookie with red sugar for the hat. Press on miniature marshmallow for the tassel. Press 2 currants for the eyes and 1 red cinnamon candy for the nose into center third of cookie. Sprinkle coconut over bottom third for the beard. About 1¹/₂ dozen cookies.

CREAMY FROSTING

1¹/₂ cups powdered sugar

¹/₂ teaspoon vanilla

2 to 3 tablespoons water

Mix all ingredients until spreading consistency.

SANTA CLAUS COOKIE POPS: After flattening balls of dough, insert wooden ice-cream stick halfway into each. Continue as directed.

⚠ **To divide dough easily, press dough evenly in the bottom of a loaf pan lined with waxed paper. Lift out the dough using the waxed paper. Cut 3 strips lengthwise and five strips crosswise, then shape into balls.**

Deluxe Sugar Cookies

These are our favorite sugar cookies! If using cookie cutters with imprints, cut the amounts of baking soda and cream of tartar in half—you'll get a more distinctive design.

1½ cups powdered sugar
1 cup (2 sticks) margarine or butter,
softened
1 teaspoon vanilla
½ teaspoon almond extract
1 egg
2½ cups all-purpose flour
1 teaspoon baking soda
1 teaspoon cream of tartar
Creamy Decorator's Frosting (below)
or Chocolate Frosting (page 20)

Mix powdered sugar, margarine, vanilla, almond extract and egg in large bowl. Stir in flour, baking soda and cream of tartar. Cover and refrigerate at least 2 hours.

Heat oven to 375°. Grease cookie sheet lightly. Divide dough in half. Roll each half ¼ inch thick on lightly floured surface. Cut into desired shapes with cookie cutters. Place on cookie sheet. Bake 7 to 8 minutes or until edges are light brown. Remove from cookie sheet. Cool on wire rack. Frost with Creamy Decorator's Frosting, and decorate as desired. About 5 dozen 2-inch cookies.

CREAMY DECORATOR'S FROSTING

1 cup powdered sugar
1 tablespoon water or 1 to 2 tablespoons
half-and-half
½ teaspoon vanilla
Few drops food color, if desired

Beat ingredients until smooth and of spreading consistency.

PAINTBRUSH COOKIES: Prepare Egg Yolk Paint (below). Before baking, paint designs on cookies using small paintbrushes.

EGG YOLK PAINT

¼ teaspoon water
1 egg yolk

Mix ingredients; divide among several small custard cups. Tint each with a different food color to make bright colors. If paint thickens while standing, stir in few drops water.

Stained Glass Cookies

1 recipe Deluxe Sugar Cookies (left)
Food colors

Prepare dough for Deluxe Sugar Cookies. Before refrigerating, divide dough in half. Divide one half into 3 to 5 parts. Tint each part with a different food color. Wrap each tinted dough and the plain dough separately. Refrigerate at least 2 hours.

Heat oven to 375°. Grease cookie sheet lightly. Roll plain dough ⅛ inch thick on lightly floured surface. Cut with bell, star, tree or other decorative cookie cutter. Place on cookie sheet. Roll each tinted dough ⅛ inch thick; cut out different shapes and arrange on plain dough shapes. Bake 7 to 8 minutes or until edges are light brown. Remove from cookie sheet. Cool on wire rack. About 5 dozen 2-inch cookies.

Magic Window Cookies

If you like, you can use tiny round hard candies in place of the ring-shaped candy, but you'll need more tubes of the round candies.

1 cup sugar

³/₄ cup shortening (part margarine or butter, softened)

1 teaspoon vanilla or ¹/₂ teaspoon lemon extract

2 eggs

2¹/₂ cups all-purpose flour

1 teaspoon baking powder

1 teaspoon salt

About 4 rolls (about 0.9 ounce each) ring-shaped hard candy

Mix sugar, shortening, vanilla and eggs in large bowl. Stir in flour, baking powder and salt. Cover and refrigerate at least 1 hour.

Heat oven to 375°. Line cookie sheet with aluminum foil. Roll dough ¹/₈ inch thick on lightly floured surface. Cut into desired shapes with cookie cutters. Place on cookie sheet. Cut out designs from cookies using smaller cutters or your own patterns. Place whole or partially crushed candy in cutouts, depending on size and shape of design. (To crush candy, place in heavy plastic bag and tap lightly with rolling pin. Because candy melts easily, leave pieces as large as possible.) If cookies are to be hung as decorations, make a hole in each, ¹/₄ inch from top with end of plastic straw.

Bake 7 to 9 minutes or until cookies are very light brown and candy is melted. If candy has not completely spread within cutout design, immediately spread with metal spatula. Cool completely before removing from cookie sheet. Remove cookies gently. About 6 dozen 3-inch cookies.

Magic Window Cookies, Deluxe Sugar Cookies (page 3); Santa Claus Cookies (page 2)

Merry Christmas Molasses Cookies

¹/₃ cup packed brown sugar

¹/₃ cup shortening

²/₃ cup molasses

1 egg

2³/₄ cups all-purpose flour

2 teaspoons ground cinnamon

1 teaspoon ground ginger

1 teaspoon baking soda

1 teaspoon salt

Baked-on Decorator's Frosting (below), if desired

Heat oven to 375°. Grease cookie sheet lightly. Mix brown sugar, shortening, molasses and egg in large bowl. Stir in flour, cinnamon, ginger, baking soda and salt. Roll dough ¹/₄ inch thick on lightly floured surface. Cut into desired shapes with cookie cutters. Place about 1 inch apart on cookie sheet. Prepare Baked-on Decorator's Frosting. Outline, write or make designs on unbaked cookies with frosting. Bake 7 to 8 minutes or until no indentation remains when touched. Remove from cookie sheet. Cool on wire rack. About 2¹/₂ dozen 3-inch cookies.

BAKED-ON DECORATOR'S FROSTING

¹/₃ cup all-purpose flour

¹/₃ cup margarine or butter, softened

1¹/₂ teaspoons hot water

2 or 3 drops food color, if desired

Mix flour and margarine until smooth. Stir in hot water and food color. Place frosting in decorating bag with a writing tip. Or place frosting in strong plastic bag; cut off a tiny tip from one corner of bag.

Clever Holiday Cookie Shapes

Something new is always a welcome sight on a tray of Christmas cookies or at a cookie exchange—you'll find the following clever shapes to be a hit. These rolled cookies do take a bit more time to make than drop or bar cookies but they can provide a fun project for family or friends. Especially unique are the angel cookies, easily made without a cookie cutter.

The cookies below can be baked ahead and frozen up to 3 to 4 months. See page 36 for details.

Chocolate-Peppermint Trees

1 recipe Bittersweet Chocolate–Cream Cheese Cookies (page 10)

48 rectangular chocolate mints (1¹/₂ × ³/₄ inches)

¹/₂ cup semisweet chocolate chips

1 tablespoon plus 1 teaspoon shortening

Heat oven to 375°. Prepare dough for Chocolate-Cream Cheese Cookies. Divide dough in half. Roll each half on lightly floured cloth-covered surface with cloth-covered rolling pin into 12-inch square, about ¹/₈ inch thick. Cut dough into 4-inch squares. Cut each square diagonally in half to make 2 triangles. Cut each mint diagonally in half. Arrange 2 mint halves to form a triangle on the center of each dough triangle (see diagram). Fold points of dough triangle to the center, overlapping slightly and with points toward the bottom. Press edges to seal. Pinch bottom points together, shaping a tree trunk on each cookie and sealing dough around mints. Place on ungreased cookie sheet.

Bake 7 to 9 minutes or until dry and set. Remove from cookie sheet. Cool on wire rack. Heat chocolate chips and shortening until melted; drizzle over cookies. Let stand about 30 minutes or until chocolate is set. 3 dozen cookies.

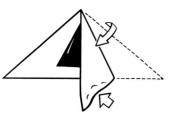

Place mint triangles to form tree in center of dough triangle; fold ends of dough to center; seal.

Easy Angels

To be sure the angel wings don't crack, shape each set of six cookies right after they are rolled out, then move on to the next group. These cheery angels are even more heavenly when decorated with colored sugar or Egg Yolk Paint before baking. Or frost after baking.

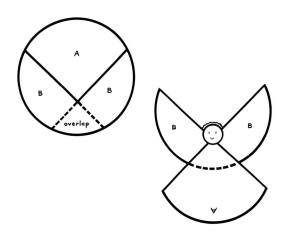

1 recipe Deluxe Sugar Cookies
   (*page 3*)

Prepare dough for Deluxe Sugar Cookies. Cover and refrigerate at least 2 hours. Heat oven to 375°. Grease cookie sheets lightly. Divide dough in half. Roll 1 half of the dough at a time ⅛ inch thick on lightly floured surface (wrap remaining dough to keep from drying out). Cut into 3-inch rounds with cookie cutter. Place 6 rounds on each cookie sheet. Shape dough as directed below for Angel or Angel in Flight.

Bake 6 to 7 minutes or until edges are light brown. Frost as desired, or decorate with colored sugar, edible glitter or Egg Yolk Paint (page 3) as desired. About 2 dozen cookies.

Angel: Make two 2-inch cuts at right angle below center of circle (see diagram). (To cut right angle easily, mark and cut along corner of piece of paper.) Fold A toward the opposite side of the circle, overlapping at B to make angel body and wings. Shape ½ teaspoon dough into ball. Flatten and place between wings for angel's head.

Angel in Flight: Make two 2-inch cuts at right angle below center of circle (see diagram). (To cut right angle easily, mark and cut along corner of piece of paper.) Fold B over A (see diagram). Move C next to the fold, pressing into fold to seal. Shape ½ teaspoon dough into ball. Flatten and place between wing and body for angel's head.

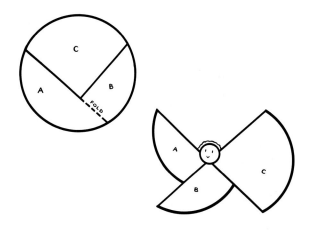

Lebkuchen

This cake-like cookie comes from Germany, and is especially popular in Nuremberg. They are often baked in decorative molds, but our version is faster, and just as tasty.

¹/₂ cup honey

¹/₂ cup molasses

³/₄ cup packed brown sugar

1 teaspoon grated lemon peel

1 tablespoon lemon juice

1 egg

2³/₄ cups all-purpose flour

1 teaspoon ground allspice

1 teaspoon ground cinnamon

1 teaspoon ground cloves

1 teaspoon ground nutmeg

¹/₂ teaspoon baking soda

¹/₃ cup chopped citron

¹/₃ cup chopped nuts

Cookie Glaze (right)

Mix honey and molasses in 3-quart saucepan. Heat to boiling, stirring occasionally; remove from heat. Cool completely. Stir in brown sugar, lemon peel, lemon juice and egg. Stir in flour, allspice, cinnamon, cloves, nutmeg and baking soda. Stir in citron and nuts. Cover and refrigerate at least 8 hours.

Heat oven to 400°. Grease cookie sheet. Roll about one-fourth of the dough at a time ¹/₄ inch thick on lightly floured surface (keep remaining dough refrigerated). Cut dough into rectangles, 2¹/₂ × 1¹/₂ inches. Place 1 inch apart on cookie sheet. Bake 10 to 12 minutes or until no indentation remains when touched lightly. Immediately remove from cookie sheet. Cool on wire rack. Brush Cookie Glaze over cookies. About 5 dozen cookies.

COOKIE GLAZE

1 cup granulated sugar

¹/₂ cup water

¹/₄ cup powdered sugar

Mix granulated sugar and water in 1-quart saucepan. Cook over medium heat to 230° on candy thermometer or just until small amount of mixture spins a 2-inch thread when dropped from a spoon; remove from heat. Stir in powdered sugar. (If glaze becomes sugary while brushing cookies, heat slightly, adding a little water, until clear again.)

Note: Store cookies in airtight container. For softer cookies, store with an apple or orange slice in airtight container, replacing slice frequently.

Easy Angels (page 7)

Bittersweet Chocolate–Cream Cheese Cookies

1 cup sugar

¹/₂ cup (1 stick) margarine or butter, softened

1¹/₂ teaspoons vanilla

1 egg

1 package (3 ounces) cream cheese, softened

3 ounces bittersweet or semisweet chocolate, melted and cooled

2¹/₂ cups all-purpose flour

¹/₂ teaspoon baking powder

¹/₂ teaspoon salt

6 ounces vanilla-flavored candy coating, melted

³/₄ cup finely crushed peppermint candies or finely chopped pistachio nuts

Heat oven to 375°. Mix sugar, margarine, vanilla, egg, cream cheese and chocolate in large bowl until smooth. Mix flour, baking powder and salt; stir into margarine mixture.

Divide dough in half. Roll each half ¹/₈ inch thick on lightly floured cloth-covered surface with cloth-covered rolling pin. Cut into desired shapes with cookie cutters. Place about 1 inch apart on ungreased cookie sheet. Bake 8 to 10 minutes or until dry and set. Remove from cookie sheet. Cool on wire rack.

Roll edge of cookies about ¹/₄ inch deep in candy coating; immediately roll in candies. Place on waxed paper. Let stand about 10 minutes or until coating is set. About 6 dozen 2¹/₂-inch cookies.

Spritz

Spritz are festive holiday cookies made with a special cookie press, available in most kitchenware stores. For even more glamour, top with currants, raisins, candies or slices of candied fruit before baking. Or after baking, decorate with edible glitter, colored sugar, nonpareils or red cinnamon candies. A drop of corn syrup will hold the decorations nicely.

1 cup (2 sticks) margarine or butter, softened

¹/₂ cup sugar

2¹/₄ cups all-purpose flour

1 teaspoon almond extract or vanilla

¹/₂ teaspoon salt

1 egg

Few drops food color, if desired

Heat oven to 400°. Mix margarine and sugar in medium bowl. Stir in remaining ingredients. Place dough in cookie press. Form desired shapes on ungreased cookie sheet. Bake 6 to 9 minutes or until set but not brown. Remove from cookie sheet. Cool on wire rack. About 5 dozen cookies.

CHOCOLATE SPRITZ: Stir 2 ounces unsweetened chocolate, melted and cooled, into margarine-sugar mixture. Omit food color.

HOLIDAY SPRITZ: Substitute rum flavoring for the almond extract. Tint dough with food colors. After baking, spread cooled cookies with Butter Rum Glaze: Heat ¹/₄ cup (¹/₂ stick) margarine or butter in 1-quart saucepan until melted; remove from heat. Stir in 1 cup powdered sugar and 1 teaspoon rum flavoring. Stir in 1 to 2 tablespoons hot water until glaze is spreading consistency. Tint glaze with food color to match cookies.

Cream Cheese Spritz Wreaths

1 cup (2 sticks) margarine or butter, softened

1 package (3 ounces) cream cheese, softened

2 cups all-purpose flour

½ cup sugar

½ teaspoon vanilla

Red and green candied cherries

Heat oven to 375°. Mix margarine and cream cheese in medium bowl. Stir in flour, sugar and vanilla. Place dough in cookie press with star plate. Form wreath shapes on ungreased cookie sheet by holding cookie press in semihorizontal position and moving press in a circular motion. Gently push ends of dough together to form wreaths. Press on bits of red and green candied cherries to form holly berries and leaves. Bake 8 to 10 minutes or until set but not brown. Immediately remove from cookie sheet. Cool on wire rack. About 4 dozen cookies.

△ **Use your microwave to soften the margarine and cream cheese. Place them together in a microwavable medium bowl; microwave uncovered on medium (50%) 2 to 3 minutes, rotating bowl ½ turn after 1 minute. Be careful not to overheat.**

Lemon Decorator Cookies

Children love to stamp these cookies, and they also love making their very own carrot press.

1 recipe Cream Cheese Spritz Wreaths (left)

1 tablespoon grated lemon peel

Carrot Press (below)

Prepare dough for Cream Cheese Spritz Wreaths —except substitute lemon peel for the vanilla. Prepare Carrot Press.

Heat oven to 375°. Shape dough into 1-inch balls. Place about 2 inches apart on ungreased cookie sheet. Flatten to about ¼-inch thickness with Carrot Press or cookie stamp dipped into sugar. Bake 7 to 9 minutes or until set but not brown. Remove from cookie sheet. Cool on wire rack. About 5 dozen cookies.

CARROT PRESS

Cut carrot, about 1½ inches in diameter, into 2-inch lengths. Cut decorative design about ⅛ inch deep in cut end of each carrot piece using small sharp knife, tip of vegetable peeler or other small sharp kitchen tool.

Berliner Kranzer

We have made these German wreath-shaped cookies a bit easier than the traditional shaping method, to speed your holiday baking.

1 cup sugar

³/₄ cup (1¹/₂ sticks) margarine or butter, softened

³/₄ cup shortening

2 teaspoons grated orange peel

2 eggs

4 cups all-purpose flour

1 egg white

2 tablespoons sugar

Red candied cherries

Green candied citron

Heat oven to 400°. Mix 1 cup sugar, the margarine, shortening, orange peel and eggs in large bowl. Mix in flour. Shape dough by rounded teaspoonfuls into ropes, 6 inches long. Form each rope into a circle, crossing ends and tucking under. (This shaping method is easier than the traditional method of tying knots.) Place on ungreased cookie sheet.

Beat egg white and 2 tablespoons sugar until foamy; brush over tops of cookies. Press bits of red candied cherries on center of knot for holly berries. Add "leaves" cut from green candied citron. Bake 10 to 12 minutes or until set but not brown. Immediately remove from cookie sheet. Cool on wire rack. About 6 dozen cookies.

Berliner Kranzer; Chocolate-Nut Fingers (page 14)

Almond-filled Crescents

1 cup powdered sugar

1 cup whipping (heavy) cream

2 eggs

3³/₄ cups all-purpose flour

1 teaspoon baking powder

¹/₂ teaspoon salt

1 package (about 8 ounces) almond paste

³/₄ cup (1¹/₂ sticks) margarine or butter, softened

Glaze (below)

Mix powdered sugar, whipping cream and eggs in large bowl. Stir in flour, baking powder and salt. (Dough will be stiff.) Cover and refrigerate about 1 hour or until firm.

Heat oven to 375°. Break almond paste into small pieces in medium bowl; add margarine. Beat on low speed until blended. Beat on high speed until fluffy (tiny bits of almond paste will remain).

Roll one-fourth of the dough at a time into 10-inch circle on lightly floured surface. Spread one-fourth of almond paste mixture (about ¹/₂ cup) over circle. Cut into 12 wedges. Roll up, beginning at rounded edge. Place on ungreased cookie sheet with points underneath. Curve cookies to form crescents. Repeat with remaining dough and almond paste mixture. Bake 14 to 16 minutes or until golden brown. Remove from cookie sheet. Cool completely on wire rack. Drizzle Glaze over crescents. 4 dozen cookies.

GLAZE

1 cup powdered sugar

6 to 7 teaspoons milk

Mix ingredients until smooth and of drizzling consistency.

Chocolate-Nut Fingers

For a different look, dip cookies halfway into the chocolate or brush the entire top of the cookie before dipping into the nuts.

> *1 cup sugar*
>
> *1 cup (2 sticks) margarine or butter, softened*
>
> *1/2 cup milk*
>
> *1 teaspoon vanilla*
>
> *1 teaspoon almond extract*
>
> *1 egg*
>
> *3 1/2 cups all-purpose flour*
>
> *1 teaspoon baking powder*
>
> *1/4 teaspoon salt*
>
> *1/2 cup semisweet chocolate chips*
>
> *1/2 cup chopped nuts*

Mix sugar, margarine, milk, vanilla, almond extract and egg in large bowl. Stir in flour, baking powder and salt. Cover and refrigerate at least 4 hours.

Heat oven to 375°. For each cookie, shape 1 teaspoon dough into 4-inch rope. (For smooth, even ropes, roll back and forth on sugared surface.) Place on ungreased cookie sheet. Bake 9 to 12 minutes or until set and very light brown. Remove from cookie sheet. Cool on wire rack. Heat chocolate chips until melted.

Dip ends of cookies into chocolate, then into nuts. Place cookies on waxed paper. Let stand about 10 minutes or until chocolate is set. About 8 dozen cookies.

ALMOND COOKIE WREATHS: Omit chocolate chips and nuts. Divide dough in half. Tint one half with 1/2 teaspoon green food color. For each cookie, shape 1 teaspoon dough from each half into 4-inch rope. Place 1 green and 1 white rope side by side; press together lightly and twist. Place on ungreased cookie sheet, and shape into circle, pressing ends together. Press on bits of candied cherries for holly berries. Bake as directed. About 4 1/2 dozen cookies.

Candy Cane Cookies

While red and white are the traditional colors for candy canes, feel free to create candy canes of different colors. Paste food color will give you more intense colors.

> *2 tablespoons crushed peppermint candies*
>
> *2 tablespoons sugar*
>
> *1 recipe Chocolate-Nut Fingers (page 14)*
>
> *1 teaspoon peppermint extract*
>
> *1/2 teaspoon red food color*

Heat oven to 375°. Mix candies and sugar; reserve. Prepare dough for Chocolate-Nut Fingers—except substitute peppermint extract for the almond extract. Divide dough in half. Tint one half with food color. For each cookie, shape 1 teaspoon dough from each half into 4-inch rope on floured surface. Place 1 red and 1 white rope side by side; press together lightly and twist. Place on ungreased cookie sheet, and curve one end of cookie to form handle of cane.

Bake 9 to 12 minutes or until set and very light brown. Immediately sprinkle reserved sugar mixture over cookies. Remove from cookie sheet. Cool on wire rack. About 4 1/2 dozen cookies.

Russian Teacakes

*1 cup (2 sticks) margarine or butter,
softened*

½ cup powdered sugar

1 teaspoon vanilla

2¼ cups all-purpose flour

¾ cup finely chopped nuts

¼ teaspoon salt

Powdered sugar

Heat oven to 400°. Mix margarine, ½ cup powdered sugar and the vanilla in large bowl. Stir in flour, nuts and salt.

Shape dough into 1-inch balls. Place about 2 inches apart on ungreased cookie sheet. Bake 8 to 9 minutes or until set but not brown. Immediately remove from cookie sheet; roll in powdered sugar. Cool completely on wire rack. Roll in powdered sugar again. About 4 dozen cookies.

Hazelnut Teacakes

*¾ cup (1½ sticks) margarine or butter,
softened*

⅓ cup powdered sugar

1¼ cups all-purpose flour

½ cup instant cocoa mix

½ cup chopped hazelnuts, toasted

Powdered sugar

Heat oven to 325°. Mix margarine and ⅓ cup powdered sugar in medium bowl. Stir in flour, cocoa mix and hazelnuts. (If dough is soft, cover and refrigerate until firm enough to shape.) Shape dough into 1-inch balls. Place about 2 inches apart on ungreased cookie sheet. Bake 12 to 15 minutes or until set. Dip tops into powdered sugar while warm; cool on wire rack. Dip tops into powdered sugar again. About 3½ dozen cookies.

Peppernuts

These spicy, crunchy morsels are Christmas favorites. The traditional German spelling is Pfeffernusse, and many people like to call them by this name.

¾ cup packed brown sugar

½ cup shortening

½ cup light molasses

1 tablespoon hot water

1 egg

*3 drops anise oil or ½ teaspoon anise
extract*

3⅓ cups all-purpose flour

½ teaspoon baking soda

½ teaspoon ground cinnamon

½ teaspoon ground cloves

¼ teaspoon salt

⅛ teaspoon white pepper

Heat oven to 350°. Mix brown sugar, shortening, molasses, water, egg and anise oil in large bowl. Stir in remaining ingredients. Knead dough until stiff enough to mold. Shape dough into ¾-inch balls. Place about 1 inch apart on ungreased cookie sheet. Bake about 12 minutes or bottoms are golden brown. Remove from cookie sheet. Cool on wire rack. About 8 dozen cookies.

Note: For traditionally hard Peppernuts, store in airtight container. For softer cookies, store with an apple or orange slice in airtight container, replacing fruit slice frequently.

Pistachio-Chocolate Checkers

1½ cups powdered sugar

*1 cup (2 sticks) margarine or butter,
    softened*

1 egg

2⅔ cups all-purpose flour

¼ teaspoon salt

¼ cup cocoa

1 tablespoon milk

⅓ cup finely chopped pistachio nuts

2 or 3 drops green food color, if desired

Mix powdered sugar, margarine and egg in large bowl. Stir in flour and salt. Divide dough in half. Stir cocoa and milk into one half; stir nuts and food color into other half.

Pat chocolate dough into rectangle, 6 × 5 inches. Cut crosswise into 8 strips, ¾ inch wide. Repeat with pistachio dough. Place 2 strips of each color of dough side by side, alternating colors. Top with 2 strips of each color of dough, alternating colors to create checkerboard. Gently press strips together. Make second stack with remaining strips. Wrap and refrigerate about 2 hours or until firm.

Heat oven to 375°. Cut rectangles crosswise into ¼-inch slices. Place about 1 inch apart on ungreased cookie sheet. Bake 8 to 10 minutes or until set. Remove from cookie sheet. Cool on wire rack. About 3 dozen cookies.

CHERRY-CHOCOLATE CHECKERS: Omit food color. Substitute finely chopped maraschino cherries, very well drained, for the pistachio nuts.

SQUARE CHOCOLATE CHECKERS: Prepare dough as directed except—use 1 strip of each color dough for each layer and make four stacks. About 6 dozen cookies.

Gingersnaps

Bring holiday cheer to everyday gingersnaps by dipping half of each cookie into melted vanilla coating for a snow-laden look.

1 cup packed brown sugar

¾ cup shortening

¼ cup molasses

1 egg

2¼ cups all-purpose flour

2 teaspoons baking soda

1 teaspoon ground cinnamon

1 teaspoon ground ginger

½ teaspoon ground cloves

¼ teaspoon salt

Granulated sugar

Mix brown sugar, shortening, molasses and egg in large bowl. Stir in flour, baking soda, cinnamon, ginger, cloves and salt. Cover and refrigerate at least 1 hour.

Heat oven to 375°. Grease cookie sheet lightly. Shape dough by rounded teaspoonfuls into balls; dip tops into granulated sugar. Place balls, sugared sides up, about 3 inches apart on cookie sheet. Bake 10 to 12 minutes or just until set. Remove from cookie sheet. Cool on wire rack. About 4 dozen cookies.

Pistachio Chocolate Checkers; Gingersnaps; Reindeer Snack (page 268)

Peppermint Pinwheels; Cookie Tarts (right)

Chocolate-Peppermint Refrigerator Cookies

1¹/₂ cups powdered sugar

1 cup (2 sticks) margarine or butter, softened

1 egg

2²/₃ cups all-purpose flour

¹/₄ teaspoon salt

¹/₄ cup cocoa

1 tablespoon milk

¹/₄ cup finely crushed peppermint candy

4 drops red food color, if desired

Mix powdered sugar, margarine and egg in large bowl. Stir in flour and salt. Divide dough in half. Stir cocoa and milk into one half; stir peppermint candy and food color into other half.

Roll chocolate dough into rectangle, 12 × 6¹/₂ inches, on waxed paper. Shape peppermint dough into roll, 12 inches long; place on chocolate dough. Wrap chocolate dough around peppermint dough using waxed paper to help lift. Press edges of chocolate dough together. Wrap and refrigerate about 2 hours or until firm.

Heat oven to 375°. Cut roll into ¹/₄-inch slices. Place about 1 inch apart on ungreased cookie sheet. Bake 8 to 10 minutes or until set. Remove from cookie sheet. Cool on wire rack. About 4 dozen cookies.

🎄 **To shape peppermint dough into a smooth roll, place in waxed paper, hold the opposite ends of the paper, and roll back and forth until even.**

Christmas Cookie Slices

1 cup (2 sticks) margarine or butter,
    softened*

1 cup granulated or packed brown sugar

1½ teaspoons vanilla

2 eggs

3 cups all-purpose flour

*½ cup chopped blanched almonds or
    black walnuts, if desired*

1 teaspoon salt

½ teaspoon baking soda

Mix margarine, sugar, vanilla and eggs in large bowl. Stir in remaining ingredients. Divide dough into 3 equal parts. Shape each part into roll, 1½ inches in diameter and about 7 inches long. Wrap in waxed paper or plastic wrap. Refrigerate at least 4 hours.

Heat oven to 400°. Cut rolls into ⅛-inch slices. Place 1 inch apart on ungreased cookie sheet. Bake 8 to 10 minutes or until edges begin to brown. Immediately remove from cookie sheet. Cool on wire rack. Drizzle with Chocolate Glaze (page 38) if desired. About 7 dozen cookies.

* Do not use tub margarine in this recipe.

CINNAMON COOKIES: Use packed brown sugar and substitute 1 tablespoon ground cinnamon for the vanilla.

COOKIE TARTS: Cut out centers of half of the unbaked slices with ¾-inch cutters, or design your own patterns. Spoon ½ teaspoon green or red jelly or jam onto uncut slices; top with cutout slices. Press edges to seal. Sprinkle with powdered sugar after baking if desired. About 3½ dozen cookies.

PEANUT BUTTER COOKIES: Decrease margarine to ½ cup and add ½ cup crunchy peanut butter. Use dark brown sugar.

PEPPERMINT PINWHEELS: Decrease vanilla to 1 teaspoon and add 1 teaspoon peppermint extract. Divide dough in half. Stir ½ teaspoon red or green food color into one half. Cover both halves and refrigerate 1 hour. Roll plain dough into rectangle, about 16 × 9 inches, on lightly floured surface. Repeat with tinted dough; place on plain dough. Roll doughs together until about ¼ inch thick. Roll up tightly, beginning at 16-inch side. Wrap and refrigerate. Continue as directed.

Chocolate Brownie Drops

Let these luscious cookies make you nutty! Try almonds, hazelnuts, macadamia nuts, mixed nuts, peanuts or pistachio nuts—whatever your family and friends love best.

> *1 cup sugar*
>
> *½ cup (1 stick) margarine or butter, softened*
>
> *⅓ cup buttermilk or water*
>
> *1 teaspoon vanilla*
>
> *1 egg*
>
> *2 ounces unsweetened chocolate, melted and cooled*
>
> *1¾ cups all-purpose flour*
>
> *1 cup chopped nuts, if desired*
>
> *½ teaspoon baking soda*
>
> *½ teaspoon salt*
>
> *Chocolate Frosting (below)*

Heat oven to 400°. Mix sugar, margarine, buttermilk, vanilla, egg and chocolate in medium bowl. Stir in flour, nuts, baking soda and salt. Drop dough by rounded teaspoonfuls about 2 inches apart onto ungreased cookie sheet.

Bake 8 to 10 minutes or until almost no indentation remains when touched. Immediately remove from cookie sheet. Cool on wire rack. Frost with Chocolate Frosting. Sprinkle with additional chopped nuts if desired. About 4½ dozen cookies.

CHOCOLATE FROSTING

> *2 ounces unsweetened chocolate*
>
> *2 tablespoons margarine or butter*
>
> *3 tablespoons water*
>
> *About 2 cups powdered sugar*

Heat chocolate and margarine in 1½-quart saucepan over low heat, stirring until melted; remove from heat. Stir in water and powdered sugar until smooth and of spreading consistency.

Brandied Fruit Drops

Nuggets of winter fruits and several spices blend nicely with the brandy flavor.

> *¾ cup packed brown sugar*
>
> *½ cup (1 stick) margarine or butter*
>
> *⅓ cup brandy or ⅓ cup water and 1 teaspoon brandy extract*
>
> *2 eggs*
>
> *2 cups all-purpose flour*
>
> *2 teaspoons baking powder*
>
> *1 teaspoon ground cardamom*
>
> *½ teaspoon ground cinnamon*
>
> *½ teaspoon ground nutmeg*
>
> *1 cup chopped pecans*
>
> *1 cup dried apricots, chopped*
>
> *½ cup golden raisins*
>
> *½ cup currants*
>
> *Browned Butter Glaze (page 25)*

Heat oven to 350°. Grease cookie sheet. Mix brown sugar, margarine, brandy and eggs in large bowl. Stir in flour, baking powder, cardamom, cinnamon and nutmeg. Stir in remaining ingredients except Browned Butter Glaze.

Drop dough by rounded teaspoonfuls about 2 inches apart onto cookie sheet. Bake 9 to 11 minutes or until light brown. Remove from cookie sheet. Cool on wire rack. Drizzle with Browned Butter Glaze. About 5 dozen cookies.

Sour Cream Cookies

1¹/₂ cups packed brown sugar

1 cup sour cream

¹/₂ cup shortening

1 teaspoon vanilla

2 eggs

2³/₄ cups all-purpose flour

¹/₂ teaspoon salt

¹/₂ teaspoon baking soda

1 cup chopped pecans, if desired

Browned Butter Glaze (page 25)

Heat oven to 375°. Mix brown sugar, sour cream, shortening, vanilla and eggs in large bowl. Stir in remaining ingredients except Browned Butter Glaze.

Drop dough by rounded teaspoonfuls about 2 inches apart onto ungreased cookie sheet. Bake 8 to 10 minutes or until almost no indentation remains when touched in center. Cool slightly before removing from cookie sheet. Cool completely on wire rack. Spread with Browned Butter Glaze. About 6 dozen cookies.

SPICE-SOUR CREAM COOKIES: Mix ¹/₂ cup granulated sugar, 1 teaspoon ground cinnamon and ¹/₄ teaspoon ground cloves; sprinkle over cookies before baking. Omit glaze.

Honey-roasted Peanut Crisps

1 cup packed brown sugar

¹/₂ cup (1 stick) margarine or butter, softened

¹/₂ cup shortening

1 teaspoon vanilla

1 egg

2 cups all-purpose flour

2 cups honey-roasted peanuts

¹/₂ teaspoon baking powder

¹/₄ teaspoon salt

Heat oven to 375°. Mix brown sugar, margarine, shortening, vanilla and egg in large bowl. Stir in remaining ingredients.

Drop dough by rounded tablespoonfuls about 2 inches apart onto ungreased cookie sheet. Flatten with greased bottom of glass dipped into sugar. Bake 9 to 11 minutes or until golden brown. Cool slightly; remove from cookie sheet. Cool on wire rack. About 4 dozen cookies.

Traditional Almond Cookies

3 cups slivered almonds, toasted

3 egg whites

1¹/₂ cups granulated sugar

1 teaspoon powdered sugar

1 teaspoon amaretto or ¹/₄ teaspoon almond extract

Granulated sugar

Heat oven to 300°. Line cookie sheet with cooking parchment paper, or grease and flour cookie sheet. Place almonds in food processor or blender. Cover and process, or blend, until finely ground but not pastelike.

Beat egg whites in medium bowl on high speed until stiff. Stir in almonds, 1¹/₂ cups granulated sugar and the powdered sugar. Stir in amaretto. Drop mixture by rounded teaspoonfuls about 2 inches apart onto cookie sheet. Sprinkle with granulated sugar. Bake 20 to 25 minutes or until brown. Remove from cookie sheet. Cool on wire rack. Drizzle with melted bittersweet chocolate if desired. About 4 dozen cookies.

Mocha Macaroons

3 egg whites

1 teaspoon freeze-dried instant coffee (dry)

¹/₄ teaspoon cream of tartar

¹/₈ teaspoon salt

¹/₂ cup sugar

2 tablespoons cocoa

2 cups flaked coconut

Heat oven to 300°. Grease cookie sheet lightly. Beat egg whites, coffee, cream of tartar and salt in medium bowl on high speed until foamy. Beat in sugar, 1 tablespoon at a time, on high speed. Continue beating until stiff. Do not underbeat. Fold in cocoa. Fold in coconut.

Drop mixture by rounded teaspoonfuls 1 inch apart onto cookie sheet. Bake 20 to 25 minutes or until set. Cool 10 minutes; remove from cookie sheet. Cool on wire rack. Sprinkle with additional cocoa or drizzle with melted chocolate if desired. About 3¹/₂ dozen cookies.

Chocolate Brownie Drops (page 20); Mocha Macaroons; Chocolate Mousse Bars (page 30)

Chocolate Chip Cookies

Turn chocolate chip cookies into tempting gifts by making cookie pops. Prepare Jumbo Chocolate Chip Cookies, but flatten the dough and insert wooden ice-cream sticks halfway into the dough before baking. These pops are nice tied to presents, or placed in a mug or pencil holder.

> *1 cup (2 sticks) margarine or butter, softened*
>
> *¾ cup granulated sugar*
>
> *¾ cup packed brown sugar*
>
> *1 egg*
>
> *2¼ cups all-purpose flour*
>
> *1 teaspoon baking soda*
>
> *½ teaspoon salt*
>
> *1 cup coarsely chopped nuts*
>
> *1 package (12 ounces) semisweet chocolate chips (2 cups)*

Heat oven to 375°. Mix margarine, sugars and egg in large bowl. Stir in flour, baking soda and salt (dough will be stiff). Stir in nuts and chocolate chips. Drop dough by rounded teaspoonfuls about 2 inches apart onto ungreased cookie sheet. Bake 8 to 10 minutes or until light brown (centers will be soft). Cool slightly; remove from cookie sheet. Cool on wire rack. Dip edges of cookies into melted semisweet chocolate if desired. Place cookies on waxed paper. Let stand about 10 minutes or until chocolate is set. About 6 dozen cookies.

CHOCOLATE CHIP BARS: Press dough in ungreased rectangular pan, 13 × 9 × 2 inches. Bake 22 to 25 minutes or until golden brown; cool. Cut into about 3 × 1½-inch bars. 24 bars.

JUMBO CHOCOLATE CHIP COOKIES: Drop dough by ¼ cupfuls about 3 inches apart onto ungreased cookie sheet. Bake 12 to 15 minutes or until edges are set. Cool completely; remove from cookie sheet. About 1½ dozen cookies.

Florentines

Want festive, professional-looking cookies? Make wavy lines in the chocolate before it is set with the tines of a table fork.

> *¾ cup whipping (heavy) cream*
>
> *¼ cup sugar*
>
> *½ cup very finely chopped blanched almonds*
>
> *4 ounces candied orange peel, very finely chopped*
>
> *¼ cup all-purpose flour*
>
> *2 bars (4 ounces each) sweet cooking chocolate or bittersweet chocolate*

Heat oven to 350°. Grease and flour cookie sheet. Mix whipping cream and sugar in medium bowl until well blended. Stir in almonds, orange peel and flour. (Dough may thicken as it stands.) Drop dough by rounded teaspoonfuls about 2 inches apart onto cookie sheet. Spread to form 2-inch circles. (Dough may be sticky.)

Bake 10 to 12 minutes or until edges are light brown. Cool 2 minutes; remove from cookie sheet to wire rack. Heat chocolate until melted. Turn cookies over; spread with chocolate. Dry several hours at room temperature until chocolate becomes firm. About 4½ dozen cookies.

Cranberry-Chip Cookies

A lovely, soft cookie bursting with cranberries and nuts. Try pistachio nuts for a unique flavor and even more color! You can use frozen cranberries, but be sure to pat them dry after chopping and don't overmix, or they may smear.

1 cup granulated sugar

³/₄ cup packed brown sugar

¹/₂ cup (1 stick) margarine or butter, softened

¹/₄ cup milk

2 tablespoons orange juice

1 egg

3 cups all-purpose flour

1 teaspoon baking powder

¹/₂ teaspoon salt

¹/₄ teaspoon baking soda

2¹/₂ cups coarsely chopped cranberries

1 cup chopped nuts

¹/₂ cup vanilla milk or semisweet chocolate chips

Browned Butter Glaze (right) or Chocolate Glaze (page 38), if desired

Heat oven to 375°. Grease cookie sheet. Mix sugars and margarine in large bowl. Stir in milk, orange juice and egg. Stir in flour, baking powder, salt and baking soda. Carefully stir in cranberries, nuts and vanilla milk chips. Drop dough by rounded teaspoonfuls about 2 inches apart on cookie sheet. Bake 10 to 15 minutes or until light brown. Remove from cookie sheet. Cool on wire rack. Spread with Browned Butter Glaze. About 5¹/₂ dozen cookies.

BROWNED BUTTER GLAZE

¹/₃ cup margarine or butter

2 cups powdered sugar

1¹/₂ teaspoons vanilla

2 to 4 tablespoons hot water

Heat margarine in 2-quart saucepan over low heat until golden brown; cool slightly. Stir in powdered sugar and vanilla. Beat in water until smooth and of spreading consistency.

🔔 **Omit the glaze, and sprinkle with grated semisweet or white chocolate while hot.**

Cranberry-Chip Cookies; Jumbo Chocolate Chip Cookies (page 23); Peppernuts (page 15)

Orange-Chocolate Cookies

1 cup sugar

²/₃ cup margarine or butter, softened

1 tablespoon grated orange peel

1 egg

1½ cups all-purpose flour

⅓ cup cocoa

¼ teaspoon salt

¼ teaspoon baking powder

¼ teaspoon baking soda

1 cup chopped pecans

1 package (6 ounces) semisweet chocolate chips (1 cup)

⅓ cup sugar

1 teaspoon grated orange peel

Heat oven to 350°. Mix 1 cup sugar, the margarine, 1 tablespoon orange peel and the egg in large bowl. Stir in flour, cocoa, salt, baking powder and baking soda. Stir in pecans and chocolate chips.

Mix ⅓ cup sugar and 1 teaspoon orange peel. Shape dough into 1½-inch balls; roll balls in sugar mixture. Place about 3 inches apart on ungreased cookie sheet. Flatten to about ½-inch thickness with bottom of glass. Bake 9 to 11 minutes or until set. Cool slightly; remove from cookie sheet. Cool on wire rack. About 2½ dozen cookies.

Glazed Fruit Bars

1 cup sugar

⅓ cup shortening

⅓ cup margarine or butter, softened

1 tablespoon grated orange peel, if desired

¼ cup orange or pineapple juice

1 egg

2½ cups all-purpose flour

1 teaspoon baking soda

½ teaspoon salt

½ teaspoon ground cinnamon

½ teaspoon ground nutmeg

1 cup raisins

1 cup chopped mixed candied fruit

½ cup chopped nuts, if desired

Powdered Sugar Glaze (below)

Heat oven to 400°. Grease jelly roll pan, 15½ × 10½ × 1 inch. Mix sugar, shortening, margarine, orange peel, orange juice and egg in large bowl. Stir in flour, baking soda, salt, cinnamon and nutmeg. Stir in raisins, candied fruit and nuts. Spread in pan.

Bake about 15 minutes or until top springs back when touched lightly; cool slightly. Spread with Powdered Sugar Glaze. Decorate with bits of candied fruit if desired. Cut into 2 × 1-inch bars. About 5 dozen bars.

POWDERED SUGAR GLAZE

1½ cups powdered sugar

¼ teaspoon vanilla

2 to 3 tablespoons milk

Beat all ingredients until smooth and of spreading consistency.

GLAZED ORANGE-RAISIN BARS: Substitute 1 cup chopped orange wedge candies (about 12) for the candied fruit.

Glazed Fruit Bars (left); Apricot-Date Bars (page 28)

Cranberry-Lime Squares

1 cup all-purpose flour

¹/₂ cup (1 stick) margarine or butter, softened

¹/₄ cup powdered sugar

1 cup granulated sugar

2 tablespoons all-purpose flour

2 tablespoons lime juice

2 teaspoons grated lime peel

¹/₂ teaspoon baking powder

¹/₄ teaspoon salt

2 eggs

2 or 3 drops green food color, if desired

¹/₃ cup coarsely chopped dried cranberries or dried cherries

Heat oven to 350°. Mix flour, margarine and powdered sugar. Press in ungreased square pan, 8 × 8 × 2 or 9 × 9 × 2 inches, building up ¹/₂-inch edges. Bake 20 minutes.

Beat remaining ingredients except cranberries on medium speed about 3 minutes or until light and fluffy. Stir in cranberries. Pour over baked layer. Bake about 25 minutes or until no indentation remains when touched in center; cool. Sprinkle with powdered sugar if desired. Cut into 1¹/₂-inch squares. About 3 dozen squares.

LIME SQUARES: Omit the dried cranberries.

Mincemeat Bars

1 cup packed brown sugar

¹/₂ cup (1 stick) margarine or butter, softened

¹/₄ cup shortening

1¹/₂ cups all-purpose flour

1 cup quick-cooking oats

1 teaspoon salt

¹/₂ teaspoon baking soda

1 jar (27 ounces) prepared mincemeat (about 3 cups)

¹/₂ cup chopped walnuts or almonds

Powdered sugar

Heat oven to 400°. Grease rectangular pan, 13 × 9 × 2 inches. Mix brown sugar, margarine and shortening in large bowl. Stir in flour, oats, salt and baking soda until crumbly. Press half of the crumbly mixture in pan. Mix mincemeat and walnuts; spread over layer in pan. Sprinkle with remaining crumbly mixture; press lightly.

Bake 25 to 30 minutes or until light brown. While warm, make a diagonal cut from corner to corner. Continue making cuts parallel to first cut, spacing them about 1¹/₂ inches apart. Repeat, cutting diagonally in opposite direction. Sprinkle with powdered sugar. About 3¹/₂ dozen bars.

APRICOT-DATE BARS: Omit mincemeat and walnuts. Mix 1¹/₂ cups chopped dried apricots, 1¹/₄ cups chopped dates, ¹/₂ cup sugar and 1¹/₂ cups water in 2-quart saucepan. Cook over medium-low heat about 10 minutes, stirring constantly, until thickened. Substitute for the mincemeat and walnut mixture.

Pumpkin-Spice Bars

4 eggs

2 cups sugar

1 cup vegetable oil

1 can (16 ounces) pumpkin

2 cups all-purpose flour

2 teaspoons baking powder

2 teaspoons ground cinnamon

1 teaspoon baking soda

¹/₂ teaspoon salt

¹/₂ teaspoon ground ginger

¹/₄ teaspoon ground cloves

¹/₂ cup raisins

Cream Cheese Frosting (below)

¹/₂ cup chopped nuts or sunflower nuts

Heat oven to 350°. Grease jelly roll pan, 15¹/₂ × 10¹/₂ × 1 inch. Beat eggs, sugar, oil and pumpkin in large bowl. Stir in flour, baking powder, cinnamon, baking soda, salt, ginger and cloves. Mix in raisins. Pour batter into pan. Bake 25 to 30 minutes or until light brown; cool. Frost with Cream Cheese Frosting. Sprinkle with nuts. Cut into 2 × 1¹/₂-inch bars. Refrigerate any remaining bars. About 4 dozen bars.

CREAM CHEESE FROSTING

1 package (3 ounces) cream cheese, softened

¹/₄ cup (¹/₂ stick) plus 2 tablespoons margarine or butter, softened

1 teaspoon vanilla

2 cups powdered sugar

Mix cream cheese, margarine and vanilla in medium bowl. Gradually beat in powdered sugar until smooth.

Almond Meringue Bars

¹/₂ cup granulated sugar

¹/₂ cup packed brown sugar

³/₄ cup (1¹/₂ sticks) margarine or butter, softened

1 teaspoon vanilla

3 eggs, separated

2 cups all-purpose flour

1 teaspoon baking powder

¹/₄ teaspoon baking soda

¹/₄ teaspoon salt

1 package (6 ounces) semisweet chocolate chips (1 cup)

1 cup flaked or shredded coconut

¹/₂ cup chopped almonds

1 cup packed brown sugar

¹/₂ cup chopped almonds

Heat oven to 350°. Grease rectangular pan, 13 × 9 × 2 inches. Beat granulated sugar, ¹/₂ cup brown sugar, the margarine, vanilla and egg yolks in large bowl on low speed until blended. Beat on medium speed about 2 minutes, scraping bowl constantly, until smooth. Stir in flour, baking powder, baking soda and salt. Press dough in pan with floured hands. Sprinkle with chocolate chips, coconut and ¹/₂ cup almonds.

Beat egg whites until foamy. Beat in 1 cup brown sugar, 1 tablespoon at a time; continue beating until stiff and glossy. Spread over top. Sprinkle with ¹/₂ cup almonds. Bake 35 to 40 minutes or until meringue is set and light brown; cool. Cut into about 3 × 1-inch bars. 3 dozen bars.

Cashew Triangles

You can cut these cookies into squares or bars. We think the triangles add a unique look!

¹/₂ cup (1 stick) margarine or butter, softened

¹/₄ cup granulated sugar

¹/₄ cup packed brown sugar

¹/₂ teaspoon vanilla

1 egg, separated

1 cup all-purpose flour

¹/₈ teaspoon salt

1 teaspoon water

1 cup chopped salted cashews, macadamia nuts or toasted almonds

1 ounce unsweetened chocolate, melted and cooled

Heat oven to 350°. Mix margarine, sugars, vanilla and egg yolk in medium bowl. Stir in flour and salt. Press dough in ungreased rectangular pan, 13 × 9 × 2 inches, with floured hands. Beat egg white and water; brush over dough. Sprinkle with cashews; press lightly into dough.

Bake about 25 minutes or until light brown; cool 10 minutes. Cut into 3-inch squares. Cut each square diagonally in half. Immediately remove from pan; cool. Drizzle with chocolate. Let stand about 2 hours or until chocolate is set. About 2 dozen bars.

Quick Praline Bars

24 graham cracker squares

¹/₂ cup packed brown sugar

¹/₂ cup (1 stick) margarine or butter

¹/₂ teaspoon vanilla

¹/₂ cup chopped pecans

Heat oven to 350°. Arrange graham crackers in single layer in ungreased jelly roll pan, 15¹/₂ × 10¹/₂ × 1 inch. Heat brown sugar and margarine to boiling. Boil and stir 1 minute; remove from heat. Stir in vanilla. Pour over crackers; spread evenly. Sprinkle with pecans. Bake 8 to 10 minutes or until bubbly. Cool slightly. Cut into 2¹/₄ × 1¹/₄-inch bars. About 4 dozen bars.

Caramel Candy Bars

2 cups all-purpose flour

2 cups quick-cooking or regular oats

1¹/₂ cups packed brown sugar

1 teaspoon baking soda

¹/₂ teaspoon salt

1 egg

1 cup (2 sticks) margarine or butter, softened

1 package (14 ounces) vanilla caramels

¹/₃ cup milk

1 package (6 ounces) semisweet chocolate chips (1 cup)

1 cup chopped walnuts or dry-roasted peanuts

Heat oven to 350°. Grease rectangular pan, 13 × 9 × 2 inches. Mix flour, oats, brown sugar, baking soda, salt and egg in large bowl. Stir in margarine with fork until mixture is crumbly. Press half of the crumbly mixture in pan. Bake 10 minutes.

Heat caramels and milk in 2-quart saucepan over low heat, stirring frequently, until smooth.

Sprinkle chocolate chips and walnuts over baked layer. Drizzle with caramel mixture. Sprinkle with remaining crumbly mixture. Bake 20 to 25 minutes or until golden brown. Cool 30 minutes. Loosen edges from sides of pan; cool completely. Cut into about 2 × 1-inch bars. 4¹/₂ dozen bars.

Chocolate Mousse Bars

For a chocolate extravaganza, use chocolate wafers, instead of vanilla, for the crust of these creamy bars. If you'd like a snowflake effect, place a paper doily on top of the bars and sprinkle with powdered sugar; remove the doily carefully.

1¹/₂ cups vanilla wafer crumbs (about 40 wafers)

¹/₄ cup (¹/₂ stick) margarine or butter, melted

³/₄ cup whipping (heavy) cream

1 package (6 ounces) semisweet chocolate chips (1 cup)

3 eggs

¹/₃ cup sugar

¹/₈ teaspoon salt

Chocolate Topping (right)

Heat oven to 350°. Mix wafer crumbs and margarine. Press in ungreased square pan, 8 × 8 × 2 or 9 × 9 × 2 inches. Bake 10 minutes.

Heat whipping cream and chocolate chips over low heat, stirring frequently, until chocolate is melted; remove from heat. Cool about 5 minutes. Beat eggs, sugar and salt in large bowl until foamy. Pour chocolate mixture into egg mixture, stirring constantly. Pour over baked layer in pan. Bake 25 to 35 minutes or until center springs back when touched lightly. Cool 15 minutes. Spread with Chocolate Topping. Refrigerate uncovered about 2 hours or until chilled. Refrigerate any remaining bars. 16 bars.

CHOCOLATE TOPPING

> *¹/₂ cup semisweet chocolate chips*
>
> *1 tablespoon shortening*

Heat ingredients over low heat, stirring frequently, until melted.

Raspberry Marbled Brownies

Cream Cheese Filling (right)
1 cup (2 sticks) margarine or butter
4 ounces unsweetened chocolate
2 cups sugar
2 teaspoons vanilla
4 eggs
1¹/₂ cups all-purpose flour
¹/₂ teaspoon salt
1 cup coarsely chopped nuts, if desired
¹/₂ cup raspberry jam or preserves

Heat oven to 350°. Grease rectangular pan, 13 × 9 × 2 inches. Prepare Cream Cheese Filling.

Heat margarine and chocolate over low heat, stirring occasionally, until melted; cool. Beat chocolate mixture, sugar, vanilla and eggs in medium bowl on medium speed 1 minute, scraping bowl occasionally. Beat in flour and salt on low speed 30 seconds, scraping bowl occasionally. Beat on medium speed 1 minute. Stir in nuts.

Spread half of the batter in pan. Spread with filling. Gently spread remaining batter over filling. Drop jam by scant teaspoonfuls randomly over batter. Gently swirl through batter, filling and jam with spoon in an over-and-under motion for marbled effect. Bake 60 to 70 minutes or until toothpick inserted in center comes out clean; cool. Cut into about 1¹/₂ × 1-inch bars. About 5 dozen bars.

CREAM CHEESE FILLING

> *¹/₂ cup sugar*
>
> *1 teaspoon ground cinnamon*
>
> *1¹/₂ teaspoons vanilla*
>
> *1 egg*
>
> *2 packages (8 ounces each) cream cheese, softened*

Beat all ingredients in small bowl on medium speed 2 minutes, scraping bowl occasionally.

Fudgy Rum Brownies

½ cup (1 stick) margarine or butter

1 package (12 ounces) semisweet chocolate chips (2 cups)

1²/₃ cups sugar

1¼ cups all-purpose flour

2 tablespoons rum or 1 teaspoon rum extract

1 teaspoon vanilla

½ teaspoon baking powder

½ teaspoon salt

3 eggs

1 cup chopped nuts, if desired

Rum Frosting (below)

Heat oven to 350°. Grease rectangular pan, 13 × 9 × 2 inches. Heat margarine and chocolate chips in 3-quart saucepan over low heat, stirring constantly, until melted. Beat in remaining ingredients except nuts and Rum Frosting until smooth. Stir in nuts. Spread in pan. Bake about 30 minutes or until center is set; cool completely. Frost with Rum Frosting. Drizzle with melted semisweet chocolate if desired. Cut into about 2 × 1½-inch bars. 3 dozen brownies.

RUM FROSTING

2 cups powdered sugar

¼ cup (½ stick) margarine or butter, softened

1 teaspoon rum or ½ teaspoon rum extract

1 to 2 tablespoons milk

Mix powdered sugar, margarine and rum. Beat in milk until smooth and of spreading consistency.

Fudgy Rum Brownies; Raspberry Marbled Brownies (page 31)

Peanut Butter Swirl Brownies

²/₃ cup granulated sugar

½ cup packed brown sugar

½ cup (1 stick) margarine or butter, softened

2 tablespoons milk

2 eggs

¾ cup all-purpose flour

½ teaspoon baking powder

¼ teaspoon salt

¼ cup peanut butter

⅓ cup peanut butter chips

⅓ cup cocoa

½ cup semisweet chocolate chips

Heat oven to 350°. Grease square pan, 9 × 9 × 2 inches. Mix sugars, margarine, milk and eggs in large bowl. Stir in flour, baking powder and salt. Divide batter in half (about 1 cup plus 2 tablespoons for each half). Stir peanut butter and peanut butter chips into 1 half. Stir cocoa and chocolate chips into remaining half.

Spoon chocolate batter into pan in 8 mounds, checkerboard-style. Spoon peanut butter batter between mounds of chocolate batter. Gently swirl through batters with knife for marbled effect. Bake 30 to 35 minutes or until toothpick inserted in center comes out clean. Cool completely. 16 brownies.

A Craving for Cookies

Nothing says Christmas like an array of freshly baked Christmas cookies. Making cookies ahead can be a lifesaver during the holidays. It frees you up for other baking and cooking, shopping, entertaining and to enjoy the festivities of the season. We've included some standard baking tips as well as guidelines for storing and mailing cookies that will be sure to make your cookie baking a success.

Mixing Cookies

❆ Measure ingredients accurately. Use liquid measuring cups for liquids, graduated dry measuring cups for dry ingredients (like flour and sugar), very thick wet ingredients (like sour cream and peanut butter) and food pieces (like chopped nuts and raisins).

❆ To measure brown sugar or shortening, spoon into cup and pack down firmly. Nuts, coconut, dried fruits or cut-up fruit should be packed lightly.

❆ Most of our cookie recipes are mixed by hand. If an electric mixer is used, a mixing speed and amount of time will be specified. If you make a recipe with a mixer when one is not specified, the cookies may spread more.

❆ Chill cookie doughs if directed. This makes the dough easier to handle with less spreading during baking. Shaping the dough into a flattened round rather than a ball will make the dough easier to work with after refrigeration. If the dough is too stiff to work with straight from the refrigerator, microwave on high for 10 seconds, adding more time if necessary. But, do not over-microwave.

❆ To roll cookie dough evenly, purchase two 15- or 18-inch rulers that are the height of the cookies in the recipe (usually $1/8$- to $1/4$-inch). Roll the dough between the rulers. With all cookies even in height, there should be no darker (thinner) or lighter (thicker) portions of the cookies.

❆ When a recipe says "drop dough by rounded teaspoonfuls (or tablespoonfuls)," use regular teaspoons and tablespoons from your everyday flatware.

❆ Make all cookies on each cookie sheet the same size to ensure uniform baking. Mixing cookie sizes will cause some to be over- or underbaked.

Baking Cookies

❆ Preheat the oven according to the recipe. On the average, this takes about 10 minutes.

❆ Use shortening when greasing cookie sheets, and only grease if specified in the recipe. Margarine or butter can cause the cookies to stick and overbrown. Regrease sheets as needed during baking.

❆ Use cookie sheets at least two inches narrower and shorter than the oven so heat will circulate around them. Shiny, bright cookie sheets are best for delicate browning. It's nice to have at least two cookie sheets on hand—while a batch is baking, you can be filling the other sheet.

❋ If using a cookie sheet with a nonstick coating, watch carefully, as cookies may brown quickly. Follow manufacturers' directions as many may suggest reducing the oven temperature by 25°.

❋ If cookie sheets are thin, consider using two together, one stacked on top of the other for added insulation.

❋ Always check cookies at minimum bake times, as even one minute can make a difference with cookies, especially those high in sugar and fat.

❋ If your cookies always turn out darker at minimum times, check the type of cookie sheets you are using. As ovens get older, the thermostat tends to swing upwards and bake hotter (both gas and electric). If you notice overbaking on a shiny aluminum cookie sheet, reduce the oven temperature by 25°. Or, correct the oven temperature by adjusting the control knob mechanism (see the oven use and care manual).

❋ Cool the cookie sheets between batches; otherwise cookie dough placed on warm cookie sheets will spread.

Decorating Cookies

❋ The most versatile cookie dough for making decorated cookies is probably rolled cookie dough. It can be cut into any shape and decorated before or after baking.

❋ Use Egg Yolk Paint, page 3, or small amounts of evaporated milk tinted with different food colors to paint on light-colored cookie dough before baking. Use Baked-On Decorators' Frosting, page 5, to paint on dark-colored cookie dough before baking.

❋ While tubes of decorating gel, available at most grocery stores, are often used on frosted cookies and cakes, try making designs with the gel on light-colored cookie dough before baking. The gel will bake into a crackled glaze, allowing the decorated cookies to be stacked easily.

❋ Bar cookies can be doily-dusted before cutting. On frosted or unfrosted bars, place a paper doily or stencil from a craft store. Depending on the color and flavor, sift powdered sugar, cocoa, powdered instant coffee or cinnamon-sugar over the bars.

❋ A decorating bag and assorted tips can make cookie decorating a snap. But if you don't have one, try a heavy plastic freezer bag with $\frac{1}{8}$-inch of one bottom corner snipped off to make a writing tip.

❋ Cookies are best baked on a rack in the center of the oven. If two cookie sheets are in the oven at the same time (placed on one oven rack in the upper third and one oven rack in the lower third of the oven), switch their positions halfway through baking time.

Keeping Cookies

❄ Cookie dough can be packaged in airtight containers and refrigerated up to 24 hours or frozen up to 6 months. Thaw frozen dough in the refrigerator.

❄ Baked, unfrosted cookies can be tightly covered and frozen for up to 12 months.

❄ Baked frosted cookies can be tightly covered and frozen for up to 3 months. Freeze them uncovered until they are firm, then pack in layers in a container lined with freezer wrap with wrap between layers. Seal tightly, label and freeze.

❄ Let frozen cookies stand uncovered on serving plate about twenty minutes before serving.

❄ Store soft cookies in containers with tight fitting lids to prevent moisture loss. A piece of bread or apple (replaced frequently) in the container helps to keep the cookies soft.

❄ Store crisp cookies in containers with loose fitting lids. This allows the flow of air to keep them crisp. If they soften, heat in a 300° oven 3 to 5 minutes to recrisp.

❄ Do not mix soft and crisp cookies in the same container or the crisp cookies will become soft.

Mailing Cookies

❄ Mail early and label your package "Open Before Christmas." The recipient can then enjoy your thoughtfulness all during the holidays!

❄ Choose sturdy cookies such as plain or lightly glazed bar cookies or rolled cookies cut with rounded (not pointed or delicately shaped) cutters to avoid crumbling and breakage.

❄ Wrap cookies in pairs, back to back, and place them flat or on end in a can, box or other sturdy container. (Cans with reusable plastic lids are particularly good choices.)

❄ Cookies may also be placed in single layers with waxed paper between.

❄ Fill each container as full as practical, padding the top with crushed waxed paper to prevent shaking and breakage.

❄ Pack containers in a foil-lined corrugated or fiberboard packing box. For fill, use crumpled newspapers, shredded paper or shredded polyethylene foam.

❄ Seal packing box with shipping tape and cover the address label with transparent tape for protection.

New Cookie Traditions

❊ *If you're short on time*, consider dressing up purchased cookies. Have plenty of ready-to-pipe or ready-to-spread frosting on hand along with chocolate or vanilla coating for melting. Stock up on assorted decorations, such as colored sugar and small decorative candies.

❊ *Hold a cookie-baking party.* Invite friends to share in mixing, baking and decorating cookies. Even the youngest helpers will be eager to join in the fun of decorating cookies. Play Christmas music and make an easy lunch or supper.

—Plan the assortment of cookies to be baked. Look for different flavors, shapes and colors.

—Ask participants to bring aprons and storage containers, extra cookie sheets, or other items.

—Set up work stations in different parts of the kitchen—mixing, shaping, baking and cooling, and decorating. If desired, plan to have the cookie doughs made ahead.

—Divide the finished cookies among the cookie bakers.

—Dip purchased vanilla wafers or other unfrosted cookies in melted chocolate or vanilla coating. Sprinkle with chopped pistachios or drizzle with a contrasting color of coating. Package in a holiday tin or on a festive paper plate and tie with raffia or ribbon and top off with an ornament.

—Attach tiny teddy bear cookies to the top of purchased chocolate covered cookies using frosting. Pipe a red hat and scarf on each bear and package attractively.

❊ *Hold a cookie exchange*, to lighten up your holiday baking. Each guest prepares only one kind of cookie or candy but ends up taking home a delicious variety. It's a wonderful social occasion especially when held at the beginning of December, before schedules become too hectic. That way, the treats are on hand for holiday entertaining.

—You may wish to invite 6 to 12 guests. Plan the cookie exchange around lunch, tea or dinner.

—Send out invitations 3 to 4 weeks in advance so everyone has time to prepare one dozen cookies for each of the guests. Let participants know what other guests are planning to bring so cookies aren't duplicated.

—Ask each guest to bring the sweets arranged on sturdy plastic or paper plates covered with plastic wrap or a plastic bag, or in other covered containers. You can also provide plates and bags for wrapping and guests can bring their treats in one container. Ask guests to label their baked goods and provide any special storage instructions.

—Provide enough space for all the plates of cookies brought by the guests.

—If recipes will be exchanged, ask for the recipes before the Cookie Exchange and make copies.

—Check with your guests to see if they would like to contribute an extra dozen cookies to a local food shelf or charity and make arrangements to deliver the goodies.

Rosettes

Making rosettes is a Christmas tradition for many, or one you may want to start in your own home! See the notes below for useful tips.

Vegetable oil

2 eggs, slightly beaten

2 tablespoons sugar

1 teaspoon salt

1 cup water or milk

1 cup all-purpose flour

2 tablespoons vegetable oil

Chocolate Glaze (right)

Heat oil (2 to 3 inches) in small, deep saucepan to 400°. Beat eggs, sugar and salt in small, deep bowl. Beat in remaining ingredients except Chocolate Glaze just until smooth. Heat rosette iron by placing in hot oil 1 minute. Tap excess oil from iron onto paper towels. Dip hot iron into batter just to top edge (don't go over top). Fry about 30 seconds or until golden brown. Immediately remove rosette; invert onto paper towels to cool. (If rosette is not crisp, batter is too thick. Stir in a small amount of water or milk.)

Heat iron in hot oil and tap on paper towels before making each rosette. (If iron is not hot enough, batter will not stick.) Drizzle rosettes with Chocolate Glaze, or just before serving, sprinkle with powdered sugar. About 3 dozen rosettes.

CHOCOLATE GLAZE

½ cup semisweet chocolate chips

2 tablespoons margarine or butter

2 tablespoons corn syrup

1 to 2 teaspoons hot water

Heat chocolate chips, margarine and corn syrup over low heat, stirring constantly, until chocolate chips are melted; cool slightly. Stir in water, 1 teaspoon at a time, until consistency of thick syrup.

TO MICROWAVE: Place chocolate chips, margarine and corn syrup in 2-cup microwavable measure. Microwave uncovered on medium (50%) 1 to 2 minutes or until chocolate can be stirred smooth. Omit water.

Notes: A table fork works well for removing fried rosettes from the iron. The bottom of the rosettes can be dipped about ¼ inch into the glazes, if desired. Draw the cookies across the edge of the bowl then turn upside down until the glaze sets. Tint the vanilla glaze with food color if desired.

- *The sugar can be omitted if you'd like to use the rosettes as an interesting base for savory foods such as chili or creamy main dishes.*
- *Rosettes may be sprinkled with cinnamon-sugar while hot, no need to add the glaze.*
- *Serve as a cookie or as a base for winter fruit compote (page 66) or ice cream and sauces.*

Rosettes, Krumkake (page 42); Pizelles (page 40)

Pizzelles

Brown sugar gives a crisp texture and caramel flavor to these pretty cookies. For holiday pizzelles, cut cookie into fourths right after baking. Dip either end into melted chocolate and sprinkle with chopped nuts or small, decorative candies.

> *2 cups all-purpose flour*
>
> *1 cup granulated or packed brown sugar*
>
> *3/4 cup (1 1/2 sticks) margarine or butter, melted and cooled*
>
> *1 tablespoon anise extract or vanilla*
>
> *2 teaspoons baking powder*
>
> *4 eggs, slightly beaten*

Heat pizzelle iron according to manufacturer's directions. Mix all ingredients. Drop 1 tablespoon batter onto each design of heated pizzelle iron; close iron. Bake about 30 seconds or until golden brown. Carefully remove pizzelle from iron. Cool on wire rack. Repeat with remaining batter. About 3 1/2 dozen cookies.

Lacy Cookie Cups

These cups are versatile as well as delicious. Try filling them with pudding, mousse or ice cream, and then top with your favorite sauces—the combinations can take you through the twelve days of Christmas, and then some!

> *1/2 cup powdered sugar*
>
> *1/4 cup (1/2 stick) butter softened**
>
> *1/2 teaspoon vanilla*
>
> *2 egg whites*
>
> *1/4 cup all-purpose flour*
>
> *1/4 teaspoon ground cinnamon*
>
> *2 cups mixed fresh strawberries and raspberries*
>
> *1/3 cup raspberry jam, melted*

Heat oven to 400°. Generously grease cookie sheet. Beat powdered sugar, butter and vanilla in medium bowl on medium speed until well blended. Beat in egg whites on low speed until mixture is well blended but not foamy. Fold in flour and cinnamon.

Drop dough by about 1 1/2 tablespoonfuls 6 inches apart onto cookie sheet. Flatten into 5-inch rounds using back of spoon dipped into cold water. Bake 5 to 6 minutes or until golden brown. Let stand 30 seconds or until firm; remove from cookie sheet. Immediately shape each cookie over inverted 6-ounce custard cup. Cool completely. Fill each cookie cup with about 1/3 cup berries. Drizzle with jam. About 6 cookie cups.

* Do not use margarine in this recipe.

Springerle

Springerle

From Germany comes this embossed Christmas cookie with centuries of tradition. A springerle rolling pin has recessed designs that make an imprint on the dough. The imprinted cookies are separated, then traditionally allowed to dry overnight, which helps set the design. We don't recommend air drying because the dough contains raw egg; if there isn't time to bake the cookies immediately, refrigerate (in a single layer, loosely covered) up to twenty-four hours. These richly flavored cookies are very hard—excellent for dunking.

1 cup sugar

2 eggs

2 cups all-purpose flour

2 teaspoons anise seed

Heat oven to 325°. Beat sugar and eggs in medium bowl on high speed about 5 minutes or until thick and lemon colored. Stir in flour and anise seed.

Divide dough in half. Roll one half at a time ¼ inch thick on floured cloth-covered surface. Roll well-floured springerle rolling pin over dough to emboss designs. Cut out cookies. Place about 1 inch apart on ungreased cookie sheet. Bake 12 to 15 minutes or until light brown. Immediately remove from cookie sheet. Cool on wire rack. About 3 dozen cookies.

Krumkake

1 cup sugar

³/₄ cup all-purpose flour

¹/₂ cup (1 stick) margarine or butter, melted

¹/₃ cup whipping (heavy) cream

2 teaspoons cornstarch

1 teaspoon vanilla

4 eggs

Heat ungreased krumkake iron over medium-high heat on smallest surface unit of range. Beat all ingredients until smooth. Test iron with a few drops of water; if they skitter around, iron is correct temperature.

Drop ¹/₂ tablespoon batter onto iron; close gently. Bake about 15 seconds on each side or until light golden brown. Keep iron over heat at all times. Remove cookie with knife. Immediately roll cookie around roller or handle of large wooden spoon. Cool on wire rack. About 6 dozen cookies.

Palmiers

¹/₂ package (17¹/₄-ounce size) frozen puff pastry, thawed

¹/₂ cup sugar

1 ounce semisweet chocolate, melted

Heat oven to 375°. Lightly grease cookie sheet. Roll pastry into rectangle, 12 × 9¹/₂ inches and ¹/₈ inch thick, on surface sprinkled with sugar. Mark a line lengthwise down center of pastry. Fold 12-inch sides toward center line, leaving ¹/₄ inch space at center. Fold pastry in half lengthwise to form strip, 12 × 2¹/₂ inches, pressing pastry together.

Cut pastry strip crosswise into ¹/₄-inch slices. Roll slices in ¹/₂ cup sugar. Place about 2 inches apart on cookie sheet. Bake 8 to 10 minutes, turning after 5 minutes, until cookies begin to turn golden brown. Immediately remove from cookie sheet. Cool completely on wire rack. Dip ends of cookies into chocolate. Place on waxed paper until chocolate is firm. About 2¹/₂ dozen cookies.

Cookie Mold Cookies

³/₄ cup packed brown sugar

¹/₂ cup (1 stick) margarine or butter, softened

¹/₄ cup molasses

¹/₂ teaspoon vanilla

1 egg

2¹/₄ cups all-purpose flour

³/₄ cup coarsely chopped sliced almonds

¹/₂ teaspoon ground allspice

¹/₄ teaspoon salt

¹/₄ teaspoon baking soda

Mix brown sugar, margarine, molasses, vanilla and egg in large bowl. Stir in remaining ingredients. Cover and refrigerate about 2 hours or until firm.

Heat oven to 350°. Lightly grease cookie sheet. Flour wooden or ceramic cookie mold(s). Tap mold to remove excess flour. Firmly press small amounts of dough into mold until mold is full and dough is uniform thickness across mold. Hold mold upright and tap edge firmly several times on hard surface (such as a counter or cutting board) to remove shaped dough. If dough does not come out, turn mold and tap another edge until dough comes out of mold. Place shaped dough on cookie sheet.

Bake 2-inch cookies 8 to 10 minutes, 5-inch cookies 10 to 12 minutes or until edges are light brown. (Time depends on thickness of cookies. Watch carefully.) About 4½ dozen 2-inch cookies or 2 dozen 5-inch cookies.

CAST-IRON COOKIE-MOLD DIRECTIONS: Grease and flour iron cookie mold(s). Press dough into mold as directed above. Bake smaller molds about 15 minutes, larger molds about 20 minutes. Cool cookies 10 minutes; remove from molds.

Holiday Cookie Mix

This multipurpose mix makes quite a large batch, but it can be easily mixed in a large roasting pan, a plastic dishpan, the vegetable bin from your refrigerator or a 6-quart mixing bowl.

8 cups all-purpose flour

4 cups packed brown sugar

1 tablespoon salt

1½ teaspoons baking soda

1½ cups shortening

Mix flour, brown sugar, salt and baking soda. Cut in shortening with pastry blender or 2 knives until mixture resembles fine crumbs. Place desired amounts of mix in storage containers (plastic containers or jars or large plastic bags). Seal tightly, label and refrigerate up to 10 weeks. To measure, dip dry-ingredient measuring cup into cookie mix; level with straight-edged spatula. 15 to 16 cups cookie mix.

Toffee Bars

4 cups Holiday Cookie Mix (left)

½ cup (1 stick) margarine or butter, softened

1 teaspoon vanilla

1 egg

4 ounces milk chocolate candy, broken into pieces

½ cup chopped nuts, if desired

Heat oven to 350°. Grease rectangular pan, 13 × 9 × 2 inches. Mix Holiday Cookie Mix, margarine, vanilla and egg. Press in pan.

Bake 25 to 30 minutes or until very light brown (layer will be soft). Remove from oven; immediately place chocolate candy on baked layer. Let stand until soft; spread evenly. Sprinkle with nuts. Cut into about 2 × 1-inch bars while warm. 4 dozen bars.

Chocolate Bonbon Cookies

These little gems are even more tempting when topped with festive treats such as flaked or shredded coconut, edible glitter, chopped candied fruit or chopped maraschino cherries.

> *4 cups Holiday Cookie Mix (page 43)*
>
> *1 cup chopped nuts*
>
> *¼ cup (½ stick) margarine or butter, softened*
>
> *1 teaspoon vanilla*
>
> *½ teaspoon almond extract*
>
> *2 eggs*
>
> *2 ounces unsweetened chocolate, melted and cooled*
>
> *Powdered sugar*
>
> *Easy Frosting (below)*

Heat oven to 375°. Mix Holiday Cookie Mix, nuts, margarine, vanilla, almond extract, eggs and chocolate. Shape dough into 1-inch balls. Place about 1 inch apart on ungreased cookie sheet. Bake 10 to 12 minutes or until set. Cool slightly before removing from cookie sheet.

Roll about 30 cookies in powdered sugar while warm; cool on wire rack. Roll in powdered sugar again. Frost remaining cookies with Easy Frosting. Decorate frosted cookies with coconut. About 5 dozen cookies.

EASY FROSTING

> *1 cup powdered sugar*
>
> *About 1 tablespoon milk*
>
> *½ teaspoon almond extract*

Mix all ingredients until smooth and of spreading consistency.

Chocolate Bonbon Cookies; Cherry-Coconut Bars

Cherry-Coconut Bars

The crackly top on these bars is easiest to cut with a wet, sharp knife.

> *4 cups Holiday Cookie Mix (page 43)*
>
> *½ cup (1 stick) margarine or butter, softened*
>
> *1½ cups sugar*
>
> *¾ cup flaked coconut*
>
> *¾ cup chopped maraschino cherries, drained*
>
> *⅓ cup all-purpose flour*
>
> *1 teaspoon vanilla*
>
> *¾ teaspoon baking powder*
>
> *½ teaspoon salt*
>
> *3 eggs, beaten*
>
> *1 cup chopped nuts*

Heat oven to 350°. Mix Holiday Cookie Mix and margarine. Press in ungreased rectangular pan, 13 × 9 × 2 inches. Bake 25 minutes. Mix remaining ingredients except nuts; spread over baked layer. Sprinkle with nuts. Bake about 25 minutes or until center is set. Cool completely. Cut into about 2 × 1-inch bars. 4 dozen bars.

Christmas Cookie Pizza

¹/₂ cup (1 stick) margarine or butter, softened

¹/₂ cup packed brown sugar

¹/₄ cup granulated sugar

1 teaspoon vanilla

1 egg

1¹/₄ cups all-purpose flour

¹/₂ teaspoon baking soda

Chocolate Pizza Sauce (below)

¹/₂ cup pecan halves

¹/₂ cup red and green candy-coated chocolate candies

¹/₄ cup shredded coconut, toasted, if desired

2 ounces vanilla-flavored candy coating, melted

Heat oven to 350°. Mix margarine, sugars, vanilla and egg in large bowl. Stir in flour and baking soda (dough will be stiff). Spread or pat dough in ungreased 12-inch pizza pan or on cookie sheet. Bake about 15 minutes or until golden brown; cool. Prepare Chocolate Pizza Sauce; spread over baked layer. Immediately sprinkle with pecan halves, candies and coconut; press lightly. Drizzle with candy coating. Let stand until set. Remove from pan if desired. Cut into wedges. 16 servings.

CHOCOLATE PIZZA SAUCE

1 package (6 ounces) semisweet chocolate chips (1 cup)

2 tablespoons margarine or butter

3 tablespoons milk

1 cup powdered sugar

Heat chocolate chips, margarine and milk over low heat, stirring occasionally, just until chocolate is melted; remove from heat. Stir in powdered sugar. Beat with wire whisk until smooth, glossy and of spreading consistency. (If not glossy, stir in a few drops hot water.)

Fruit Jumbles

4 cups Holiday Cookie Mix (page 43)

³/₄ cup sour cream

1 teaspoon vanilla

2 eggs

1¹/₂ cups candied cherries, cut in half

1¹/₂ cups chopped dates

1 cup chopped pecans

Pecan halves, if desired

Heat oven to 375°. Mix Holiday Cookie Mix, sour cream, vanilla and eggs in large bowl. Stir in cherries, dates and chopped pecans. Drop dough by rounded teaspoonfuls about 2 inches apart onto ungreased cookie sheet. Place pecan half on each cookie. Bake about 8 minutes or until almost no indentation remains when touched. Immediately remove from cookie sheet. Cool on wire rack. About 6 dozen cookies.

🎄 **A miniature spring-handled ice cream scoop (No. 40) makes shaping these cookies quick work.**

The Homemade Candy Shop

*T*urn your kitchen into a branch of Santa's workshop when you make these luscious candies. Tempting truffles, mouthwatering fudge, wonderfully fast microwave candies and other goodies all make delightful presents for family and friends–or to keep for yourself!

Rum-Raisin Fudge

¹/₂ cup raisins

2 tablespoons rum

2 cups sugar

¹/₃ cup milk

¹/₃ cup half-and-half

2 tablespoons light corn syrup

2 tablespoons rum

2 tablespoons margarine or butter

Butter loaf pan, 9 × 5 × 3 inches. Mix raisins and 2 tablespoons rum; reserve. Cook remaining ingredients except margarine in 3-quart saucepan over medium heat, stirring constantly, until sugar is dissolved. Cook, stirring occasionally, to 234° on candy thermometer. Remove saucepan from heat. Stir in margarine.

Cool mixture without stirring to 120°. (Bottom of saucepan will be lukewarm.) Beat vigorously and continuously with spoon or heavy electric mixer 5 to 10 minutes or until candy is thick and no longer glossy. (Mixture will hold its shape when dropped from a spoon.) Quickly stir in raisin-rum mixture. Spread in pan; cool. Cut into 1-inch squares. About 2¹/₂ dozen candies.

HAZELNUT FUDGE: Omit raisins and rum. Add 2 tablespoons hazelnut liqueur with the corn syrup. Stir ¹/₂ cup chopped hazelnuts (filberts), toasted, into mixture before spreading in pan. Top with whole hazelnuts if desired.

Fudge Meltaways

1³/₄ cups graham cracker crumbs (about 20 squares)

1 cup flaked coconut

¹/₄ cup cocoa

2 tablespoons granulated sugar

¹/₂ cup (1 stick) margarine or butter, melted

2 tablespoons water

2 cups powdered sugar

¹/₄ cup (¹/₂ stick) margarine or butter, softened

1 tablespoon milk

1 teaspoon vanilla

Mix cracker crumbs, coconut, cocoa and granulated sugar in medium bowl. Stir in ¹/₂ cup margarine and the water. Press in ungreased square pan, 9 × 9 × 2 inches; refrigerate.

Meanwhile, mix remaining ingredients. (If necessary, stir in additional 1 to 2 teaspoons milk until smooth and of spreading consistency.) Spread over layer in pan. Refrigerate 1 hour. Cut into 1-inch squares. Decorate with chopped red and green candied cherries if desired. About 5 dozen candies.

Easy Chocolate Fudge

1 cup granulated sugar

¹/₄ cup cocoa

¹/₄ cup (¹/₂ stick) margarine or butter

¹/₃ cup milk

1 tablespoon light corn syrup

1 teaspoon vanilla

¹/₂ cup chopped nuts, if desired

2 to 2¹/₄ cups powdered sugar

Line loaf pan, 9 × 5 × 3 inches, with aluminum foil, leaving 1 inch of foil overhanging on opposite sides. Grease foil. Mix granulated sugar and cocoa in 2-quart saucepan. Stir in margarine, milk and corn syrup. Heat to boiling over medium heat, stirring frequently. Boil and stir 1 minute; remove from heat. Cool without stirring about 45 minutes or until bottom of pan is lukewarm. Stir in vanilla and nuts. Stir in powdered sugar until mixture is very stiff. Press in pan. Refrigerate about 30 minutes or until firm. Remove from pan, using foil to lift. Cut into 1-inch squares. About 2¹/₂ dozen candies.

PEANUT BUTTER FUDGE: Omit cocoa and margarine. Stir in ¹/₂ cup peanut butter with the milk. Substitute salted peanuts for the nuts.

NUT ROLL: Do not use pan. Shape candy into 12-inch roll, and roll in ¹/₂ cup finely chopped nuts. Wrap and refrigerate until firm. Cut roll into ¹/₄-inch slices. About 4 dozen candies.

PENUCHE: Substitute 1 cup packed brown sugar for the granulated sugar and omit cocoa. Substitute walnuts for the nuts.

🔔 **Line your fudge pan with buttered aluminum foil. When fudge is firm, remove it from the pan, using the foil to lift. Peel the aluminum "sides" away, and cut the fudge easily.**

Nut Roll; Penuche; Hazelnut Fudge (page 47)

Truffles

6 ounces semisweet chocolate, cut up

2 tablespoons margarine or butter

¹/₄ cup whipping (heavy) cream

1 cup semisweet or milk chocolate chips or vanilla milk chips

1 tablespoon shortening

Heat semisweet chocolate in heavy 2-quart saucepan over low heat, stirring constantly, until melted; remove from heat. Stir in margarine. Stir in whipping cream. Refrigerate 10 to 15 minutes, stirring frequently, *just* until thick enough to hold a shape.

Line cookie sheet with aluminum foil. Drop refrigerated mixture by teaspoonfuls onto cookie sheet. Shape into balls. (If mixture is too sticky, refrigerate until firm enough to shape.) Freeze 30 minutes.

Heat chocolate chips and shortening over low heat, stirring constantly, until chocolate is melted and mixture is smooth; remove from heat. Dip 1 truffle at a time into chocolate, using fork, until coated. Place on foil-covered cookie sheet.

Immediately sprinkle some of the truffles with finely chopped nuts if desired. Or drizzle some of the truffles with a mixture of ¹/₄ cup powdered sugar and ¹/₂ teaspoon milk if desired. Refrigerate truffles about 10 minutes or until chocolate is set. Serve at room temperature. Store in airtight container. About 15 candies.

LIQUEUR TRUFFLES: Stir 2 tablespoons flavored liqueur or brandy (almond, apricot, cherry, coffee, etc.) into whipping cream.

Chestnut Truffles

1 pound chestnuts*
4 cups water
2 cups milk
1/3 cup margarine or butter, softened
1 cup sugar
1 tablespoon cocoa
1/4 teaspoon vanilla
1 ounce semisweet chocolate, grated

Make a shallow crisscross cut on flat side of each chestnut with the tip of pointed, sharp knife. Heat chestnuts and water to boiling; reduce heat. Cover and simmer 15 minutes. Remove about one-fourth of the chestnuts at a time from the water. Peel off shell and skin while chestnuts are warm.

Heat chestnuts and milk to boiling; reduce heat slightly. Gently boil uncovered 15 minutes. Remove milk skin from surface; drain chestnuts thoroughly. Place chestnuts in food processor.** Cover and process until smooth.

Beat margarine in medium bowl on high speed until fluffy. Beat in chestnuts, sugar, cocoa and vanilla until smooth paste forms. Shape into 1-inch balls; roll balls in chocolate. Refrigerate at least 1 hour. About 2½ dozen candies.

* 1 can (16 ounces) chestnuts, drained, can be substituted for the fresh chestnuts. Do not make crisscross cut or boil in water.

** Using a blender for this recipe is not recommended.

Bourbon Balls

Bourbon balls are especially nice for busy people, as the cookies don't need to be baked and can be prepared before the holiday crush begins. In fact, the longer they sit, the better the flavor! If you like, you can substitute brandy or rum for the bourbon.

3 cups finely crushed vanilla wafers
  (about 75)
2 cups powdered sugar
1 cup finely chopped pecans or walnuts
1/4 cup cocoa
1/2 cup bourbon
1/4 cup light corn syrup
Granulated or powdered sugar

Mix crushed wafers, powdered sugar, pecans and cocoa in large bowl. Stir in bourbon and corn syrup. Shape mixture into 1-inch balls. Roll in granulated sugar. Cover tightly and refrigerate several days before serving. About 5 dozen candies.

🔔 **Use a food processor to crush the vanilla wafers quickly or purchase packaged vanilla wafer crumbs.**

Bourbon Balls; Peanut Brittle (page 61); Walnut Caramels (page 55)

Traditional Marzipan

Although marzipan is generally molded into fruit shapes, feel free to use Christmas shapes for inspiration—angels, Christmas trees, snowmen, teddy bears—or whatever you like best. The shaping and coloring techniques below will guide you in forming your Christmas marzipan.

1 package (about 8 ounces) almond paste
³/₄ cup powdered sugar
2 tablespoons margarine or butter
¹/₂ teaspoon almond extract
Food colors

Beat all ingredients except food colors on low speed until smooth paste forms. Cover and refrigerate 1 hour. Divide dough into 8 equal parts; use 1 part dough for each fruit below if desired. Add food colors and shape dough as directed below. Store in refrigerator or at room temperature. About 3¹/₂ dozen candies.

APPLES: Mix red food color into dough. Shape into 1-inch balls. Insert chocolate shot in top for stem. Brush with red or green food color diluted with water.

BANANAS: Mix yellow food color into dough. Shape into 3-inch rolls, tapering ends to resemble bananas; curve slightly. Brush on characteristic markings with brown food color.

CHERRIES: Mix red food color into dough. Roll into ¹/₂-inch balls. Use stems from maraschino cherries or chocolate shot for stems.

LIMES: Mix green food color into dough. Shape into 1-inch balls. Prick with blunt end of toothpick to resemble texture of lime.

ORANGES: Mix red and yellow food color into dough. Shape into 1-inch balls. Insert chocolate shot in top for stem. Prick balls with blunt end of toothpick to resemble texture of orange.

PEACHES: Mix red and yellow food color into dough. Shape into 1-inch balls. Make crease down 1 side with toothpick. Brush on brown or dark green food color for stem. Brush with red food color diluted with water for peach "blush."

PEARS: Mix yellow food color into dough. Shape into 1-inch balls, then into cone shapes, rounding narrow end of each. Brush with green food color at stem end. Insert chocolate shot in top for stem. Brush with red food color diluted with water for "cheeks" of pears.

STRAWBERRIES: Mix red food color into dough. Shape into 1-inch balls, then into heart shapes. Prick with blunt end of toothpick to resemble texture of strawberry. Brush top with green food color for stem or shape green-tinted dough into small leaves. Roll in red sugar.

Traditional Marzipan

Chocolate-Coconut Candies

1 cup warm or cold mashed potatoes

1 pound powdered sugar (4 cups)

1 teaspoon almond extract

1 pound flaked coconut (about 4 cups)

1 package (12 ounces) semisweet chocolate chips (2 cups)

2 tablespoons shortening

Mix potatoes, powdered sugar and almond extract in large bowl. Stir in coconut. Drop mixture by rounded teaspoonfuls onto waxed paper; shape into balls. (If mixture is too soft to shape, refrigerate 30 to 60 minutes or until firm.)

Heat chocolate chips and shortening in 1-quart saucepan over low heat, stirring frequently, until melted. Dip 1 ball at a time into chocolate, using fork or tongs, until coated; place on waxed paper. (Keep chocolate over low heat while dipping balls.) Refrigerate balls about 1 hour or until firm. About 4 dozen candies.

COCONUT BARS: Press coconut mixture in ungreased rectangular pan, 13 × 9 × 2 inches. Spread with melted chocolate. Refrigerate 30 to 60 minutes or until firm. Cut into 2 × 1-inch bars. About 4 dozen bars.

Almond-Orange Candy

10 thick-skinned large oranges

1 cup honey

2³/₄ cups slivered almonds, toasted

Thinly cut peel from oranges in about ¹/₂-inch strips, removing only outer orange layer. Trim any excess white membrane. Cut strips crosswise into slivers to yield 3¹/₂ cups. Cover orange peel with cold water. Cover and refrigerate 48 hours, draining and covering with fresh cold water every 12 hours; drain.

Cook orange peel and honey in heavy 12-inch skillet over medium heat about 30 minutes, stirring occasionally, until honey is absorbed and mixture is sticky. Stir in almonds until evenly distributed. Spread in shallow 6-cup dish or ungreased round pan, 9 × 1¹/₂ inches. Refrigerate about 3 hours or until chilled and firm. Cut into about 2-inch pieces. About 2 dozen candies.

Taffy

1 cup sugar

1 tablespoon cornstarch

²/₄ cup light corn syrup

²/₃ cup water

2 tablespoons margarine or butter

1 teaspoon salt

2 teaspoons vanilla

Butter square pan, 8 × 8 × 2 inches. Mix sugar and cornstarch in 2-quart saucepan. Stir in corn syrup, water, margarine and salt. Heat to boiling over medium heat, stirring constantly. Cook, without stirring, to 265° on candy thermometer or until small amount of mixture dropped into very cold water forms a hard ball that holds its shape but is pliable; remove from heat. Stir in vanilla. Pour into pan.

When just cool enough to handle, pull taffy with lightly buttered hands until satiny, light in color and stiff. Pull into long strips ¹/₂ inch wide. Cut strips into 1¹/₂-inch pieces, using scissors. (For ease in cutting, wipe scissors with vegetable oil.) Wrap pieces individually in plastic wrap or waxed paper (candy must be wrapped to hold its shape). About 4 dozen candies.

Brandied Stuffed Dates

1 pound pitted dates

1 cup brandy or orange juice

About 1 cup pecan halves or blanched whole almonds

Sugar, if desired

Soak dates in brandy about 24 hours, turning occasionally, until most of the brandy is absorbed. Place 1 pecan half in each date; press to close. Roll in sugar. Store in airtight container in refrigerator. About 1 pound candies.

Toffee

1 cup chopped pecans

³/₄ cup packed brown sugar

¹/₂ cup (1 stick) margarine or butter

¹/₂ cup semisweet chocolate chips

Butter square pan, 9 × 9 × 2 inches. Spread pecans in pan. Heat brown sugar and margarine to boiling over medium heat, stirring constantly. Boil 7 minutes, stirring constantly. Immediately spread evenly over pecans. Sprinkle with chocolate chips. Cover pan with cookie sheet. Let stand about 1 minute or until chips soften. Spread softened chocolate over candy. While hot, cut into 1¹/₂-inch squares. Refrigerate until firm. 3 dozen candies.

Walnut Caramels

To make these scrumptious caramels even more special, try using black walnuts.

1 can (14 ounces) sweetened condensed milk

1 cup light corn syrup

¹/₈ teaspoon salt

2 tablespoons margarine or butter

1 teaspoon vanilla

¹/₂ cup finely chopped walnuts

Line square pan, 8 × 8 × 2 inches, with aluminum foil, leaving 1 inch of foil overhanging on opposite sides. Butter foil that lines bottom of pan. Heat milk, corn syrup and salt to boiling in heavy 1¹/₂-quart saucepan over medium heat, stirring constantly. Cook over medium heat, stirring frequently, to 245° on candy thermometer or until small amount of mixture dropped into very cold water forms a firm ball. Stir in margarine, vanilla and walnuts until margarine is melted. Immediately spread in pan; cool. Remove from pan, using foil to lift. Cut into 1 × ¹/₂-inch pieces. Wrap pieces individually in plastic wrap or waxed paper if desired. About 10 dozen candies.

Microwave Candies

The microwave can help you make fabulous Christmas candies in a matter of minutes! The delectable recipes that follow use a variety of cooking and melting techniques. (When you make Mixed Maple Brittle be sure to use a microwavable casserole or bowl that can withstand high temperatures.) We think these special treats will find a permanent home on your list of favorite candies and food gifts for the Christmas season.

❄ Use a bowl or container that is microwavable. Be sure it's large enough so food can be mixed easily and won't boil over. Do not cover the dish unless directed.

❄ Stir as directed to evenly distribute the heat and avoid boilover.

❄ Always use potholders.

Maple–Mixed Nut Brittle

1 cup packed brown sugar

1/2 cup maple-flavored syrup

1 can (about 12 ounces) lightly salted mixed nuts (2 cups)

1 tablespoon margarine or butter

1 teaspoon baking soda

Generously butter large cookie sheet; keep warm in 200° oven. Mix brown sugar and syrup in 8-cup microwavable measure. Microwave uncovered on high 5 minutes. Stir in nuts. Microwave uncovered 5 to 7 minutes or until syrup is bubbling and nuts are toasted. Syrup will be very hot. Stir in margarine. Microwave uncovered 1 minute longer.

Quickly and thoroughly stir in baking soda until light and foamy. Pour onto cookie sheet and quickly spread candy. Cool 30 to 60 minutes or until hard. Break into pieces. About 2 pounds candy.

Peanut Clusters

1 cup sugar

1/3 cup evaporated milk

1/4 cup (1/2 stick) margarine or butter

1/4 cup crunchy peanut butter

1/2 teaspoon vanilla

2 cups quick-cooking or regular oats

1/2 cup Spanish peanuts

1/2 cup semisweet chocolate chips

Line cookie sheet with waxed paper. Mix sugar, milk and margarine in 2-quart microwavable casserole. Microwave uncovered on high 2 to 3 minutes or until boiling. Stir in peanut butter and vanilla until blended. Stir in remaining ingredients. Drop by tablespoonfuls onto cookie sheet. (If mixture becomes too stiff, stir in 1 or 2 drops milk.) Refrigerate about 30 minutes or until firm. About 2 dozen candies.

Cappuccino-Pecan Nuggets

Taste these luscious nuggets, and they will no doubt become a holiday tradition and reap rave reviews when served or given as gifts. Don't be fooled by this recipe—it may look long, but you'll find it quite efficient.

$\frac{1}{4}$ cup packed brown sugar

1 tablespoon instant espresso coffee (dry)

$\frac{2}{3}$ cup sweetened condensed milk

12 ounces vanilla-flavored candy coating, chopped

12 vanilla or chocolate caramels

$\frac{1}{4}$ cup semisweet chocolate chips

1 tablespoon whipping (heavy) cream

72 large pecan halves (about $1\frac{1}{2}$ cups)

10 to 12 ounces semisweet, bittersweet or milk chocolate, broken or chopped

3 tablespoons shortening

Line square pan, $8 \times 8 \times 2$ or $9 \times 9 \times 2$ inches, with aluminum foil, leaving 1 inch of foil overhanging on opposite sides. Spray foil with nonstick cooking spray. Mix brown sugar and espresso in 8-cup microwavable measure. Stir in milk. Microwave uncovered on high 2 to 3 minutes, stirring every minute, until boiling. Stir in candy coating until melted. Pour into pan. Refrigerate uncovered about 30 minutes or until firm. Remove from pan, using foil to lift. Cut into 36 squares.

Place caramels, chocolate chips and whipping cream in 2-cup microwavable measure. Microwave uncovered on medium (50%) $1\frac{1}{2}$ to $2\frac{1}{2}$ minutes, stirring every minute, until mixture is almost melted. Stir until smooth. Refrigerate uncovered about 15 minutes, stirring once or twice, until mixture holds its shape and is cool enough to handle.

Line cookie sheet with waxed paper. For each nugget, roll $\frac{1}{2}$ teaspoon caramel-chocolate mixture into ball. Press 2 pecan halves on ball in sandwich shape, flattening ball slightly between bottom sides of pecan halves. Flatten slightly and shape 1 square espresso mixture evenly around pecan cluster; roll between hands to form ball. If espresso mixture gets sticky, dust very lightly with powdered sugar. Place on cookie sheet. Refrigerate about 15 minutes or until firm.

Place chocolate and shortening in dry microwavable 4-cup measure or bowl. (Any water in the measure will cause chocolate to seize, or harden, when melted.) Microwave uncovered on medium (50%) 3 to 4 minutes, stirring every minute, until chocolate is almost melted. Stir until smooth. Dip 1 nugget at a time into chocolate, using fork, until coated. (When removing nugget from measure, lightly tap bottom of fork on edge of measure and draw fork across measure to remove excess chocolate.) Place on foil-lined cookie sheet. Immediately sprinkle some of the nuggets with finely chopped pecans or equal amounts of instant espresso coffee and cocoa mixed together if desired. (One tablespoon each of instant expresso coffee and cocoa will cover entire recipe.)

Drizzle some of the nuggets with remaining melted chocolate if desired. Refrigerate about 10 minutes or just until set. Serve at room temperature. Store in airtight container. 3 dozen candies.

CAPPUCCINO-DATE NUGGETS: Substitute 36 whole pitted dates, cut in half, for the pecans.

Peppermint Bark

This holiday candy is both quick and delicious! There are several brands of candy coating, and you'll find each melts a bit differently. The white color varies, and some are thinner than others. Take a minute to note the brand you prefer, so your candy is exactly as you like it.

1 package (16 ounces) vanilla-flavored candy coating, broken into pieces
24 hard peppermint candies

Line cookie sheet with waxed paper, aluminum foil or cooking parchment paper. Place candy coating in 8-cup microwavable measure or 2-quart microwavable casserole. Microwave uncovered on high 2 to 3 minutes, stirring every 30 seconds, until almost melted. Stir until smooth.

Place peppermint candies in heavy plastic bag; crush with rolling pin or bottom of small heavy saucepan. Pour crushed candies into wire strainer. Shake strainer over melted coating until all of the tiniest candy pieces fall into the coating; reserve the larger candy pieces. Stir coating to mix well. Spread coating evenly on cookie sheet. Sprinkle with remaining candy pieces. Let stand about 1 hour or until cool and hardened. Break into pieces. About 1 pound candy.

CHOCOLATE-PEPPERMINT BARK: Substitute chocolate-flavored candy coating for the vanilla candy coating.

DRIZZLED PEPPERMINT BARK: Heat 1/2 cup semisweet chocolate chips or vanilla milk chips and 1 teaspoon shortening until melted. Drizzle over Peppermint Bark before letting stand 1 hour.

Deluxe Christmas Fudge

If you delight in creamy chocolate fudge, just leave out the pistachios and the cherries for a smooth, rich chocolate treat.

1 1/2 packages (12-ounce size) semisweet chocolate chips (3 cups)
2 cups miniature marshmallows or 16 large marshmallows, cut in half
1 can (14 ounces) sweetened condensed milk
1 teaspoon vanilla
1 cup pistachio nuts
1/2 cup chopped candied cherries

Line square pan, 9 × 9 × 2 inches, with aluminum foil; butter foil. Place chocolate chips, marshmallows and milk in 8-cup microwavable measure. Microwave uncovered on high 3 to 5 minutes, stirring every minute, until marshmallows and chips are melted and can be stirred smooth. Stir in vanilla, nuts and cherries. Immediately pour into pan. Drizzle with melted vanilla-flavored candy coating if desired. Refrigerate about 2 hours or until firm. Cut into 1-inch squares. About 6 dozen candies.

Christmas Mice

These charming mice are a hit with both adults and children. For problem-free mice, caramels should be soft enough to shape easily and candy coating thick enough to drizzle but not run. If candy coating is too thin, let it stand at room temperature until it cools slightly and thickens, then fill plastic bag.

12 large pretzel twists

12 vanilla caramels

¹/₂ package (11¹/₂-ounce size) milk chocolate chips (1 cup)

3 tablespoons vanilla milk chips

¹/₄ teaspoon shortening

Line two 10-inch microwavable plates with plastic wrap or spray with nonstick cooking spray. Arrange 6 pretzels in circle on each plate. Place a caramel with a corner down on center triangle of each pretzel. Microwave uncovered on high 15 to 30 seconds or until caramels soften slightly. Carefully press each caramel to fit triangle space and pinch into shape of a mouse nose (you can be as creative as you like).

Place chocolate chips in 1-cup microwavable measure. Microwave uncovered on medium (50%) 3 to 4 minutes, stirring every minute, until chips are almost melted. Stir until smooth. Spoon and spread 2 level teaspoons melted chocolate evenly over caramel and center pretzel triangle. Refrigerate about 15 minutes or until firm.

Meanwhile, place vanilla milk chips and shortening in small microwavable bowl. Microwave uncovered on medium (50%) 1 to 2 minutes, stirring every minute, until almost melted. Stir until smooth. Place melted chips in strong plastic bag; cut off a tiny tip from one corner of bag. Decorate as desired, piping on eyes and whiskers. 1 dozen candies.

🔔 To fill plastic bag without mess, place one corner of bag down into a mug. Open and pull the bag around the outside of the mug. After filling the bag, lift out of mug and tightly twist top of bag to just above melted chips. Snip off corner to decorate.

Orange-Date Balls

2 packages (8 ounces each) chopped dates

¹/₂ cup (1 stick) margarine or butter

¹/₃ cup sugar

1 egg, well beaten

¹/₄ teaspoon salt

2 teaspoons grated orange peel

2 tablespoons orange juice

1 teaspoon vanilla

¹/₂ cup chopped nuts

¹/₂ cup graham cracker crumbs

4 cups toasted whole-grain wheat flake cereal

1¹/₄ cups finely chopped nuts

Mix dates, margarine and sugar in 3-quart microwavable casserole. Cover tightly and microwave on high 4 minutes. Stir in egg and salt. Cover tightly and microwave on medium-high (70%) 3 to 4 minutes or until slightly thickened. Stir in orange peel, orange juice, vanilla, ¹/₂ cup nuts and the cracker crumbs.

Let stand 10 minutes or until cool. Stir in cereal. Shape into 1-inch balls, using buttered hands. Roll balls in finely chopped nuts. About 5 dozen candies.

Peanut Brittle

The trick to making thin, tender peanut brittle is keeping the cookie sheets warm. You'll be able to spread the candy to ¼ inch thickness without it setting up.

> *1½ teaspoons baking soda*
> *1 teaspoon water*
> *1 teaspoon vanilla*
> *1½ cups sugar*
> *1 cup water*
> *1 cup light corn syrup*
> *3 tablespoons margarine or butter*
> *1 pound shelled unroasted peanuts*

Butter 2 cookie sheets, 15½ × 12 inches; keep warm in 200° oven. Mix baking soda, 1 teaspoon water and the vanilla; reserve. Mix sugar, 1 cup water and the corn syrup in 3-quart saucepan. Cook over medium heat, stirring occasionally, to 240° on candy thermometer or until small amount of syrup dropped into very cold water forms a soft ball that flattens when removed from water.

Stir in margarine and peanuts. Cook, stirring constantly, to 300° or until small amount of mixture dropped into very cold water separates into hard, brittle threads. (Watch carefully so mixture does not burn.) Immediately remove from heat. Quickly stir in baking soda mixture until light and foamy.

Pour half the candy mixture onto each cookie sheet; quickly spread about ¼ inch thick. Cool; break into pieces. About 2 pounds candy.

Oven Caramel Corn

You'll want to make batches of this tempting caramel corn to give as gifts, serve at open houses and sell at Christmas bazaars. Store tightly covered, especially if you make it a week or two ahead of time.

> *15 cups popped popcorn*
> *1 cup packed brown sugar*
> *½ cup (1 stick) margarine or butter*
> *¼ cup light corn syrup*
> *½ teaspoon salt*
> *½ teaspoon baking soda*

Heat oven to 200°. Divide popcorn between 2 ungreased rectangular pans, 13 × 9 × 2 inches. Heat brown sugar, margarine, corn syrup and salt in 3-quart saucepan over medium heat, stirring occasionally, until bubbly around edges. Cook 5 minutes, stirring occasionally; remove from heat. Stir in baking soda. Pour over popcorn; stir until well coated. Bake 1 hour, stirring every 15 minutes. About 15 cups snack.

NUTTY CARAMEL CORN: Decrease popcorn to 12 cups. Add 1½ cups walnut halves, pecan halves, peanuts or unblanched whole almonds to each pan of popcorn before stirring in brown sugar mixture.

Peppermint Bark (page 58); Cappuccino-Pecan Nuggets (page 57)

Popcorn Balls

Try a fun, new shape for old-fashioned popcorn balls. Shape the popcorn mixture into pinecone shapes, then drizzle with melted chocolate-flavored candy coating.

> *¹/₂ cup sugar*
> *¹/₂ cup light corn syrup*
> *¹/₄ cup (¹/₂ stick) margarine or butter*
> *¹/₄ teaspoon salt*
> *Few drops food color*
> *8 cups popped popcorn*

Heat all ingredients except popcorn to boiling in Dutch oven over medium-high heat, stirring constantly. Add popcorn. Cook about 3 minutes, stirring constantly, until popcorn is well coated. Cool slightly.

Dip hands into cold water. Shape mixture into 2¹/₂-inch balls. Place on waxed paper; cool. Wrap individually in plastic wrap, or place in plastic bags and seal. 8 or 9 popcorn balls.

CHRISTMAS POPCORN CUTOUTS: Do not shape mixture into balls. Press evenly in lightly buttered jelly roll pan, 15¹/₂ × 10¹/₂ × 1 inch. Cut into holiday shapes with 1-inch-deep metal cookie cutters. Heat 4 ounces vanilla- or chocolate-flavored candy coating until melted. Spread cut edges of shapes with candy coating. Before coating dries, sprinkle with colored sugar or candy sprinkles. Place on waxed paper until coating is set.

🔔 **Use the microwave to pop popcorn, or you can also buy already popped corn.**

Popcorn Balls

The Dessert Tray

Desserts come into their own in the Christmas season, and the enticing collection here will end your holiday meals in style. A warm and cozy pie, elegant tart, pretty cake, classic plum pudding or any of the other desserts will delight your family and friends and complete your meal deliciously.

Christmas Coconut Cake

Tutti-Frutti Filling (right)

2 cups all-purpose flour

1½ cups granulated sugar

½ cup shortening

1 cup milk

3½ teaspoons baking powder

1 teaspoon salt

1 teaspoon vanilla

4 egg whites

⅔ cup flaked coconut

1 cup whipping (heavy) cream

¼ cup powdered sugar

¾ teaspoon almond extract

Prepare Tutti-Frutti Filling. Heat oven to 350°. Grease and flour 2 round pans, 9 × 1½ inches. Beat flour, granulated sugar, shortening, milk, baking powder, salt and vanilla in large bowl on low speed 30 seconds, scraping bowl constantly. Beat on high speed 2 minutes, scraping bowl occasionally. Add egg whites; beat on high speed 2 minutes, scraping bowl occasionally. Stir in coconut. Pour into pans.

Bake 30 to 35 minutes or until toothpick inserted in center comes out clean. Remove from pans; cool on wire rack. Fill layers and frost top of cake to within 1 inch of edge with Tutti-Frutti Filling. Beat whipping cream, powdered sugar and almond extract in chilled medium bowl until stiff. Spread over side and top edge of cake. Refrigerate until serving time. Refrigerate any remaining cake. 16 servings.

TUTTI-FRUTTI FILLING

2 egg yolks

⅔ cup sour cream

⅔ cup sugar

1 cup finely chopped pecans

⅔ cup flaked coconut

½ to 1 cup finely chopped raisins

½ to 1 cup finely chopped candied cherries

Mix egg yolks and sour cream in 2-quart saucepan. Stir in sugar. Cook over low heat, stirring constantly, until mixture begins to simmer. Simmer, stirring constantly, until mixture begins to thicken; remove from heat. Stir in remaining ingredients; cool.

Raspberry–White Chocolate Cream Cake

Raspberry Filling (right)
3 ounces white baking bar, chopped
2¼ cups all-purpose flour
1½ cups sugar
2¼ teaspoons baking powder
½ teaspoon salt
1⅔ cups whipping (heavy) cream
3 eggs
1 teaspoon almond extract
White Chocolate Frosting (right)

Prepare Raspberry Filling. Heat oven to 350°. Grease and flour 2 round pans, 8 × 1½ or 9 × 1½ inches. Heat white baking bar over low heat, stirring occasionally, until melted; cool. Mix flour, sugar, baking powder and salt; reserve. Beat whipping cream in chilled large bowl until stiff; reserve. Beat eggs about 5 minutes or until thick and lemon colored; beat in melted baking bar and almond extract.

Fold egg mixture into whipped cream. Add flour mixture, about ½ cup at a time, folding gently after each addition until blended. Pour into pans. Bake 8-inch rounds 35 to 40 minutes, 9-inch rounds 30 to 35 minutes or until toothpick inserted in center comes out clean. Cool 10 minutes; remove from pans. Cool completely on wire racks.

Fill layers with Raspberry Filling. Prepare White Chocolate Frosting; spread over side and top of cake. 16 servings.

RASPBERRY FILLING

¼ cup sugar
2 tablespoons cornstarch
⅛ teaspoon salt
1 cup raspberry-flavored wine cooler or sparkling raspberry juice
1 tablespoon margarine or butter
⅛ teaspoon almond extract
2 or 3 drops red food color, if desired

Mix sugar, cornstarch and salt in 1½-quart saucepan. Stir in wine cooler. Cook over medium heat, stirring constantly, until mixture thickens and boils. Boil and stir 1 minute; remove from heat. Stir in remaining ingredients. Cover and refrigerate until chilled.

WHITE CHOCOLATE FROSTING

3 ounces white baking bar, chopped
3½ cups powdered sugar
3 to 4 tablespoons plus 2 teaspoons raspberry-flavored wine cooler or water
¼ cup margarine or butter, softened
½ teaspoon almond extract

Heat white baking bar over low heat, stirring occasionally, until melted; cool. Beat melted baking bar and remaining ingredients in medium bowl on medium speed until smooth and of spreading consistency. If necessary, stir in additional wine cooler, 1 teaspoon at a time.

Raspberry-White Chocolate Cream Cake

Angel Food Cake with Winter Compote

Winter Compote (right)

1½ cups powdered sugar

1 cup cake flour

1½ cups egg whites (about 12)

1½ teaspoons cream of tartar

1 cup granulated sugar

1½ teaspoons vanilla

½ teaspoon almond extract

¼ teaspoon salt

Prepare Winter Compote. Move oven rack to lowest position. Heat oven to 375°. Mix powdered sugar and flour; reserve. Beat egg whites and cream of tartar in medium bowl on medium speed until foamy. Beat in granulated sugar on high speed, 2 tablespoons at a time, adding vanilla, almond extract and salt with the last addition of sugar; continue beating until stiff and glossy. Do not underbeat.

Sprinkle sugar-flour mixture, ¼ cup at a time, over meringue, folding in just until sugar-flour mixture disappears. Spread batter in ungreased tube pan, 10 × 4 inches. Cut gently through batter with metal spatula.

Bake 30 to 35 minutes or until cracks in cake feel dry and top springs back when touched lightly. Immediately turn pan upside down onto glass bottle or metal funnel. Let hang about 2 hours or until cake is completely cool. Remove cake from pan by sliding a stiff knife or spatula firmly against the side of pan and moving it in up-and-down strokes, being careful not to damage cake. Serve cake with compote. Garnish with plain yogurt or crème fraîche if desired. 16 servings.

WINTER COMPOTE

1 two-inch stick cinnamon

6 whole cloves

¼ cup sugar

½ cup port, sweet red wine or apple juice

½ cup water

2 tablespoons lemon juice

2 packages (6 ounces each) dried mixed fruit

2 bananas, sliced

Tie cinnamon stick and cloves in cheesecloth bag. Heat cheesecloth bag, sugar, port, water and lemon juice to boiling in 2-quart saucepan. Stir in dried fruit. Heat to boiling; reduce heat. Simmer uncovered 10 to 15 minutes, stirring occasionally, until fruit is plump and tender. Refrigerate uncovered about 3 hours, stirring occasionally, until chilled. Remove cheesecloth bag. Stir bananas into fruit mixture until coated with syrup.

🔔 **Instead of baking the angel food cake from scratch, try an angel food cake mix or a purchased cake.**

Bûche de Noël (page 68)

Bûche de Noël

3 eggs

1 cup sugar

1/3 cup water

1 teaspoon vanilla

3/4 cup all-purpose flour

1 teaspoon baking powder

1/4 teaspoon salt

1 cup whipping (heavy) cream

2 tablespoons sugar

*1 1/2 teaspoons freeze-dried or powdered
    instant coffee (dry)*

Chocolate Buttercream Frosting (right)

Meringue Mushrooms (right)

Heat oven to 375°. Line jelly roll pan, 15½ × 10½ × 1 inch, with aluminum foil or waxed paper; grease. Beat eggs in small bowl on high speed about 5 minutes or until very thick and lemon colored. Pour eggs into large bowl; gradually beat in 1 cup sugar. Beat in water and vanilla on low speed. Gradually add flour, baking powder and salt, beating just until batter is smooth. Pour into pan, spreading batter to corners.

Bake 12 to 15 minutes or until toothpick inserted in center comes out clean. Immediately loosen cake from edges of pan; invert onto towel generously sprinkled with powdered sugar. Carefully remove foil. Trim off stiff edges of cake if necessary. While hot, carefully roll cake and towel from narrow end. Cool on wire rack at least 30 minutes.

Beat whipping cream, 2 tablespoons sugar and the coffee in chilled medium bowl until stiff. Unroll cake; remove towel. Spread whipped cream mixture over cake. Roll up cake. For tree stump, cut off a 2-inch diagonal slice from one end. Attach stump to one long side using 1 tablespoon frosting. Frost with Chocolate Buttercream Frosting. Make strokes in frosting to resemble tree bark, using tines of fork. Garnish with Meringue Mushrooms. 10 servings.

CHOCOLATE BUTTERCREAM FROSTING

1/3 cup cocoa

1/3 cup margarine or butter, softened

2 cups powdered sugar

1 1/2 teaspoons vanilla

1 to 2 tablespoons hot water

Thoroughly mix cocoa and margarine in medium bowl. Beat in powdered sugar on low speed. Stir in vanilla and hot water. Beat until smooth and of spreading consistency.

MERINGUE MUSHROOMS

2 egg whites

1/4 teaspoon cream of tartar

1/2 cup sugar

Cocoa

Chocolate Decorator's Frosting (right)

Cover 2 cookie sheets with cooking parchment paper or heavy brown paper. Beat egg whites and cream of tartar in small bowl on medium speed until foamy. Beat in sugar on high speed, 1 tablespoon at a time; continue beating about 5 minutes or until stiff and glossy. Do not underbeat.

Heat oven to 200°. Place meringue in decorating bag with plain tip with 1/4-inch opening (No. 10 or 11). Or place meringue in strong plastic bag; cut off a tiny tip from one corner of bag. Pipe meringue in about 55 mushroom-cap shapes, each 1 to 1 1/4 inches in diameter, onto 1 cookie sheet. Sift cocoa over mushroom caps. Bake 45 to 50 minutes or until firm. Immediately turn mushroom caps upside down and make an indentation in bottom of each cap. Brush off excess cocoa with soft-bristled brush.

Pipe about fifty-five 3/4-inch upright cone shapes onto second cookie sheet for mushroom stems. Stems should have peaks that fit into indentations in mushroom caps. Bake 40 to 45 minutes or until firm; cool. Prepare Chocolate Decorator's Frosting. To assemble mushrooms, spread small amount of frosting in indentation of each mushroom cap; insert peak end of stem into frosting. Place upside down to dry. Store uncovered at room temperature. About 55 candies.

CHOCOLATE DECORATOR'S FROSTING

1 ounce unsweetened chocolate

1 teaspoon margarine or butter

1 cup powdered sugar

1 tablespoon hot water

Heat chocolate and margarine until melted; remove from heat. Beat in powdered sugar and hot water until smooth and of spreading consistency. If necessary, stir in additional hot water, 1 teaspoon at a time.

🔔 **Instead of taking the time to make the tree stump and Meringue Mushrooms, garnish the "log" with chopped pistachio nuts and candied red cherries.**

White Chocolate Bûche de Noël

We've created this contemporary version of the Christmas classic. We hope you enjoy the results!

Tutti-Frutti Filling (page 63)

White Chocolate Bark (right)

Cake from Bûche de Noël (page 68)

White Chocolate Frosting (page 64)

Prepare Tutti-Frutti Filling and White Chocolate Bark.

Prepare and bake cake from Bûche de Noël as directed—except carefully roll cake and towel

from long end. Cool on wire rack at least 30 minutes. While cake is cooling, prepare White Chocolate Frosting.

Unroll cake; remove towel. Spread Tutti-Frutti Filling over cake. Roll up cake. For tree stumps, cut cake as shown in diagram.

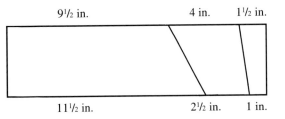

Attach one stump to each long side of cake using 1 tablespoon frosting. You may have to turn the stump around to find the position you prefer. (See photograph, page 70, for placement.) Secure stumps with wooden skewers.

Frost with White Chocolate Frosting, leaving coiled ends unfrosted. While frosting is still soft, and working quickly so chocolate doesn't melt, carefully place White Chocolate Bark lengthwise on the log to resemble tree bark. Decorate with fresh rosemary, pomegranate seeds and lemon peel, and dust with powdered sugar if desired. 10 servings.

WHITE CHOCOLATE BARK

Heat 6 ounces vanilla-flavored candy coating or 1 package (6 ounces) white baking bars until melted. Using metal spatula, spread melted coating in thin layer on 2 ungreased large cookie sheets. Refrigerate coating about 10 minutes or *just* until coating is firm. *Do not refrigerate until hard or coating will break.* If coating becomes too hard, let stand at room temperature.

Using metal pastry scraper or long side of metal spatula, scrape large shavings from coating by pushing scraper away from your body down the cookie sheet. Scraping with different tools will make shavings of different widths. Refrigerate until ready to use.

🔔 **Omit White Chocolate Bark and tree stumps.**

Chocolate Nesselrode Cake

2 cups all-purpose flour

2 cups sugar

¹/₂ cup shortening

³/₄ cup water

³/₄ cup buttermilk

1 teaspoon baking soda

1 teaspoon salt

¹/₂ teaspoon baking powder

1 teaspoon vanilla

2 eggs

*4 ounces unsweetened chocolate, melted
    and cooled*

Nesselrode Filling (right)

Cocoa Fluff (right)

Heat oven to 350°. Grease and flour 3 round pans, 8 × 1¹/₂ inches, or 2 round pans, 9 × 1¹/₂ inches. Beat all ingredients except Nesselrode Filling and Cocoa Fluff in large bowl on low speed 30 seconds, scraping bowl constantly. Beat on high speed 3 minutes, scraping bowl occasionally. Pour into pans.

Bake 30 to 35 minutes or until toothpick inserted in center comes out clean. Remove from pans; cool on wire rack. Fill layers and frost top of cake with Nesselrode Filling. (If using 9-inch pans, split cakes to make 4 layers.) Frost side of cake with Cocoa Fluff. Refrigerate until serving time. Refrigerate any remaining cake. 16 servings.

NESSELRODE FILLING

1 cup whipping (heavy) cream

¹/₄ cup powdered sugar

¹/₄ cup Nesselrode*

Beat whipping cream and powdered sugar in chilled medium bowl until stiff. Fold in Nesselrode.

COCOA FLUFF

1 cup whipping (heavy) cream

¹/₄ cup powdered sugar

2 tablespoons cocoa

Beat all ingredients in chilled medium bowl until stiff.

* ¹/₄ cup finely chopped candied fruit and 1 teaspoon rum flavoring can be substituted for the Nesselrode.

White Chocolate Bûche de Noël (*page 69*)

Hazelnut-Chocolate Torte

6 eggs, separated

1 tablespoon grated orange peel

³/₄ teaspoon ground cinnamon

¹/₂ cup granulated sugar

1 teaspoon cream of tartar

¹/₂ cup granulated sugar

3 cups very finely ground hazelnuts
  (filberts)

¹/₂ cup all-purpose flour

Chocolate Butter Frosting (right)

1 cup whipping (heavy) cream

¹/₂ cup powdered sugar

¹/₄ cup cocoa

2 teaspoons grated orange peel

¹/₂ cup finely chopped hazelnuts (filberts)

Heat oven to 325°. Grease bottom only of spring-form pan, 9 × 3 inches. Line bottom with waxed paper; grease generously. Beat egg yolks, 1 tablespoon orange peel and the cinnamon in small bowl on high speed about 6 minutes or until very thick and light colored. Gradually beat in ¹/₂ cup granulated sugar, 1 tablespoon at a time; reserve. Wash beaters. Beat egg whites and cream of tartar in large bowl on high speed until soft peaks form. Gradually beat in ¹/₂ cup granulated sugar, 1 tablespoon at a time; continue beating until stiff peaks form. Fold egg yolk mixture into meringue. Mix 3 cups ground hazelnuts and the flour. Sprinkle about one-third of the hazelnut mixture over meringue; fold in. Repeat twice with remaining hazelnut mixture. Spread in pan.

Bake 55 to 60 minutes or until toothpick inserted in center comes out clean. Cool in pan on wire rack 15 minutes. Loosen side of cake from pan

with metal spatula. Carefully remove side of pan. Invert cake onto wire rack; remove bottom of pan. Turn cake right side up. Cool cake completely. Wrap tightly and refrigerate at least 4 hours.

Prepare Chocolate Butter Frosting; reserve 1 cup for decorating. Beat whipping cream, powdered sugar and cocoa in chilled small bowl until stiff. Fold in 2 teaspoons orange peel. Carefully split cake horizontally to make 3 layers. (To split, mark side of cake with toothpicks and cut with long, thin straight-edged knife.) Spread 1 layer with half of the whipped cream mixture. Top with second layer; spread with remaining whipped cream mixture. Top with remaining layer. Frost side and top of torte with Chocolate Butter Frosting. Press ¹/₂ cup chopped hazelnuts around side. Place reserved 1 cup frosting in decorating bag with large open star tip (No. 4B). Or place frosting in strong plastic bag; cut off a tip from one corner of bag. Pipe rosettes on top of cake. Garnish with whole hazelnuts if desired. Refrigerate at least 8 hours. Cut with sharp, straight-edged knife. Refrigerate any remaining torte. 16 servings.

CHOCOLATE BUTTER FROSTING

¹/₂ cup (1 stick) margarine or butter,
  softened

3 ounces unsweetened chocolate, melted
  and cooled, or ¹/₂ cup cocoa

3 cups powdered sugar

1 tablespoon brandy, if desired

2 teaspoons vanilla

About 3 tablespoons milk

Mix margarine and chocolate in large bowl. Beat in remaining ingredients until mixture is smooth and of spreading consistency.

Hazelnut Chocolate Torte; Peppermint Cream Pinwheel (page 75)

Fudge-Pecan Torte

*1¹/₂ cups pecan shortbread cookie crumbs
(about twelve 2-inch cookies)*

1¹/₂ cups sugar

1 cup (2 sticks) margarine or butter

1 cup water

*1 pound semisweet chocolate, cut into
pieces*

8 eggs

¹/₂ cup all-purpose flour

1 cup chopped pecans

Soft Cream (below)

Heat oven to 350°. Press cookie crumbs on bottom of ungreased springform pan, 9 × 3 inches.* Bake 10 to 12 minutes or until light golden brown.

Heat sugar, margarine, water and chocolate in 3-quart saucepan over low heat, stirring constantly, until melted and smooth. Beat eggs slightly in large bowl. Gradually stir chocolate mixture into eggs. Stir in flour and pecans. Pour over crust in pan. Bake 1 to 1¹/₄ hours or until toothpick inserted in center comes out clean. Cool 30 minutes.

Loosen torte from side of pan with knife if necessary; remove side of pan. Cover with plastic wrap and refrigerate about 4 hours or until chilled. Serve with Soft Cream. Refrigerate any remaining torte. 24 servings.

SOFT CREAM

1 cup whipping cream

2 tablespoons packed brown sugar

*1 tablespoon praline liqueur or bourbon,
if desired*

Beat all ingredients in chilled medium bowl until soft peaks form.

*If springform pan does not seal tightly, wrap aluminum foil around outside bottom of pan to prevent any dripping onto oven floor.

Espresso-Praline Torte

4 egg whites

¹/₄ teaspoon cream of tartar

1 cup sugar

Almond Praline (below)

1¹/₂ cups whipping (heavy) cream

1 tablespoon sugar

1 teaspoon instant espresso coffee (dry)

¹/₄ teaspoon almond extract

Cover 3 cookie sheets with cooking parchment paper or heavy brown paper. Heat oven to 225°. Beat egg whites and cream of tartar in large bowl on medium speed until foamy. Beat in 1 cup sugar, 1 tablespoon at a time on high speed; continue beating until stiff and glossy. Do not underbeat. Shape meringue into three 8-inch circles on brown paper. Bake 1 hour. Turn oven off and leave meringues in oven with door closed 1 hour. Finishing cooling at room temperature. Remove from paper to wire rack with spatula.

Prepare Almond Praline. Beat whipping cream, 1 tablespoon sugar, the espresso and almond extract in chilled medium bowl until stiff. Reserve 1 to 2 tablespoons praline for garnish. Fold remaining praline into whipped cream. Stack meringues, spreading whipped cream mixture between layers and over top. Sprinkle with reserved praline. Refrigerate at least 2 hours. Cover and refrigerate any remaining torte. 12 servings.

ALMOND PRALINE

¹/₂ cup sliced almonds

¹/₄ cup sugar

Grease cookie sheet. Cook ingredients in 1-quart saucepan over low heat, stirring occasionally, until sugar is melted and golden brown. Pour onto cookie sheet; cool. Crush coarsely in blender, or place in plastic bag and crush with wooden mallet.

Peppermint Cream Pinwheel

You can make this pretty dessert even more festive by using a decorating bag to pipe the whipped cream over the top of the pinwheel. Try a star tip and pipe the whipped cream to look like a snowflake.

4 eggs

1 cup granulated sugar

1/3 cup water

1 teaspoon vanilla

3/4 cup all-purpose flour or 1 cup cake flour

1/4 cup cocoa

1 teaspoon baking powder

1/4 teaspoon salt

Powdered sugar

2 1/2 cups whipping (heavy) cream

1/2 cup crushed hard peppermint candies (about 18 candies)

Heat oven to 375°. Line jelly roll pan, 15 1/2 × 10 1/2 × 1 inch, with aluminum foil, waxed paper or cooking parchment paper; grease aluminum foil or waxed paper generously. Beat eggs in small bowl on high speed about 5 minutes or until very thick and lemon colored. Pour eggs into medium bowl. Gradually beat in granulated sugar. Beat in water and vanilla on low speed. Gradually add flour, cocoa, baking powder and salt, beating just until batter is smooth. Pour into pan, spreading batter to corners.

Bake 12 to 15 minutes or until toothpick inserted in center comes out clean. Immediately loosen cake from edges of pan; invert onto towel generously sprinkled with powdered sugar. Carefully remove foil. Trim off stiff edges of cake if necessary. While hot, carefully roll cake and towel from narrow end. Cool on wire rack at least 30 minutes.

Beat whipping cream in chilled large bowl until stiff. Reserve 2 cups whipped cream. Fold crushed candies into remaining whipped cream. Unroll cake and remove towel. Spread cake with peppermint topping. Cut cake lengthwise evenly into 6 strips. Roll up one of the strips, and place it cut side up in center of 10-inch serving plate. Coil remaining strips tightly around center roll, with topping side toward center. Smooth top with spatula if necessary. Frost top and side of torte with reserved whipped cream. Drizzle with chocolate syrup or sprinkle with crushed hard peppermint candies if desired. Refrigerate at least 2 hours. Refrigerate any remaining dessert. 12 servings.

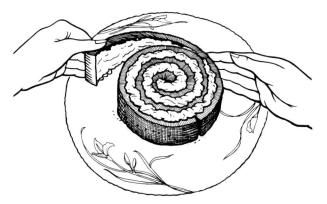

Roll up one of the strips and place on the serving plate. Coil remaining strips tightly around center roll.

COCONUT CREAM PINWHEEL: Substitute 1 cup flaked coconut for the peppermint candies. Sprinkle pinwheel with additional coconut if desired.

HAZELNUT CREAM PINWHEEL: Substitute 3/4 cup finely chopped hazelnuts (filberts), toasted, for the peppermint candies; reserve 1/4 cup to sprinkle on top.

🌲 **Substitute 1 container (12 ounces) frozen whipped topping for the whipping cream.**

Triple Ginger Pound Cake

Pound cake is one of the most versatile cakes you can keep on hand. It freezes well, tightly covered, up to 4 months.

2³/₄ cups sugar

1¹/₄ cups (2¹/₂ sticks) margarine or butter, softened

1 tablespoon grated gingerroot

1 teaspoon vanilla

5 eggs

3 cups all-purpose flour

2 teaspoons ground ginger

1 teaspoon baking powder

¹/₄ teaspoon salt

1 cup milk or evaporated milk

¹/₂ cup finely chopped crystallized ginger

Pineapple Cream (right)

Heat oven to 350°. Grease and flour 12-cup bundt cake pan or tube pan, 10 × 4 inches, or 2 loaf pans, 9 × 5 × 3 inches. Beat sugar, margarine, gingerroot, vanilla and eggs in large bowl on low speed 30 seconds, scraping bowl constantly. Beat on high speed 5 minutes, scraping bowl occasionally. Mix flour, ground ginger, baking powder and salt. Beat into sugar mixture alternately with milk on low speed. Fold in crystallized ginger until evenly mixed. Spread in pan(s).

Bake bundt or tube pan 1 hour 10 minutes to 1 hour 20 minutes, loaf pans 1 hour to 1 hour 10 minutes or until toothpick inserted in center comes out clean. Cool 20 minutes; remove from pan(s). Cool completely on wire rack. Serve with Pineapple Cream. 24 servings.

PINEAPPLE CREAM

2 cups whipping (heavy) cream

2 tablespoons powdered sugar

1 can (20 ounces) crushed pineapple, well drained

Beat whipping cream and powdered sugar in chilled large bowl on high speed until stiff. Fold in pineapple. Refrigerate any remaining Pineapple Cream.

COCONUT POUND CAKE: Omit gingerroot, ground ginger, crystallized ginger and Pineapple Cream. Fold 1 tablespoon coconut extract and 1 cup flaked coconut into batter before spreading in pan(s).

GRATED CHOCOLATE POUND CAKE: Omit gingerroot, ground ginger, crystallized ginger and Pineapple Cream. Fold 2 ounces unsweetened chocolate, grated, and ¹/₂ cup chopped nuts into batter before spreading in pan(s).

🔔 **Instead of making the Pineapple Cream, serve the pound cake slices with pineapple yogurt.**

Pistachio-Lime Cake

Pistachio-Lime Cake

3 cups Bisquick® Original baking mix

¹/₂ cup granulated sugar

1 cup water

¹/₂ cup vegetable oil

1 teaspoon grated lime or lemon peel

4 eggs

1 package (4-serving size) pistachio instant pudding and pie filling

1 cup coarsely chopped pistachio nuts or pecans

1¹/₃ cups powdered sugar

1 to 2 tablespoons lime or lemon juice

Heat oven to 350°. Grease and flour 12-cup bundt cake pan. Beat baking mix, granulated sugar, water, oil, lime peel, eggs and pudding and pie filling (dry) on low speed 30 seconds, scraping bowl constantly. Beat on medium speed 4 minutes, scraping bowl occasionally. Stir in nuts. Pour into pan.

Bake 40 to 45 minutes or until toothpick inserted in center comes out clean. Cool 10 minutes; remove from pan. Cool completely. Mix powdered sugar and lime juice until smooth; drizzle over cake. Sprinkle with grated lime peel if desired. 16 servings.

Date-Pecan Upside-down Cake

¹/₄ cup (¹/₂ stick) plus 2 tablespoons margarine or butter

²/₃ cup packed brown sugar

12 pitted dates

1 cup coarsely chopped pecans

1 cup all-purpose flour

³/₄ cup granulated sugar

¹/₃ cup shortening

³/₄ cup milk

1¹/₂ teaspoons baking powder

1 teaspoon vanilla

¹/₂ teaspoon salt

1 egg

Whipped cream

Heat oven to 350°. Heat margarine in 10-inch ovenproof skillet or square pan, 9 × 9 × 2 inches, in oven until melted. Sprinkle evenly with brown sugar. Arrange dates on top so that each serving will include one date. Sprinkle with pecans.

Beat remaining ingredients except whipped cream in large bowl on low speed 30 seconds, scraping bowl constantly. Beat on high speed 3 minutes, scraping bowl occasionally. Pour evenly over dates and pecans.

Bake 40 to 45 minutes or until toothpick inserted in center comes out clean. Loosen side of cake from skillet with knife. Invert onto heatproof platter; leave skillet over cake a few minutes. Serve warm with whipped cream. 12 servings.

Wild Rice–Nut Cake

2¹/₂ cups all-purpose flour

2 cups packed brown sugar

³/₄ cup (1¹/₂ sticks) margarine or butter, softened

1 cup buttermilk

1 teaspoon baking powder

1 teaspoon baking soda

1 teaspoon vanilla

¹/₂ teaspoon salt

¹/₂ teaspoon ground nutmeg

¹/₂ teaspoon maple flavoring

3 eggs

2 cups cooked wild rice, well drained

2 cups chopped nuts, toasted, if desired

Maple Whipped Cream (below)

Move oven rack to lowest position. Heat oven to 350°. Generously grease and flour 12-cup bundt cake pan or tube pan, 10 × 4 inches. Beat all ingredients except wild rice, nuts and Maple Whipped Cream in large bowl on low speed 30 seconds, scraping bowl constantly. Beat on high speed 3 minutes, scraping bowl occasionally. Stir in wild rice and nuts. Pour into pan.

Bake 55 to 60 minutes or until toothpick inserted in center comes out clean. Cool 20 minutes. Invert onto wire rack; cool completely. Serve with Maple Whipped Cream or Divine Caramel Sauce (page 246) if desired. 24 servings.

MAPLE WHIPPED CREAM

2 cups whipping (heavy) cream

¹/₄ cup packed brown sugar

¹/₂ teaspoon maple flavoring

Beat all ingredients in chilled medium bowl until soft peaks form.

Jeweled Fruitcake

³/₄ cup all-purpose flour

³/₄ cup sugar

¹/₂ teaspoon baking powder

¹/₂ teaspoon salt

1¹/₂ teaspoons vanilla

3 eggs

2 cups dried apricots (about 11 ounces)

2 cups pitted dates (about 12 ounces)

1¹/₂ cups Brazil nuts (about 8 ounces)

1 cup red and green candied pineapple, chopped (about 7 ounces)

1 cup red and green maraschino cherries, drained (about 12 ounces)

Heat oven to 300°. Line loaf pan, 9 × 5 × 3 or 8¹/₂ × 4¹/₂ × 2¹/₂ inches, with aluminum foil; grease. Mix flour, sugar, baking powder, salt, vanilla and eggs in large bowl until smooth. Stir in remaining ingredients. Spread in pan. Bake about 1³/₄ hours or until toothpick inserted in center comes out clean. If necessary, cover with aluminum foil during last 30 minutes of baking to prevent excessive browning. Remove from pan; cool on wire rack. Wrap in plastic wrap; store in refrigerator no longer than 2 months. 32 servings.

PETITE FRUITCAKES: Line 24 medium muffin cups, 2¹/₂ × 1¹/₄ inches, with foil liners. Divide batter evenly among cups (about ¹/₃ cup each). Bake 35 to 40 minutes or until toothpick inserted in center comes out clean. Remove from pan; cool on wire rack. 24 servings.

MINI LOAVES: Generously grease 7 or 8 miniature loaf pans, 4¹/₂ × 2³/₄ × 1¹/₄ inches, or line with aluminum foil and grease. Divide batter evenly among pans (about 1 cup each). Bake about 1 hour or until toothpick inserted in center comes out clean. Remove from pans; cool on wire rack. 7 or 8 mini loaves.

Festive Fruitcake Bars

1 cup all-purpose flour

³/₄ cup packed brown sugar

¹/₂ cup (1 stick) margarine or butter, softened

1 teaspoon grated orange peel

¹/₂ teaspoon baking soda

¹/₂ teaspoon ground cinnamon

¹/₄ teaspoon salt

1 egg

¹/₄ cup all-purpose flour

16 ounces fruitcake mix

8 ounces dates, cut up

1 cup chopped pecans or chopped filberts

Orange Glaze (below)

Heat oven to 350°. Grease and flour rectangular pan, 13 × 9 × 2 inches. Mix 1 cup flour, the brown sugar, margarine, orange peel, baking soda, cinnamon, salt and egg in large bowl. Mix ¹/₄ cup flour, the fruitcake mix, dates and pecans; stir into brown sugar mixture. Spread in pan. Bake about 35 minutes or until toothpick inserted in center comes out clean; cool. Drizzle with Orange Glaze. Cut into about 2 × ¹/₂-inch bars. 3 dozen bars.

ORANGE GLAZE

¹/₃ cup sugar

2 tablespoons orange juice

Heat ingredients in 1-quart saucepan over medium heat, stirring occasionally, until mixture thickens slightly.

Black and Gold Fruitcake

3 cups Bisquick® Original baking mix

1 cup sugar

6 eggs

1 teaspoon almond extract

1¹/₂ cups dried apricots (about 8 ounces)

1 cup candied pineapple

1 cup golden raisins

1 teaspoon ground cinnamon

2 teaspoons vanilla

3 ounces semisweet chocolate, melted and cooled

1 cup candied cherries

2 packages (8 ounces each) pitted dates

Heat oven to 300°. Grease and flour two 6-cup bundt cake pans or ring molds, or 2 loaf pans, 8¹/₂ × 4¹/₂ × 2¹/₂ or 9 × 5 × 3 inches. Beat baking mix, sugar and eggs in large bowl on low speed until blended. Beat on medium speed 2 minutes. Pour half of the batter into large bowl; beat in almond extract until smooth. Stir in apricots, pineapple and raisins.

Beat cinnamon, vanilla and chocolate into remaining half of batter, using same beaters, until smooth. Stir in cherries and dates. Divide chocolate batter between pans; spread evenly. Divide gold batter between pans, carefully spooning over chocolate batter; spread evenly. Bake bundt pans about 1 hour 20 minutes to 1 hour 30 minutes, loaf pans about 1 hour 30 minutes to 1 hour 40 minutes or until toothpick inserted in center comes out clean. Cool 5 minutes. Invert bundt cakes onto wire rack; turn loaves out of pans and place top sides up on wire rack. Cool completely. Wrap tightly and refrigerate 1 day before slicing. 2 loaves (16 slices each).

Black and Gold Fruitcake; Petite Fruitcakes (page 79)

Pumpkin-Pecan Cheesecake

1¹/₄ cups pecan shortbread cookie crumbs (about ten 2-inch cookies)

2 tablespoons margarine or butter, melted

3 packages (8 ounces each) cream cheese, softened

1 cup sugar

1 teaspoon ground cinnamon

1 teaspoon ground ginger

¹/₂ teaspoon ground cloves

1 can (16 ounces) pumpkin

4 eggs

2 tablespoons sugar

16 pecan halves

³/₄ cup whipping (heavy) cream

Heat oven to 350°. Mix cookie crumbs and margarine. Press evenly on bottom of ungreased springform pan, 9 × 3 inches. Bake 10 minutes; cool. Reduce oven temperature to 300°. Beat cream cheese, 1 cup sugar, the cinnamon, ginger and cloves in large bowl on medium speed until smooth and fluffy. Beat in pumpkin. Beat in eggs, one at a time, on low speed. Pour over baked layer. Bake about 1¹/₄ hours or until center is firm. Cover and refrigerate at least 3 hours until chilled.

Cook 2 tablespoons sugar and the pecan halves over medium heat, stirring frequently, until sugar is melted and pecans are coated. Immediately spread on dinner plate or aluminum foil; cool. Carefully break nuts apart to separate if necessary.

Loosen cheesecake from side of pan; remove side of pan. Beat whipping cream in chilled small bowl until stiff. Serve cheesecake with whipped cream and garnish with pecans. Refrigerate any remaining cheesecake. 16 servings.

Chocolate Swirl Cheesecake with Raspberry Topping

The remaining Thick Yogurt is delicious spread on toast or bagels, or to top fresh fruit.

2 cups Thick Yogurt (right)

4 chocolate wafers, crushed (about 1/4 cup)

1 package (8 ounces) cream cheese, softened

2/3 cup sugar

1/4 cup milk

2 tablespoons all-purpose flour

2 teaspoons vanilla

3 egg whites

1 tablespoon cocoa

1 teaspoon chocolate extract

Raspberry Topping (right)

Prepare Thick Yogurt. Heat oven to 300°. Spray springform pan, 9 × 3 inches, with nonstick cooking spray. Sprinkle chocolate wafer crumbs on bottom of pan. Beat Thick Yogurt and cream cheese in medium bowl on medium speed until smooth. Add sugar, milk, flour, vanilla and egg whites. Beat on medium speed about 2 minutes or until smooth.

Place 1 cup batter in small bowl. Beat in cocoa and chocolate extract until blended. Carefully spread vanilla batter over crumbs in pan. Drop chocolate batter by spoonfuls onto vanilla batter. Swirl through batter with metal spatula for marbled effect, being careful not to touch bottom. Bake 1 hour. Turn off oven; leave cheesecake in oven 30 minutes. Remove from oven; cool 15 minutes. Prepare Raspberry Topping; spread over cheesecake. Cover and refrigerate at least 3 hours. Loosen cheesecake from side of pan; remove side of pan. Refrigerate any remaining cheesecake. 12 servings.

THICK YOGURT

Line 6-inch strainer with basket-style paper coffee filter or double-thickness cheesecloth. Place strainer over bowl. Spoon 4 cups plain yogurt into strainer. Cover strainer and bowl and refrigerate at least 12 hours, draining liquid from bowl occasionally.

RASPBERRY TOPPING

1 package (10 ounces) frozen raspberries, thawed, drained and juice reserved

1/4 cup sugar

2 tablespoons cornstarch

Add enough water to reserved juice to measure 1 1/4 cups. Mix sugar and cornstarch in 1 1/2-quart saucepan. Stir in juice mixture and raspberries. Heat to boiling over medium heat, stirring frequently. Boil and stir 1 minute; cool.

Chocolate Swirl Cheesecake with Raspberry Topping

Cheesecake Squares

1 cup all-purpose flour

1/2 cup (1 stick) margarine or butter, softened

1/4 cup sugar

1 tablespoon grated lemon peel

1 egg yolk

5 packages (8 ounces each) cream cheese, softened

1 3/4 cups sugar

3 tablespoons all-purpose flour

1 tablespoon grated orange peel

1 tablespoon grated lemon peel

1/4 teaspoon salt

5 eggs

2 egg yolks

1/4 cup whipping (heavy) cream

3/4 cup whipping (heavy) cream

1/2 cup slivered almonds, toasted, if desired

Move oven rack to lowest position. Heat oven to 400°. Lightly grease rectangular pan, 13 × 9 × 2 inches. Mix 1 cup flour, the margarine, 1/4 cup sugar, 1 tablespoon lemon peel and 1 egg yolk with hands. Press evenly in bottom of pan. Bake about 15 minutes or until golden brown; cool.

Increase oven to 475°. Beat cream cheese, 1 3/4 cups sugar, 3 tablespoons flour, the orange peel, 1 tablespoon lemon peel, the salt and 2 of the eggs in large bowl until smooth. Continue beating, adding remaining eggs and 2 egg yolks, one at a time, until blended. Beat in 1/4 cup whipping cream on low speed. Pour over baked layer. Bake 15 minutes.

Reduce oven temperature to 200°. Bake about 45 minutes or until center is set. Turn off oven and leave cheesecake in oven 15 minutes. Remove from oven; cool 15 minutes. Cover and refrigerate at least 12 hours but no longer than 48 hours.

Beat 3/4 cup whipping cream in chilled bowl until stiff. Spread whipped cream over top of cheesecake. Sprinkle with almonds. Cut into 2 1/2-inch squares. Refrigerate any remaining squares. 20 squares.

Favorite Pastry

One-Crust Pie and Baked Pie Shell

9-inch

1/3 cup plus 1 tablespoon shortening or 1/3 cup lard

1 cup all-purpose flour

1/4 teaspoon salt

2 to 3 tablespoons cold water

Two-Crust Pie

9-inch

2/3 cup plus 2 tablespoons shortening or 2/3 cup lard

2 cups all-purpose flour

1 teaspoon salt

4 to 5 tablespoons cold water

Cut shortening into flour and salt until particles are size of small peas. Sprinkle in water, 1 tablespoon at a time, tossing with fork until all flour is moistened and pastry almost cleans side of bowl (1 to 2 teaspoons water can be added if necessary).

Gather pastry into a ball. Shape into flattened round on lightly floured cloth-covered board. (For Two-Crust Pie, divide pastry in half and shape into 2 rounds.)

Roll pastry 2 inches larger than inverted pie plate with floured cloth-covered rolling pin. Fold pastry into fourths; place in pie plate. Unfold and ease into plate, pressing firmly against bottom and side.

For One-Crust Pie: Trim overhanging edge of pastry 1 inch from rim of plate. Fold and roll pastry under, even with plate; flute (below). Fill and bake as directed in recipe.

For Baked Pie Shell: Heat oven to 475°. Trim overhanging edge of pastry 1 inch from rim of plate. Fold and roll pastry under, even with plate; flute (below). Prick bottom and side thoroughly with fork. Bake 8 to 10 minutes or until light brown; cool.

For Two-Crust Pie: Turn desired filling into pastry-lined pie plate. Trim overhanging edge of pastry ¹/₂ inch from rim of plate. Roll other round of pastry. Fold into fourths and cut slits so steam can escape.

Place over filling and unfold. Trim overhanging edge of pastry 1 inch from rim of plate. Fold and roll top edge under lower edge, pressing on rim to seal; flute (below). Or if desired, prepare Lattice Top (right).

Fluted Pastry Edge: Place index finger of one hand on inside of pastry edge and knuckles (or thumb and index finger) of other hand on outside. Pinch pastry into V shape; pinch again to sharpen. Continue around pastry edge.

Lattice Top: Prepare pastry as directed for Two-Crust Pie (left)—except leave 1-inch overhang on lower crust. After rolling circle for top crust, cut into strips about ¹/₂ inch wide. (Use a pastry wheel for decorative strips.)

Place 5 to 7 strips (depending on size of pie) across filling in pie plate. Weave a cross-strip through center by first folding back every other strip going the other way. Continue weaving until lattice is complete, folding back alternate strips each time cross-strip is added. (To save time, do not weave strips. Simply lay second half of strips across first strips.) Trim ends of strips.

Fold trimmed edge of lower crust over ends of strips, building up a high edge. Seal and flute (left). (A juicy fruit pie with a lattice top is more likely to bubble over than a two-crust pie, so be sure to build up a high pastry edge.)

Note: If possible, hook fluted edge over edge of pie plate to prevent shrinking and help pastry retain its shape.

Use your food processor for speedy pastry. Measure 2 tablespoons water (for One-Crust Pie) or 4 tablespoons water (for Two-Crust Pie) into small bowl. Place shortening, flour and salt in food processor. Cover and process, using quick on and off motions, until mixture is crumbly. With food processor running, pour water all at once through feed tube just until dough leaves side of bowl. (Dough should not form a ball.) Continue as directed above.

Mincemeat-Pear Pie

Pastry for 9-inch One-Crust Pie (page 84)

1/4 cup all-purpose flour

1/3 cup sugar

1/8 teaspoon salt

1 tablespoon margarine or butter

1/4 cup water

2 tablespoons red cinnamon candies

1 jar (20 1/2 ounces) prepared mincemeat (about 2 cups)

3 medium pears or tart apples

Heat oven to 425°. Prepare pastry. If desired, use pastry scraps to make tiny cutouts and overlap around edge of pastry. Sprinkle 2 tablespoons of the flour in pastry-lined pie plate. Mix remaining flour, the sugar, salt and margarine until crumbly. Heat water and cinnamon candies, stirring constantly, until candies are dissolved; remove from heat. Spread mincemeat over pastry in pie plate.

Peel pears; cut into fourths. Cut fourths into wedges, 1/2 inch thick at outer side. Arrange pear wedges on mincemeat, overlapping wedges in 2 circles. Sprinkle with sugar mixture. Spoon cinnamon syrup over top, moistening as much of sugar mixture as possible.

Cover edge of pastry with 2- to 3-inch strip of aluminum foil to prevent excessive browning; remove foil last 15 minutes of baking. Bake 40 to 50 minutes or until crust is golden brown. 8 servings.

Della Robbia Apple Pie

Pastry for 9-inch Two-Crust Pie (page 84)

4 cups diced peeled tart apples (about 4 medium)

1/4 cup lemon juice

1/2 cup chopped dates

1/2 cup maraschino cherries, cut into fourths

1/2 cup coarsely chopped walnuts

1/2 cup sugar

1/4 cup all-purpose flour

1/4 cup half-and-half

1/4 teaspoon salt

Traditional Marzipan (page 52) or Della Robbia Wreath (below)

Heat oven to 425°. Prepare pastry. Mix apples and lemon juice in large bowl. Stir in remaining ingredients except Traditional Marzipan. Turn into pastry-lined pie plate. Cover with top crust that has slits cut in it; seal and flute. Cover edge with 2- to 3-inch strip of aluminum foil to prevent excessive browning; remove foil during last 15 minutes of baking. Bake 50 to 60 minutes or until crust is brown and juice begins to bubble through slits in crust; cool. Garnish with wreath of marzipan fruits and cranberries, hazelnuts and sprigs of fresh rosemary if desired. 8 servings.

DELLA ROBBIA WREATH

Mold process cheese into small apple and pear shapes. Sprinkle tops with red sugar. Arrange cheese fruits, green and red maraschino cherries and dates on pie in the shape of a wreath.

Mincemeat-Pear Pie; Classic Pumpkin Pie (page 88) with Divine Caramel Sauce (page 246)

Cranberry-Apple Pie

A nice blend of flavors for those who find cranberries alone a bit too intense.

Pastry for 9-inch Two-Crust Pie
  (page 84)

1³/₄ to 2 cups sugar

¹/₄ cup all-purpose flour

*3 cups sliced peeled tart apples (about 3
  medium)*

*2 cups fresh or frozen (thawed)
  cranberries*

2 tablespoons margarine or butter

Heat oven to 425°. Prepare pastry. Mix sugar and flour. Arrange half of the apples in pastry-lined pie plate. Top with cranberries. Sprinkle sugar mixture over cranberries. Top with remaining apples. Dot with margarine. Cover with top crust that has slits cut in it; seal and flute. Cover edge with 2- to 3-inch strip of aluminum foil to prevent excessive browning; remove foil during last 15 minutes of baking. Bake 40 to 50 minutes or until crust is brown and juice begins to bubble through slits in crust. Serve warm with ice cream if desired. 8 servings.

Classic Pumpkin Pie

Pastry for 9-inch One-Crust Pie
  (page 84)

2 eggs

¹/₂ cup sugar

1 teaspoon ground cinnamon

¹/₂ teaspoon salt

¹/₂ teaspoon ground ginger

¹/₈ teaspoon ground cloves

1 can (16 ounces) pumpkin

1 can (12 ounces) evaporated milk

Heat oven to 425°. Prepare pastry. Beat eggs slightly with hand beater or wire whisk in medium bowl. Beat in remaining ingredients. To prevent spilling, place pastry-lined pie plate on oven rack. Pour filling into pie plate. Bake 15 minutes.

Reduce oven temperature to 350°. Bake about 45 minutes longer or until knife inserted in center comes out clean. Refrigerate about 4 hours or until chilled. Serve with whipped cream or ice cream and Divine Caramel Sauce (page 246) if desired. Refrigerate any remaining pie. 8 servings.

PRALINE PUMPKIN PIE: Prepare pie as directed—except decrease second bake time to 35 minutes. Mix ¹/₃ cup packed brown sugar, ¹/₃ cup chopped pecans and 1 tablespoon margarine or butter, softened. Sprinkle over pie. Bake about 10 minutes longer or until knife inserted in center comes out clean.

🎄 **The pastry can be prepared, rolled and shaped in the pie plate the day before baking. Cover tightly with plastic wrap and refrigerate. Uncover and pour in filling when ready to bake.**

Peppermint Stick Pie

For a refreshing change of pace, try serving this dessert frozen.

Chocolate Cookie Crust (right)
32 large marshmallows
1/2 cup milk
1 teaspoon vanilla
1/8 teaspoon salt
6 drops peppermint extract
6 drops red or green food color
1 1/2 cups whipping (heavy) cream
2 tablespoons crushed hard peppermint candies

Prepare Chocolate Cookie Crust. Heat marshmallows and milk in 3-quart saucepan over low heat, stirring constantly, just until marshmallows are melted; remove from heat. Stir in vanilla, salt, peppermint extract and food color. Refrigerate about 20 minutes, stirring occasionally, until mixture mounds slightly when dropped from a spoon.

Beat whipping cream in chilled medium bowl until stiff. Stir marshmallow mixture until blended; fold into whipped cream. Mound into crust. Refrigerate at least 12 hours. Just before serving, sprinkle with crushed candies. Serve with whipped cream if desired. 8 servings.

CHOCOLATE COOKIE CRUST

1 1/2 cups chocolate wafer crumbs
1/4 cup (1/2 stick) margarine or butter, melted

Heat oven to 350°. Mix ingredients. Press firmly against bottom and side of ungreased pie plate, 9 × 1 1/4 inches. Bake 10 minutes; cool.

GRASSHOPPER PIE: Omit peppermint extract and peppermint candy. Stir 1/2 cup crème de menthe and 3 tablespoons white crème de cacao into marshmallow mixture after refrigerating.

INDIVIDUAL TARTS. Omit Chocolate Cookie Crust. Line 12 medium muffin cups, 2 1/2 × 1 1/4 inches, with paper baking cups. Heat 1 package (12 ounces) semisweet chocolate chips (2 cups) and 2 tablespoons shortening over medium heat 3 to 4 minutes, stirring constantly, until chocolate is melted. Swirl 1 tablespoon chocolate in each cup with back of spoon, coating bottom and side. Refrigerate until firm. Fill in thin areas with remaining chocolate. Refrigerate until firm. Carefully remove paper cups from chocolate shells. Return shells to muffin cups. Divide filling among shells. Refrigerate 2 to 3 hours or until set. Garnish with whipped cream if desired. 12 servings.

Chocolate Nesselrode Pie

Pastry for 9-inch Baked Pie Shell (page 84)

6 egg yolks, slightly beaten

1/2 cup sugar

1/4 cup cornstarch

2 cups milk

4 teaspoons unflavored gelatin

1/2 teaspoon salt

1 bar (4 ounces) sweet cooking chocolate, grated

1 teaspoon vanilla

1/2 teaspoon rum flavoring

1 jar (10 ounces) Nesselrode

3 cups whipping (heavy) cream

Bake pie shell; cool. Mix egg yolks, sugar, cornstarch, milk, gelatin and salt in 2-quart saucepan. Cook over medium heat, stirring constantly, until mixture thickens and boils. Boil and stir 1 minute. Pour 1 1/2 cups of the hot mixture into a bowl; cool completely. Reserve 2 tablespoons of the chocolate for topping. Stir remaining chocolate and the vanilla into hot mixture in saucepan; cool.

Line pie plate, 9 × 1 1/4 inches, with waxed paper. Stir rum flavoring and Nesselrode into 1 1/2 cups mixture in bowl. Beat 2 cups of the whipping cream in chilled medium bowl until stiff. Fold half of the whipped cream into Nesselrode mixture and half into chocolate mixture. Pour chocolate mixture into baked pie shell. Pour Nesselrode mixture onto waxed paper in pie plate. Refrigerate both mixtures at least 2 hours until firm.

Just before serving, loosen edge of Nesselrode layer from waxed paper with spatula; invert onto chocolate layer and remove waxed paper. Beat remaining 1 cup whipping cream in chilled small bowl until stiff. Spread over pie, covering surface completely. Sprinkle with reserved chocolate. Serve immediately. Refrigerate any remaining pie. 8 servings.

Brownie Fudge Pie

Specialty ice cream stores are a bonanza of ideas, and choosing just the right flavor for this pie can be a family outing. Peppermint, peanut butter, cookies and cream, raspberry sherbet, or frozen yogurt are wonderful for starters. Have fun choosing the ice cream for this pie—the more imaginative the better!

Hot Fudge Sauce (page 246)

4 eggs

1/4 cup (1/2 stick) margarine or butter, melted

1 bar (4 ounces) sweet cooking chocolate, melted and cooled

1/2 cup packed brown sugar

1/2 cup granulated sugar

1/2 cup Bisquick® Original baking mix

3/4 cup chopped nuts

1/2 gallon any flavor ice cream, softened

Prepare Hot Fudge Sauce; cool. Heat oven to 350°. Grease pie plate, 9 × 1 1/4 inches. Beat eggs, margarine and chocolate until smooth, 10 seconds in blender on high speed or 30 seconds with hand beater. Add sugars and baking mix. Beat until smooth, 1 minute in blender on high speed, stopping blender occasionally to scrape sides, or 2 minutes with hand beater. Pour into pie plate. Sprinkle with nuts.

Bake about 35 minutes or until knife inserted in center comes out clean. Cool completely in pie plate on wire rack. Spread 1 1/2 cups Hot Fudge Sauce over pie. Spoon ice cream onto pie, mounding and packing firmly. Freeze at least 4 hours until firm. Heat remaining sauce; serve with pie. Freeze any remaining pie. 8 servings.

Brownie Fudge Pie

Stained Glass Tart

Cookie Tart Pastry (right)
¼ cup sliced almonds
1 package (4-serving size) French vanilla instant pudding and pie filling
1 cup milk
1 cup whipping (heavy) cream
½ teaspoon almond extract
1 cup whipping (heavy) cream
Assorted colors of jellies and jams

Heat oven to 400°. Prepare Cookie Tart Pastry as directed—except add almonds. Bake 12 to 14 minutes. Cool completely.

Beat pudding and pie filling (dry), milk, 1 cup whipping cream and the almond extract on low speed until smooth. Pour into baked pastry; spread evenly. Beat 1 cup whipping cream in chilled medium bowl until stiff. Place whipped cream in decorating bag fitted with open star tip (No. 5). Or place whipped cream in strong plastic bag; cut off ½-inch tip from one corner of bag.

Pipe 8 teardrop-shaped loops, triangles or a combination of both onto pudding mixture as shown below in diagram (be sure that whipped cream is completely sealed to pudding mixture). Stir jelly until smooth; spoon 1 tablespoon jelly into each loop. Spoon jelly into areas between loops around edge of pan if desired. Refrigerate at least 1 hour but no longer than 4 hours. Refrigerate any remaining tart. 8 servings.

COOKIE TART PASTRY

1½ cups all-purpose flour
⅔ cup margarine or butter, softened
¼ cup packed brown sugar
1 egg

Heat oven to 400°. Mix all ingredients until dough forms. Press firmly and evenly against bottom and side of ungreased 11-inch tart pan with removable bottom. Bake 10 to 12 minutes or until light brown.

⚠ **Prepare the crust and filling up to 24 hours before serving; cover the filling by placing plastic wrap directly over the top. Add whipped cream and jelly within 4 hours of serving.**

Apricot-Chocolate Wafer Tart

This luscious tangy tart is spectacular served with whipped cream and chocolate leaves.

1½ cups chocolate wafer crumbs
¼ cup (½ stick) margarine or butter, melted
2 packages (6 ounces each) dried apricots
½ cup sugar
1 cup orange juice
1 cup whipping (heavy) cream, whipped

Heat oven to 350°. Mix crumbs and margarine; reserve 3 tablespoons for topping. Press remaining crumb mixture against bottom and side of 9-inch tart pan with removable bottom. Bake 10 minutes; cool.

Cook apricots, sugar and orange juice in 2-quart saucepan over medium heat 10 minutes, stirring occasionally, until apricots are soft. Place apricot mixture in blender or food processor. Cover and blend, or process, until smooth; cool 15 minutes. Fold apricot mixture into whipped cream; spoon into tart shell. Sprinkle with reserved chocolate wafer crumbs.

Cover and refrigerate 1 hour. Remove rim of pan before serving. Refrigerate any remaining tart. 8 servings.

Cranberry–Sour Cream Tart

The filling in this tart has a lovely, light pink color from the cranberries.

> *Cookie Tart Pastry (page 92)*
>
> *1 cup sugar*
>
> *1 tablespoon plus 1¹/₂ teaspoons cornstarch*
>
> *¹/₂ teaspoon ground cardamom*
>
> *¹/₈ teaspoon salt*
>
> *1¹/₂ cups sour cream*
>
> *1¹/₂ cups dried cranberries or dried cherries*
>
> *1 tablespoon lemon juice*
>
> *3 egg yolks*
>
> *Meringue (right)*

Mix sugar, cornstarch, cardamom and salt in 2-quart saucepan. Stir in sour cream. Stir in cranberries, lemon juice and egg yolks. Cook over medium heat, constantly stirring, until mixture thickens and boils. Boil and stir 1 minute. Pour into baked pastry.

Prepare Meringue; spoon onto hot filling. Spread meringue over filling, carefully sealing meringue to edge of crust to prevent shrinking or weeping. Bake about 5 minutes or until meringue is light brown. Immediately refrigerate about 3 hours or until chilled. Refrigerate any remaining tart. 12 servings.

MERINGUE

> *3 egg whites*
>
> *¹/₄ teaspoon cream of tartar*
>
> *6 tablespoons granulated or packed brown sugar*
>
> *¹/₂ teaspoon vanilla*

Beat egg whites and cream of tartar in medium bowl until foamy. Beat in sugar, 1 tablespoon at a time; continue beating until stiff and glossy. Do not underbeat. Beat in vanilla.

RAISIN-SOUR CREAM PIE: Substitute 9-inch Baked Pie Shell (page 84) for the Cookie Tart Pastry. Substitute raisins for the dried cranberries and ³/₄ teaspoon ground nutmeg for the cardamom. Continue as directed—except bake pie about 10 minutes. 8 servings.

Little Cheese Tarts

While these little tarts are enticing by themselves, they are also delicious when dusted with nutmeg and served on top of Cranberries Jubilee (page 105). Or serve with Winter Compote (page 66) or accompany them with sliced kiwifruit drizzled with chocolate sauce.

Tart Dough (right)

1/3 cup golden raisins

2 tablespoons almond-flavored liqueur or rum*

1 container (15 ounces) ricotta cheese

1/2 cup sugar

2 teaspoons grated lemon peel

4 egg yolks

1/2 cup all-purpose flour

1/2 cup finely chopped candied fruit

2 egg whites

Prepare Tart Dough. Mix raisins and amaretto. Let stand 30 minutes.

Heat oven to 400°. Mix cheese, sugar and lemon peel in medium bowl. Stir in egg yolks, one at a time. Stir in raisin mixture, flour and candied fruit. Beat egg whites in medium bowl on high speed until stiff. Fold cheese mixture into egg whites.

Roll refrigerated dough 1/8 inch thick on lightly floured surface. Cut into sixteen 4-inch circles. Ease dough circles into ungreased 3-inch tart pans or 6-ounce custard cups. Divide cheese mixture evenly among tart pans (about 1/4 cup each). Bake 20 to 25 minutes or until crust is golden brown and filling is set. Serve warm or cold. Sprinkle with powdered sugar if desired. Immediately refrigerate any remaining tarts. 16 tarts.

* 2 tablespoons water plus 1 teaspoon almond or rum extract can be substituted for the almond-flavored liqueur or rum.

TART DOUGH

2 cups plus 2 tablespoons all-purpose flour

1/2 cup sugar

1/2 cup (1 stick) plus 2 tablespoons margarine or butter, softened

2 teaspoons grated lemon peel

1/2 teaspoon salt

1 egg

1 egg yolk

Mix all ingredients until dough forms. Knead 3 minutes on unfloured surface. Shape into a ball. Cover and refrigerate about 2 hours or until chilled.

Macadamia-Pineapple Tart

Cookie Tart Pastry (page 92)

¾ cup coarsely chopped macadamia nuts

*¾ cup coarsely chopped candied
    pineapple*

½ cup sugar

⅓ cup margarine or butter, melted

¾ cup corn syrup

¼ cup coffee liqueur, if desired

¼ teaspoon salt

3 eggs

Bake Cookie Tart Pastry. Reduce oven temperature to 375°. Sprinkle nuts and pineapple evenly in baked pastry. Beat remaining ingredients until smooth. Pour over nuts and pineapple. Bake about 30 minutes or until set. Serve warm or cool and, if desired, with whipped cream or dusted with powdered sugar. 12 servings.

🔔 **Use a food processor to make the pastry. Place all ingredients in food processor. Cover and process, using quick on and off motions, until dough forms a ball. Continue as directed above.**

Brandied Plum Pastry

5 cups thinly sliced plums

3 tablespoons brandy or apple juice

Pastry Dough (right)

½ cup granulated or packed brown sugar

⅓ cup all-purpose flour

1 tablespoon margarine or butter

½ cup powdered sugar

2 teaspoons brandy or apple juice

1 to 2 teaspoons milk

Heat oven to 350°. Toss plums and 3 tablespoons brandy; reserve. Prepare Pastry Dough. Roll dough into 15-inch circle on lightly floured surface. Fold dough into fourths. Carefully place on ungreased cookie sheet and unfold (reshape if necessary). Mix granulated sugar and flour; toss with plums. Spoon plum mixture onto center of dough to within 3 inches of edge. Dot with margarine. Bring edge of dough up and over plum mixture, stretching slightly to make 4-inch opening in center.

Bake about 40 minutes or until crust is golden brown and plums are tender. Cool 15 minutes on cookie sheet; remove to wire rack. Mix powdered sugar, 2 teaspoons brandy and the milk until smooth and consistency of thick syrup; drizzle over warm crust. Serve warm or cool. 12 servings.

PASTRY DOUGH

*1 package regular or quick-acting active
    dry yeast*

½ cup warm water (105° to 115°)

2 to 2¼ cups all-purpose flour

*½ cup (1 stick) margarine or butter,
    softened*

⅓ cup sugar

¼ teaspoon salt

Dissolve yeast in warm water in large bowl. Add 1 cup of the flour and the remaining ingredients. Beat until smooth. Stir in enough remaining flour to make dough easy to handle. Turn dough onto lightly floured surface; gently roll in flour to coat. Knead 1 minute.

BRANDIED APPLE PASTRY: Substitute 5 cups thinly sliced peeled tart apples for the plums.

Pear Tart Tatin

2 tablespoons margarine or butter

1/2 cup packed brown sugar

6 medium pears or tart apples (about 3 pounds), peeled, cored and cut into eighths

1/2 package (17 1/4-ounce size) frozen puff pastry, thawed

Pear Chantilly Cream (below)

Heat margarine and brown sugar in 10-inch oven-proof skillet over medium heat, stirring constantly, until melted. Stir in pears. Cook 20 to 25 minutes, stirring frequently, until syrup thickens; remove from heat. If desired, use two forks and arrange pear slices overlapping in a pinwheel pattern.

Heat oven to 400°. Roll pastry into 10 1/2-inch square on lightly floured surface. Cut into 10 1/2-inch circle. Fold pastry into fourths; cut slits so steam can escape. Place over pears in skillet and unfold; carefully tuck edge down around pears. Bake 15 to 20 minutes or until pastry is brown. Let stand 5 minutes; invert onto heatproof serving plate. Serve with Pear Chantilly Cream. 8 servings.

PEAR CHANTILLY CREAM

1 cup whipping (heavy) cream

1 tablespoon pear liqueur, pear brandy, apple brandy or apple juice

Beat ingredients in chilled medium bowl until soft peaks form.

Glazed Oranges

This dessert looks pretty on a clear dessert plate, served with a knife and fork.

6 large seedless oranges

1 cup sugar

1/2 cup dry white wine or water

1/4 cup light corn syrup

1 tablespoon orange-flavored liqueur or 1 teaspoon orange extract

2 tablespoons slivered almonds, toasted

Cut slivers of peel from 1 orange, using vegetable peeler or sharp knife, being careful not to cut into white membrane; reserve peel. Peel all oranges, cutting only deep enough to remove all the white membrane.

Mix sugar, wine and corn syrup in 2-quart saucepan. Cook over medium heat, stirring occasionally, to 230° to 234° on candy thermometer or until syrup forms a 2-inch thread when dropped from a spoon. Stir in reserved slivered peel and the liqueur. Place peeled oranges in syrup; turn to coat all sides. Remove oranges to shallow dish or pan. Spoon syrup over oranges until they are well glazed. Refrigerate at least 2 hours until chilled, occasionally spooning syrup over oranges.

To serve, place each orange in dessert dish. Pour syrup over oranges. Sprinkle with almonds. Serve with crème fraîche or sour cream if desired. 6 servings.

Pear Tart Tatin

Raisin-Pineapple Flambé

1 cup brandy*
½ cup golden raisins
¼ cup (½ stick) margarine or butter
1 pineapple, peeled, cored and cut into 6
    rings, about ¾ inch thick
½ cup sugar

Pour brandy over raisins. Let stand 30 minutes.

Heat margarine in 12-inch skillet over medium heat. Arrange pineapple rings in single layer in skillet. Sprinkle with half of the sugar. Cook uncovered 4 minutes. Turn pineapple; sprinkle with remaining sugar. Add raisins and brandy; push raisins off pineapple into liquid. Heat over high heat until brandy is hot; carefully ignite. Serve hot after flame dies. 6 servings.

* ¾ cup apple juice and 2 teaspoons brandy extract can be substituted for the brandy. Mixture will not flame.

Individual Cranberry-Orange Desserts

3 egg whites
1 egg yolk
½ cup milk
2 teaspoons grated orange peel
¼ cup orange juice
1 cup sugar
⅓ cup all-purpose flour
¼ teaspoon salt
¾ cup cranberry halves

Heat oven to 350°. Beat egg whites in large bowl on high speed until stiff peaks form; reserve.

Beat egg yolk slightly in medium bowl on medium speed. Beat in milk, orange peel and orange juice. Beat in sugar, flour and salt until smooth. Stir in cranberry halves. Fold egg yolk mixture into egg whites. Divide among 4 ungreased 10-ounce ramekins or custard cups.

Place ramekins in rectangular pan, $13 \times 9 \times 2$ inches, on oven rack. Pour very hot water into pan until 1 inch deep. Bake about 30 minutes or until golden brown. Serve warm or cold. Sprinkle with powdered sugar if desired. 4 servings.

Pear-Fig Strudel with Eggnog Sauce

2 pounds ripe pears, peeled and coarsely chopped (about 4 large)

1 teaspoon grated lemon peel

2 tablespoons lemon juice

1/2 cup coarsely chopped pistachio nuts

1/3 to 1/2 cup sugar

1/2 teaspoon ground cinnamon

1/4 teaspoon ground ginger

1/8 teaspoon ground cloves

1 package (8 ounces) dried figs, stems removed and figs cut in half

1/3 cup unseasoned dry bread crumbs

Eggnog Sauce (right)

6 frozen phyllo sheets, 18 × 12 inches, thawed

1/2 cup (1 stick) margarine or butter, melted

Powdered sugar, if desired

Heat pears, lemon peel and lemon juice in 10-inch skillet over medium heat about 5 minutes, stirring occasionally, until pears are soft; remove from heat. Stir in nuts, sugar, cinnamon, ginger, cloves and figs, mixing well. Stir in bread crumbs. Prepare Eggnog Sauce.

Heat oven to 400°. Line jelly roll pan, 15½ × 10½ × 1 inch, with cooking parchment pa-per or aluminum foil. Place damp towel on work surface, long side facing you. Cover with plastic wrap or waxed paper. Place phyllo sheets on plastic wrap. Cover with plastic wrap. Fold sheets with plastic wrap crosswise in half to the right.

Unfold phyllo sheets one at a time, brushing each half sheet with margarine. Fold sheets with plastic wrap crosswise in half to the left. Repeat unfolding and brushing with margarine. Remove top sheet of plastic wrap. Spread pear mixture evenly over bottom third of sheet, leaving 2-inch border. Fold in 2-inch border on all sides. Roll strudel, starting at end with pear mixture, using plastic wrap to help roll. Place seam side down diagonally in pan. Brush with margarine. Bake about 30 minutes, brushing with margarine every 10 minutes, until golden brown. Cool slightly; dust with powdered sugar. Cut into slices to serve. Serve with Eggnog Sauce. 8 to 10 servings.

EGGNOG SAUCE

2 cups prepared eggnog

1 tablespoon cornstarch

Mix ingredients with wire whisk in 2-quart saucepan. Heat over medium heat to boiling, stirring constantly. Boil and stir 1 minute or until slightly thickened. Cover and refrigerate about 1 hour or until chilled. Refrigerate any remaining sauce.

Raspberry Trifle

Pumpkin Flan

³/₄ cup sugar

¹/₄ cup water

1 cup canned pumpkin

³/₄ cup sugar

1 teaspoon ground cinnamon

¹/₂ teaspoon ground ginger

¹/₄ teaspoon ground allspice

¹/₄ teaspoon ground nutmeg

6 eggs

1 cup half-and-half

1 cup whipping (heavy) cream

Heat oven to 350°. Heat ³/₄ cup sugar and the water to boiling in heavy 2-quart saucepan over low heat, stirring constantly. Boil, without stirring, until syrup is deep golden brown.

Place quiche dish, 9 × 1¹/₂ or 10 × 1¹/₄ inches, in hot water until warm (to prevent dish from cracking when pouring hot syrup into it); dry completely. Pour syrup into dish; immediately rotate dish until syrup covers bottom.

Beat remaining ingredients except half-and-half and whipping cream in large bowl until well blended. Beat in half-and-half and whipping cream. Pour over syrup. Place dish in shallow roasting pan on oven rack. Pour very hot water into pan until 1 inch deep. Bake 1 to 1¹/₄ hours or until knife inserted in center comes out clean.

Remove dish from water; cool 15 minutes. Refrigerate about 3 hours or until chilled. Loosen side of flan from dish with knife; unmold. Refrigerate any remaining flan. 12 servings.

Raspberry Trifle

You'll find the size and number of ladyfingers can vary in the 3-ounce package. If you have at least 12, they can be sandwiched around the raspberry jam and arranged perpendicular to the side of the bowl—see the photo at left.

½ cup sugar

3 tablespoons cornstarch

¼ teaspoon salt

3 cups milk

½ cup dry sherry, ½ cup dry white wine or ⅓ cup orange juice plus 2 tablespoons sherry flavoring

3 egg yolks, beaten

3 tablespoons stick margarine or butter*

1 tablespoon vanilla

2 packages (3 ounces each) ladyfingers

½ cup raspberry preserves

1 package (12 ounces) frozen raspberries, thawed

1 cup whipping (heavy) cream

2 tablespoons sugar

2 tablespoons slivered almonds, toasted

Mix ½ cup sugar, the cornstarch and salt in 3-quart saucepan. Gradually stir in milk and sherry. Heat to boiling over medium heat, stirring constantly. Boil and stir 1 minute. Gradually stir at least half of the hot mixture into egg yolks; stir back into hot mixture in saucepan. Boil and stir 1 minute; remove from heat. Stir in margarine and vanilla. Cover and refrigerate at least 3 hours.

Split ladyfingers lengthwise in half; spread each half with raspberry preserves. Layer one-fourth of the ladyfingers, cut sides up, half of the raspberries and half of the pudding in 2-quart serving bowl; repeat. Arrange remaining ladyfingers around edge of bowl in upright position with cut sides toward center. (It may be necessary to gently ease ladyfingers down into pudding about 1 inch so they remain upright.)

Beat whipping cream and 2 tablespoons sugar in chilled medium bowl until stiff; spread over dessert. Sprinkle with almonds. Cover and refrigerate until serving time. Refrigerate any remaining dessert. 10 servings.

* Do not use tub margarine in this recipe.

Fig Bread Pudding

½ pound French bread, torn into 1-inch pieces

4 ounces fresh or dried figs, cut into fourths

1½ cups milk

1 cup whipping (heavy) cream

¼ cup (½ stick) margarine or butter

½ cup sugar

1 teaspoon vanilla

3 eggs

2 tablespoons sugar

Heat oven to 350°. Grease square baking dish, 8 × 8 × 2 inches. Sprinkle bread pieces and figs evenly in dish. Heat milk, whipping cream and margarine in 2-quart saucepan over medium heat until margarine is melted and milk is hot. Beat ½ cup sugar, the vanilla and eggs in 4-cup measure or medium bowl. Stir in milk mixture. Pour over bread pieces and figs. Sprinkle with 2 tablespoons sugar. Place dish in shallow roasting pan on oven rack. Pour very hot water into pan until 1 inch deep.

Bake 40 to 45 minutes or until knife inserted 1 inch from edge comes out clean. Serve warm with whipped cream if desired. 9 servings.

Peanut Brittle Bread Pudding

4 cups soft bread cubes (4 to 5 slices bread)

¹/₂ cup coarsely broken peanut brittle

¹/₂ cup semisweet chocolate chips

1 egg

¹/₂ cup milk

¹/₃ cup packed brown sugar

¹/₄ cup (¹/₂ stick) margarine or butter, melted

1 cup whipping (heavy) cream

¹/₄ cup chocolate-flavored syrup

Heat oven to 350°. Grease 1-quart casserole. Place half of the bread cubes in casserole. Sprinkle with half of the peanut brittle and half of the chocolate chips. Repeat with remaining bread cubes, peanut brittle and chocolate chips. Beat egg in small bowl. Stir in milk, brown sugar and margarine; pour over bread mixture. Bake 30 minutes or until center is set. Beat whipping cream and syrup in chilled small bowl until soft peaks form. Serve with warm pudding and sprinkle with crushed peanut brittle if desired. 6 servings.

Christmas Steamed Pudding

1 cup boiling water

1 cup chopped cranberries or chopped raisins

2 tablespoons shortening

1¹/₂ cups all-purpose flour

¹/₂ cup sugar

1 teaspoon baking soda

1 teaspoon salt

¹/₂ cup molasses

1 egg

Creamy Sauce (below) or Rum Hard Sauce (below)

Generously grease 6-cup mold. Pour boiling water on cranberries; stir in shortening. Mix flour, sugar, baking soda and salt in medium bowl. Stir in cranberry mixture, molasses and egg. Pour into mold. Cover tightly with aluminum foil. Place mold on rack in Dutch oven or steamer; pour boiling water into Dutch oven halfway up mold. Cover Dutch oven. Keep water boiling over low heat about 2 hours or until toothpick inserted in center of pudding comes out clean. Remove mold from Dutch oven. Let stand 5 minutes; unmold. Serve warm or cool with Creamy Sauce or Rum Hard Sauce. 8 servings.

CREAMY SAUCE

¹/₂ cup powdered sugar

¹/₂ cup (1 stick) margarine or butter, softened

¹/₂ cup whipping (heavy) cream

Mix powdered sugar and margarine in 1-quart saucepan until smooth and creamy. Stir in whipping cream. Heat to boiling, stirring occasionally. Serve warm.

RUM HARD SAUCE

¹/₂ cup (1 stick) margarine or butter, softened

1 cup powdered sugar

1 tablespoon rum or 2 teaspoons vanilla

Beat margarine in small bowl on high speed about 5 minutes or until smooth. Gradually beat in powdered sugar and rum. Cover and refrigerate 1 hour.

Steamed Christmas Pudding with Rum Hard Sauce

Hazelnut Meringues

6 egg whites

1 teaspoon vanilla

1 teaspoon white vinegar

2 cups granulated sugar

¼ cup powdered sugar

½ cup hazelnuts (filberts)

1 cup whipping (heavy) cream

2 tablespoons powdered sugar

1 teaspoon cocoa

Heat oven to 275°. Grease and flour 2 cookie sheets or line with cooking parchment paper. Beat egg whites, vanilla and vinegar in large bowl on high speed until foamy. Beat in granulated sugar and ¼ cup powdered sugar, 1 tablespoon at a time, until stiff and glossy.

Place egg white mixture in decorating bag with star or drop-flower tip. Pipe mixture into 2-inch rounds (about 24) onto cookie sheet. Bake 45 minutes. Turn off oven; leave in oven with door closed 1 hour. Finish cooling meringues at room temperature.

Heat oven to 400°. Bake hazelnuts in ungreased pan 5 minutes or until skins begin to crack. Wrap hazelnuts in clean towel; let stand 2 minutes. Rub hazelnuts in towel to remove skins. Chop hazelnuts. Return to pan. Bake about 8 minutes, stirring occasionally, until golden brown; cool.

Beat whipping cream, 2 tablespoons powdered sugar and the cocoa in chilled medium bowl until stiff. Fold in hazelnuts. Put meringues together in pairs with about 3 tablespoons whipped cream mixture. Cover and refrigerate about 2 hours or until firm. Refrigerate any remaining meringues. About 12 servings.

Angel Meringue Torte

Angel Meringue Torte

The meringue can also be spread in a 9-inch circle on a buttered cookie sheet.

6 egg whites

¹/₂ teaspoon cream of tartar

¹/₄ teaspoon salt

1¹/₂ cups sugar

¹/₂ teaspoon vanilla

¹/₂ teaspoon almond extract

1 cup whipping (heavy) cream

Cranberries Jubilee (right) or sweetened sliced strawberries

Heat oven to 275°. Butter bottom only of springform pan, 9 × 3 inches, or tube pan, 10 × 4 inches. Beat egg whites, cream of tartar and salt in large bowl on medium speed until foamy. Beat in sugar, 2 tablespoons at a time, on high speed; continue beating until stiff and glossy. Do not underbeat. Beat in vanilla and almond extract. Spread evenly in pan. Bake 1¹/₂ hours. Turn oven off and leave pan in oven with door closed 1 hour. Finish cooling at room temperature on wire rack.

Loosen side of meringue from pan with knife; invert onto serving plate. Beat whipping cream in chilled medium bowl until stiff. Frost meringue with whipped cream. Refrigerate at least 4 hours. Cut into wedges. Serve with Cranberries Jubilee. 12 servings.

CRANBERRIES JUBILEE

³/₄ teaspoon grated orange peel

¹/₂ cup orange juice

¹/₂ cup water

2 cups sugar

2 cups cranberries

2 tablespoons water

2 teaspoons cornstarch

¹/₄ cup brandy, if desired

Mix orange peel, orange juice, ¹/₂ cup water and the sugar in 2-quart saucepan. Heat to boiling; boil 5 minutes. Stir in cranberries. Heat to boiling; boil rapidly 5 minutes, stirring occasionally. Mix 2 tablespoons water and the cornstarch; stir into cranberry mixture. Cook, stirring constantly, until mixture thickens and boils. Boil and stir 1 minute. Pour into chafing dish; keep warm. Heat brandy in small, long-handled pan or metal ladle just until warm. Carefully ignite and pour flaming brandy over cranberry mixture. Serve hot after flame dies.

Champagne Cream Torte

Champagne Cream (below)
Cream Puff Dough (right)
1 cup whipping (heavy) cream
1 tablespoon light corn syrup
1/4 cup sliced almonds, toasted
Powdered sugar

Prepare Champagne Cream.

Heat oven to 400°. Prepare Cream Puff Dough. Spoon dough into 10-inch ring, about 2 inches wide, on ungreased cookie sheet; spread evenly. Bake 35 to 40 minutes or until puffed and golden. Cool away from draft. Split ring horizontally to make 2 rings. Pull out any filaments of soft dough.

Beat whipping cream in chilled medium bowl until stiff. Fold Champagne Cream into whipped cream. Place bottom of cream puff ring on serving plate. Fill with whipped cream mixture. Top with remaining cream puff ring. Heat corn syrup until warm. Lightly brush over top of ring. Sprinkle with almonds and powdered sugar. Refrigerate any remaining torte. 12 servings.

CHAMPAGNE CREAM

1/3 cup sugar
1 tablespoon plus 1 1/2 teaspoons cornstarch
1 cup champagne, sparkling white wine or sparkling white grape juice
2 eggs
2 tablespoons margarine or butter

Mix sugar and cornstarch in 1 1/2-quart saucepan. Stir in champagne. Cook over medium heat, stirring constantly, until mixture thickens and boils. Boil and stir 1 minute. Beat eggs on medium speed until well blended. Gradually stir at least half of the hot mixture into eggs; stir back into hot mixture in saucepan (mixture may look slightly curdled). Boil and stir 1 minute; remove from heat. Stir in margarine. Cover and refrigerate about 1 1/2 hours or until chilled.

APRICOT CREAM TORTE: Substitute apricot nectar for the champagne in Champagne Cream. Fold 1/3 cup finely chopped dried apricots into whipped cream mixture before filling cream puff ring.

Fudgy Ice-Cream Puffs

Cream Puff Dough (below)
12 scoops peppermint, coffee, eggnog or rum-raisin ice cream (3 pints)
Hot Fudge Sauce (page 246)

Heat oven to 400°. Prepare Cream Puff Dough. Drop dough by scant 1/4 cupfuls about 3 inches apart onto ungreased cookie sheet. Bake 35 to 40 minutes or until puffed and golden. Cool away from draft. Cut off tops and pull out any filaments of soft dough. Fill puffs with ice cream. Replace tops and freeze until serving time. Prepare Hot Fudge Sauce and serve over Ice-Cream Puffs. Freeze any remaining puffs. 12 puffs.

CREAM PUFF DOUGH

1 cup water
1/2 cup (1 stick) margarine or butter
1 cup all-purpose flour
4 eggs

Heat water and margarine to rolling boil in 2 1/2-quart saucepan. Stir in flour; reduce heat to low. Stir vigorously about 1 minute or until mixture forms a ball; remove from heat. Beat in eggs, all at once; continue beating until smooth.

Cardamom Cream Crepes

Crepes (below)
¾ cup whipping (heavy) cream
¼ cup packed brown sugar
¼ teaspoon ground cardamom
⅓ cup sour cream
1 container (16 ounces) lingonberries or whole berry cranberry sauce

Prepare Crepes. Beat whipping cream, brown sugar and cardamom in chilled small bowl about 2 minutes or just until soft peaks form. Fold in sour cream. Spoon about 2 tablespoons cream mixture onto each crepe; roll up. Place 2 crepes, seam sides down, on each dessert plate. Top with lingonberries. 8 servings.

CREPES

1½ cups all-purpose flour
1 tablespoon sugar
½ teaspoon baking powder
½ teaspoon salt
2 cups milk
2 tablespoons margarine or butter, melted
½ teaspoon vanilla
2 eggs

Mix flour, sugar, baking powder and salt in medium bowl. Stir in remaining ingredients. Beat with hand beater until smooth. Lightly butter 6-inch crepe pan or skillet; heat over medium heat until bubbly. For each crepe, pour scant ¼ cup of the batter into skillet. *Immediately* rotate skillet until thin film covers bottom.

Cook until light brown. Run wide spatula around edge to loosen; turn and cook other side until light brown. Stack crepes, placing waxed paper between each; keep covered. 16 crepes.

Crepes Jubilee

1 can (16½ ounces) pitted dark sweet cherries, drained and ¼ cup syrup reserved
¼ cup rum
Crepes (left)
¾ cup currant jelly
1 teaspoon grated orange peel
¼ cup brandy
1 quart vanilla ice cream

Mix reserved cherry syrup and the rum; pour over cherries. Refrigerate at least 4 hours.

Prepare Crepes; keep warm. Heat jelly in chafing dish or 10-inch skillet over low heat, stirring occasionally, until melted. Stir in cherry mixture and orange peel. Cook, stirring occasionally, until mixture simmers. Heat brandy in small, long-handled pan or metal ladle just until warm.

Carefully ignite and pour flaming brandy over cherry mixture. Stir when flame dies. Fold crepes into fourths; top with ice cream. Spoon cherry mixture over ice cream. 6 servings.

Chocolate-Almond Cream

Add flavored almonds for delicious crunch to this velvety dessert. Cook ½ cup sliced or slivered almonds and ¼ cup almond-flavored liqueur in a 10-inch skillet over medium heat, stirring often, until no liquid remains. Cool on aluminum foil, then break into pieces.

Hot Fudge Sauce (page 246)

About 18 ladyfingers

⅓ cup amaretto or 1 teaspoon almond extract mixed with ¼ cup water

3 tablespoons water

3 cups whipping (heavy) cream

¼ cup amaretto or 1 teaspoon almond extract

Prepare Hot Fudge Sauce. Remove 1 cup of the sauce; cool. Cover and refrigerate remaining sauce. Split ladyfingers lengthwise in half. Arrange ladyfingers, cut sides toward center, on bottom and upright around side of ungreased springform pan, 9 × 3 inches. Mix ⅓ cup amaretto and 3 tablespoons water; brush over ladyfingers. Beat whipping cream in chilled large bowl until stiff. Mix 1 cup cooled Hot Fudge Sauce and ¼ cup amaretto; fold into whipped cream. Spoon into pan; smooth top. Freeze about 8 hours or until firm.

Place in refrigerator at least 1 hour but no longer than 2 hours before serving. Heat refrigerated Hot Fudge Sauce, stirring occasionally, just until warm. Loosen dessert from side of pan; remove side of pan. Cut dessert into wedges. Serve with sauce. Refrigerate any remaining dessert. 16 servings.

Peppermint Bavarian

1 envelope unflavored gelatin

¼ cup cold water

3 eggs

¼ cup sugar

⅓ cup crushed hard peppermint candies

¼ teaspoon salt

1 cup milk

1 cup whipping (heavy) cream

3 tablespoons sugar

Few drops red food color

Sprinkle gelatin on cold water to soften. Mix eggs, ¼ cup sugar, the crushed candies and salt in heavy 2-quart saucepan. Gradually stir in milk. Cook over medium heat 7 to 10 minutes, stirring constantly, until mixture thickens and *just* begins to boil; remove from heat. Stir in softened gelatin until dissolved.

Place saucepan in ice and water about 15 minutes or in refrigerator about 30 minutes, stirring occasionally, until mixture mounds when dropped from spoon. (If mixture is too thick, place saucepan in warm water; stir mixture until smooth. Refrigerate about 10 minutes or until mixture mounds when dropped from spoon.)

Beat whipping cream and 3 tablespoons sugar in chilled medium bowl until stiff. Fold gelatin mixture into whipped cream. Gently fold in food color just until streaked with color. Pour into 4-quart mold. Cover and refrigerate 5 hours or until set. Quickly dip mold into hot water; unmold onto serving plate. Refrigerate any remaining bavarian. 8 servings.

Chocolate Almond Cream and Christmas Tortoni (page 110)

Christmas Tortoni

*⅔ cup macaroon cookie or vanilla wafer
crumbs (about 12 cookies)*

½ cup chopped salted almonds

¼ cup chopped red candied cherries

*1 quart vanilla ice cream, slightly
softened*

Red and green candied cherries

Line 8 medium muffin cups, 2½ × 1¼ inches, with paper baking cups. Mix cookie crumbs, almonds and ¼ cup candied cherries; fold into ice cream. Divide ice-cream mixture among muffin cups. Decorate with candied cherries. Freeze about 4 hours or until firm. 8 servings.

Hot Chocolate Soufflé

⅓ cup sugar

⅓ cup cocoa

¼ cup all-purpose flour

1 cup milk

3 egg yolks

*2 tablespoons margarine or butter,
softened*

1 teaspoon vanilla

4 egg whites

¼ teaspoon cream of tartar

⅛ teaspoon salt

3 tablespoons sugar

Cream Sauce (page 102)

Mix ⅓ cup sugar, the cocoa and flour in 1½-quart saucepan. Gradually stir in milk. Heat to boiling, stirring constantly; remove from heat. Beat egg yolks with fork in small bowl. Beat in about one-third of the cocoa mixture. Gradually stir in remaining cocoa mixture. Stir in margarine and vanilla; cool slightly.

Move oven rack to lowest position. Heat oven to 350°. Butter 6-cup soufflé dish; sprinkle with sugar. Make 4-inch band of triple-thickness aluminum foil 2 inches longer than circumference of dish. Butter one side of band; sprinkle with sugar. Extend height of dish by securing band, buttered side in, around outside edge, using tape.

Beat egg whites, cream of tartar and salt in medium bowl until foamy. Beat in 3 tablespoons sugar, 1 tablespoon at a time; continue beating until stiff and glossy. Do not underbeat. Stir about one-fourth of the egg whites into cocoa mixture. Fold cocoa mixture into remaining egg whites. Carefully pour into soufflé dish. Place dish in square pan, 9 × 9 × 2 inches, on oven rack. Pour very hot water into pan until 1 inch deep. Bake 1¼ hours. While soufflé is baking, prepare Creamy Sauce. Immediately serve soufflé with Creamy Sauce. 6 servings.

Beautiful Breads

Bountiful loaves of bread, fresh coffee cakes, sweet and savory muffins are all welcome additions to the holiday bread basket. And Christmas breads such as Stollen or cheerful Snowman Buns add a warm, special touch to celebrations of the season.

Banana Bread

For a spicier banana bread, stir in 1 teaspoon ground cinnamon, ¼ teaspoon ground cloves and ¼ teaspoon ground nutmeg with the flour.

1¼ cups sugar

½ cup (1 stick) margarine or butter, softened

2 eggs

1½ cups mashed ripe bananas (3 to 4 medium)

½ cup buttermilk

1 teaspoon vanilla

2½ cups all-purpose flour

1 teaspoon baking soda

1 teaspoon salt

1 cup chopped nuts, if desired

Move oven rack to lowest position. Heat oven to 350°. Grease bottoms only of 2 loaf pans, 8½ × 4½ × 2½ inches, or 1 loaf pan, 9 × 5 × 3 inches. Mix sugar and margarine in large bowl. Stir in eggs until well blended. Add bananas, buttermilk and vanilla. Beat until smooth. Stir in flour, baking soda and salt just until moistened. Stir in nuts. Pour into pans. Bake 8-inch loaves about 1 hour, 9-inch loaf about 1 hour 15 minutes or until toothpick inserted in center comes out clean. Cool 5 minutes. Loosen sides of loaves from pans; remove from pans. Cool completely on wire rack before slicing. Wrap tightly and store at room temperature up to 4 days, or refrigerate up to 10 days. 2 loaves (24 slices each).

TO MICROWAVE: Generously grease 12-cup microwavable bundt cake dish. Prepare batter as directed. Pour into dish. Microwave uncovered on high 12 to 14 minutes, rotating dish ¼ turn every 4 minutes, until top springs back when touched lightly. Let stand on heatproof surface (not wire rack) 10 minutes. Remove from dish; cool.

MACADAMIA-COCONUT BANANA BREAD: Substitute 1 jar (3½ ounces) macadamia nuts, chopped and toasted, and ½ cup flaked coconut for the chopped nuts.

MINI BANANA BREADS: Grease bottoms only of 10 miniature loaf pans, 4½ × 2¾ × 1¼ inches. Divide batter among pans (about ½ cup each). Bake 30 to 35 minutes. 10 loaves (8 slices each).

Holiday Nut Bread

2½ cups all-purpose flour

½ cup granulated sugar

½ cup packed brown sugar

3 teaspoons baking powder

1 teaspoon salt

½ teaspoon baking soda

¼ cup shortening

1¼ cups buttermilk*

2 eggs

1 cup chopped nuts

Heat oven to 350°. Grease bottom only of loaf pan, 9 × 5 × 3 inches. Beat all ingredients except nuts in large bowl on low speed 15 seconds. Beat on medium speed 30 seconds, scraping bowl constantly. Stir in nuts. Pour into pan. Bake 60 to 65 minutes or until toothpick inserted in center comes out clean. Immediately remove from pan. Cool completely on wire rack before slicing. Garnish top of nut bread with maraschino cherries and sliced green candied pineapple if desired. For best results, wrap and refrigerate at least 8 hours before slicing. 1 loaf (about 20 slices).

* 1¼ cups milk and 1 tablespoon white vinegar can be substituted for the buttermilk; mix and let stand 5 minutes.

CHERRY-NUT BREAD: Decrease buttermilk to 1 cup and add ¼ cup maraschino cherry juice. After beating, stir in ½ cup chopped drained maraschino cherries. Bake 1 hour 10 minutes to 1 hour 15 minutes.

DATE-NUT BREAD: Omit buttermilk. Pour 1½ cups boiling water over 1½ cups chopped dates; stir and let cool. Beat date mixture with remaining ingredients. Bake 1 hour 5 minutes to 1 hour 10 minutes.

PUMPKIN-NUT BREAD: Omit buttermilk. Beat 1 cup canned pumpkin, ⅔ cup milk, ½ teaspoon ground cinnamon, ½ teaspoon ground cloves and ½ teaspoon ground nutmeg with remaining ingredients. Bake 1 hour 15 minutes.

🔔 **Purchase chopped nuts for this quick bread, or use your food processor to chop a large quantity of nuts. Freeze in 1-cup amounts to have ready for use any time.**

Eggnog–Poppy Seed Bread

2½ cups all-purpose flour

1 cup sugar

¼ cup poppy seed

1¼ cups prepared eggnog

1 tablespoon plus 1 teaspoon grated orange peel

3 tablespoons vegetable oil

3½ teaspoons baking powder

1 teaspoon salt

1 teaspoon ground nutmeg

1 egg

Heat oven to 350°. Grease bottom only of loaf pan, 9 × 5 × 3 inches, or 2 loaf pans, 8½ × 4½ × 2½ inches. Mix all ingredients; beat 30 seconds. Pour into pan(s). Bake 9-inch loaf 55 to 65 minutes, 8-inch loaves 55 to 60 minutes or until toothpick inserted in center comes out clean; cool slightly. Loosen sides of loaf from pan; remove from pan. Cool completely on wire rack before slicing. Wrap and refrigerate up to 1 week. 1 large loaf (24 slices) or 2 small loaves (16 slices each).

Cherry Nut Bread, Eggnog–Poppy Seed Bread; Mini Banana Breads (page 111)

Cranberry-Orange Nut Bread

Our classic nut bread, but with a twist—chocolate! Once you try it, you too will become a fan of the combination of tart cranberries and sweet chocolate.

> 2 cups all-purpose flour
> ³/₄ cup sugar
> 1¹/₂ teaspoons baking powder
> ³/₄ teaspoon salt
> ¹/₂ teaspoon baking soda
> ¹/₄ cup (¹/₂ stick) margarine or butter, softened
> 1 tablespoon grated orange peel
> ³/₄ cup orange juice
> 1 egg
> 1 cup fresh or frozen cranberries, chopped
> ¹/₂ cup chopped nuts
> ¹/₂ cup miniature chocolate chips, if desired

Heat oven to 350°. Grease bottom only of loaf pan, 9 × 5 × 3 inches. Mix flour, sugar, baking powder, salt and baking soda in large bowl. Stir in margarine until mixture is crumbly. Stir in orange peel, orange juice and egg just until all flour is moistened. Stir in cranberries, nuts and chocolate chips. Spread in pan.

Bake 55 to 65 minutes or until toothpick inserted in center comes out clean. Loosen sides of loaf from pan; remove from pan. Cool completely on wire rack before slicing. 1 loaf (24 slices).

🔔 Use a foil pan to bake the bread—no pan to wash, and it's an excellent way to freeze bread for use later.

Toasted Nut Loaf

> 2 cups all-purpose flour
> 1 cup chopped nuts, toasted*
> ¹/₂ cup whole wheat flour
> ¹/₂ cup granulated sugar
> ¹/₂ cup packed brown sugar
> 1¹/₄ cups milk
> ¹/₃ cup vegetable oil
> 3 teaspoons baking powder
> ¹/₂ teaspoon salt
> 2 eggs

Heat oven to 350°. Grease bottom only of loaf pan, 9 × 5 × 3 inches, or 2 loaf pans, 8¹/₂ × 4¹/₂ × 2¹/₂ inches. Mix all ingredients; beat 30 seconds. Pour into pan. Bake 9-inch loaf 55 to 65 minutes, 8-inch loaves 55 to 60 minutes or until toothpick inserted in center comes out clean. Cool 5 minutes. Loosen sides of loaf from pan; remove from pan. Cool completely on wire rack before slicing. 1 or 2 loaves (24 slices each).

* To toast nuts, bake in ungreased pan in 350° oven about 8 minutes, stirring occasionally, until golden brown.

Gingered Pear Bread

*3 cups chopped unpeeled pears (about 3
  medium)*
1¹/₄ cups sugar
¹/₂ cup vegetable oil
1 tablespoon finely chopped gingerroot
3 eggs
3 cups all-purpose flour
3¹/₂ teaspoons baking powder
1 teaspoon salt

Heat oven to 350°. Grease bottoms only of 2 loaf
pans, 8¹/₂ × 4¹/₂ × 2¹/₂ or 9 × 5 × 3 inches. Mix
pears, sugar, oil, gingerroot and eggs in large
bowl. Stir in remaining ingredients. Pour into
pans.

Bake 8-inch loaves about 65 minutes, 9-inch
loaves about 50 minutes or until toothpick inserted in center comes out clean. Cool 10 minutes. Loosen sides of loaves from pans; remove
from pans.

Cool completely on wire rack before slicing.
Store tightly wrapped in refrigerator up to 1
week. 2 loaves (24 slices each).

Cardamom-Fig Bread

2¹/₂ cups all-purpose flour
1 cup sugar
1 cup chopped dried figs
1¹/₄ cups buttermilk
¹/₃ cup vegetable oil
1 teaspoon baking powder
¹/₂ teaspoon baking soda
¹/₂ teaspoon ground cardamom
¹/₂ teaspoon salt
2 eggs

Heat oven to 350°. Grease bottoms only of 2
loaf pans, 8¹/₂ × 4¹/₂ × 2 inches, or 1 loaf pan,
9 × 5 × 3 inches. Mix all ingredients; beat 30 seconds. Pour into pans.

Bake 8-inch loaves 45 to 50 minutes, 9-inch loaf
55 to 60 minutes or until toothpick inserted in
center comes out clean. Cool 10 minutes. Loosen
sides of loaves from pans; remove from pans.

Cool completely on wire rack before slicing.
Store tightly wrapped in refrigerator up to 1
week. 2 loaves (12 slices each) or 1 loaf (24
slices).

Toasted Coconut-Banana Coffee Cake

2¹/₂ cups all-purpose flour

1¹/₄ cups sugar

1 cup coconut, toasted*

1 cup mashed ripe bananas (about 2 medium)

³/₄ cup (1¹/₂ sticks) margarine or butter, softened

¹/₂ cup plain yogurt

1¹/₄ teaspoons baking powder

1 teaspoon baking soda

1 teaspoon vanilla

¹/₄ teaspoon salt

2 eggs

Browned Butter Glaze (below)

Heat oven to 350°. Grease 12-cup bundt cake pan or tube pan, 10 × 4 inches. Mix all ingredients except Browned Butter Glaze on low speed until blended. Beat on medium speed 2 minutes, scraping bowl occasionally. Spread in pan.

Bake 50 to 55 minutes or until toothpick inserted near center comes out clean. Cool 20 minutes. Remove from pan. Cool completely on wire rack. Drizzle with Browned Butter Glaze. 16 servings.

BROWNED BUTTER GLAZE

2 tablespoons butter**

1¹/₂ cups powdered sugar

¹/₂ teaspoon vanilla

1 to 2 tablespoons milk

Heat butter in 1¹/₂-quart saucepan over medium heat until light brown. Stir in remaining ingredients until smooth and drizzling consistency. If frosting becomes too thick, stir in hot water, a few drops at a time.

* To toast coconut, bake in ungreased pan in 350° oven 5 to 7 minutes, stirring occasionally, until golden brown.

** Do not use margarine for this glaze.

Poppy Seed–Walnut Coffee Cake

Poppy Seed Filling (below)

2 cups all-purpose flour

³/₄ cup packed brown sugar

¹/₃ cup margarine or butter, softened

1 cup milk

2¹/₂ teaspoons baking powder

¹/₂ teaspoon salt

¹/₂ teaspoon ground cinnamon

¹/₄ teaspoon ground nutmeg

1 egg

¹/₂ cup chopped walnuts

¹/₄ cup chopped walnuts

Heat oven to 350°. Grease square pan, 9 × 9 × 2 inches. Prepare Poppy Seed Filling; reserve. Beat remaining ingredients except walnuts in large bowl on low speed until blended. Beat on medium speed 1 minute, scraping bowl occasionally. Stir in ¹/₂ cup walnuts. Spread half of the batter in pan. Spoon filling by small spoonfuls onto batter; carefully spread over batter.

Spoon remaining batter onto filling; carefully spread to cover filling. Sprinkle with ¹/₄ cup walnuts. Bake 40 to 45 minutes or until toothpick inserted in center comes out clean. Serve warm or let stand until cool. Sprinkle with powdered sugar if desired. 9 servings.

POPPY SEED FILLING

¹/₃ cup poppy seed

¹/₃ cup walnuts

¹/₄ cup milk

¹/₄ cup honey

Place all ingredients in blender or food processor. Cover and blend on medium speed, stopping blender frequently to scrape sides, or process, until milk is absorbed.

Sour Cream Coffee Cake

This coffee cake is perfect to serve a crowd! When baked in loaf pans, you can serve one, and give the other as a gift.

1¹/₂ cups sugar

³/₄ cup (1¹/₂ sticks) margarine or butter, softened

1¹/₂ teaspoons vanilla

3 eggs

3 cups all-purpose or whole wheat flour

1¹/₂ teaspoons baking powder

1¹/₂ teaspoons baking soda

³/₄ teaspoon salt

1¹/₂ cups sour cream

Filling (right)

Light Brown Glaze (right)

Heat oven to 350°. Grease tube pan, 10 × 4 inches, 12-cup bundt cake pan or 2 loaf pans, 9 × 5 × 3 inches. Beat sugar, margarine, vanilla and eggs in large bowl on medium speed 2 minutes, scraping bowl occasionally. Beat in flour, baking powder, baking soda and salt alternately with sour cream on low speed. Prepare Filling.

For tube or bundt cake pan, spread one-third of the batter (about 2 cups) in pan and sprinkle with one-third of the Filling (about 6 tablespoons); repeat twice. For loaf pans, spread one-fourth of the batter (about 1¹/₂ cups) in each pan and sprinkle each with one-fourth of the Filling (about 5 tablespoons); repeat once. Bake about 1 hour or until toothpick inserted near center comes out clean. Cool slightly; remove from pan to wire rack. Cool 10 minutes. Drizzle Light Brown Glaze over warm coffee cake. Serve warm or cool. 14 to 16 servings.

FILLING

¹/₂ cup packed brown sugar

¹/₂ cup finely chopped nuts

1¹/₂ teaspoons ground cinnamon

Mix all ingredients.

LIGHT BROWN GLAZE

¹/₄ cup (¹/₂ stick) margarine or butter

2 cups powdered sugar

1 teaspoon vanilla

1 to 2 tablespoons milk

Heat margarine in 1¹/₂-quart saucepan over medium heat until light brown; remove from heat. Stir in powdered sugar and vanilla. Stir in milk, 1 tablespoon at a time, until smooth and of drizzling consistency.

Raspberry-Marzipan Coffee Cake

Marzipan and almond paste are both made from blanched, ground almonds and a liquid, such as glycerin or pasturized egg whites to help hold its shape. Almond paste is usually less sweet and slightly coarser than marzipan, and may have almond extract added for extra flavor. Chopping is easier if marzipan is frozen about 30 minutes before chopping.

> *Streusel (right)*
> *2 cups all-purpose flour*
> *³/₄ cup sugar*
> *¹/₄ cup (¹/₂ stick) margarine or butter, softened*
> *1 cup milk*
> *2 teaspoons baking powder*
> *1 teaspoon vanilla*
> *¹/₂ teaspoon salt*
> *1 egg*
> *¹/₂ package (7-ounce size) almond paste, finely chopped*
> *1 cup fresh or unsweetened frozen (thawed) raspberries*

Heat oven to 350°. Grease square pan, 9 × 9 × 2 inches. Prepare Streusel. Beat remaining ingredients except almond paste and raspberries on low speed 30 seconds. Beat on medium speed 2 minutes, scraping bowl occasionally.

Spread half of the batter in pan. Sprinkle with half each of the almond paste, raspberries and Streusel. Repeat with remaining batter, almond paste, raspberries and Streusel. Bake about 50 minutes or until toothpick inserted in center comes out clean. Serve warm or cool. 12 servings.

STREUSEL

> *¹/₃ cup all-purpose flour*
> *¹/₄ cup sugar*
> *¹/₄ cup (¹/₂ stick) firm margarine or butter*
> *¹/₃ cup slivered almonds*

Mix flour and sugar. Cut in margarine until crumbly. Stir in almonds.

RASPBERRY-CHOCOLATE COFFEE CAKE: Substitute 1 package (6 ounces) semisweet chocolate chips (1 cup) for the almond paste.

APRICOT-MARZIPAN COFFEE CAKE: Substitute 8 ounces dried apricots, cut into fourths (1 cup) for the raspberries.

Raspberry-Marzipan Coffee Cake; Orange-Cheese Braid (page 120)

Orange-Cheese Braid

1 package (3 ounces) cream cheese

¹⁄₄ cup (¹⁄₂ stick) firm margarine or butter

2¹⁄₂ cups Bisquick® Original baking mix

¹⁄₂ cup orange juice

1 package (8 ounces) cream cheese, softened

¹⁄₃ cup orange marmalade

Chocolate Drizzle (below)

Heat oven to 400°. Cut 3-ounce package cream cheese and the margarine into baking mix. Stir in orange juice. Turn dough onto surface well dusted with baking mix; gently roll in baking mix to coat. Knead 10 times. Roll into rectangle, 15 × 9 inches. Place on large ungreased cookie sheet.

Beat 8-ounce package cream cheese and the marmalade until smooth. Spread in 4-inch strip lengthwise down center of rectangle. Make cuts 2¹⁄₂ inches long at 1-inch intervals on each 15-inch side of rectangle. Fold strips over filling, overlapping and crossing in center. Bake about 20 minutes or until golden brown. Cool 10 minutes. Carefully remove from cookie sheet to wire rack. Cool completely. Drizzle with Chocolate Glaze. Refrigerate any remaining coffee cake. 1 coffee cake (12 slices).

CHOCOLATE DRIZZLE

¹⁄₂ cup powdered sugar

2 tablespoons cocoa

¹⁄₄ teaspoon vanilla

3 to 4 teaspoons milk

Mix all ingredients until smooth and of drizzling consistency.

Skillet Chile-Cheese Corn Bread

A down-home favorite, perfect served right from the skillet. For festive flair, just before baking arrange thin slices of red or green bell peppers in the shape of Christmas trees on top of the batter.

1¹⁄₂ cups cornmeal

¹⁄₂ cup all-purpose flour

¹⁄₂ cup shredded Cheddar cheese (2 ounces)

¹⁄₄ cup shortening

1¹⁄₂ cups buttermilk

2 teaspoons baking powder

1 teaspoon sugar

1 teaspoon salt

¹⁄₂ teaspoon baking soda

¹⁄₂ teaspoon chile powder

2 eggs

1 can (4 ounces) chopped green chiles, well drained

Heat oven to 450°. Grease 10-inch ovenproof skillet, round pan, 9 × 1¹⁄₂ inches, or square pan, 8 × 8 × 2 inches. Mix all ingredients; beat vigorously 30 seconds. Pour into skillet or pan. Bake skillet about 20 minutes, round or square pan 25 to 30 minutes or until golden brown. Serve warm. 12 servings.

CHILE-CHEESE CORN STICKS: Fill 18 greased corn stick pans about seven-eighths full. Bake 12 to 15 minutes. 18 corn sticks.

Basil-Pepper Biscuits

¹/₄ cup shortening

2 cups all-purpose or whole wheat flour

*2 tablespoons chopped fresh or 2
    teaspoons dried basil leaves*

1 tablespoon sugar, if desired

3 teaspoons baking powder

1 teaspoon salt

1 teaspoon cracked black pepper

About ³/₄ cup milk

Heat oven to 450°. Cut shortening into remaining ingredients except milk with pastry blender in medium bowl until mixture resembles fine crumbs. Stir in just enough milk so dough leaves side of bowl and rounds up into a ball. (Too much milk makes dough sticky, not enough makes biscuits dry.)

Turn dough onto lightly floured surface; gently roll in flour to coat. Knead lightly 20 to 25 times. Roll or pat ¹/₂ inch thick. Cut with floured 2¹/₂-inch biscuit cutter. Place on ungreased cookie sheet about 1 inch apart for crusty sides, touching for soft sides. Bake 10 to 12 minutes or until golden brown. Immediately remove from cookie sheet. Serve warm. About 10 biscuits.

CORNMEAL–BASIL-PEPPER BISCUITS: Substitute ¹/₂ cup yellow, white or blue cornmeal for ¹/₂ cup of the flour. Sprinkle cornmeal over biscuits before baking if desired.

Cinnamon Popovers

This recipe can easily be doubled, so you can be sure of having plenty of popovers to eat with the satisfying Apple Spread.

2 eggs

1 cup milk

1 cup all-purpose flour

¹/₂ teaspoon salt

¹/₂ teaspoon ground cinnamon

Apple Spread (below)

Heat oven to 450°. Generously grease 6-cup popover pan, six 6-ounce custard cups or 8 medium muffin cups, 2¹/₂ × 1¹/₄ inches. Beat eggs and milk slightly in medium bowl. Stir in flour, salt and cinnamon with fork or wire whisk just until smooth (do not overbeat). Fill popover or custard cups one-half full, muffin cups three-fourths full.

Bake 25 minutes. Reduce oven temperature to 350°. Bake 15 to 20 minutes longer or until deep golden brown. Immediately remove from pan. Serve hot with Apple Spread. 6 or 8 popovers.

APPLE SPREAD

*¹/₄ cup (¹/₂ stick) margarine or butter,
    softened*

*2 tablespoons Spirited Apple Butter (page
    253), apple butter or applesauce*

Beat ingredients in small bowl on high speed until blended.

POPOVERS: Omit cinnamon.

⚠ **You can bake popovers well ahead of time, to fit your schedule. Poke a hole in each popover just after baking to release steam, then cool on a wire rack. Store loosely covered no longer than 2 days. Heat uncovered in 300° oven about 10 minutes before serving.**

Lemon Oat Scones; Basil-Pepper Biscuits (page 121); Plum Preserves (page 251)

Lemon-Oat Scones

¹/₃ cup margarine or butter

1¹/₄ cups all-purpose flour

¹/₂ cup quick-cooking oats

3 tablespoons sugar

2¹/₂ teaspoons baking powder

2 teaspoons grated lemon peel

¹/₂ teaspoon salt

1 egg, beaten

¹/₂ cup chopped almonds, toasted

4 to 6 tablespoons half-and-half

1 egg, beaten

Heat oven to 400°. Cut margarine into flour, oats, sugar, baking powder, lemon peel and salt with pastry blender in medium bowl until mixture resembles fine crumbs. Stir in 1 egg, the almonds and just enough half-and-half so dough leaves side of bowl.

Turn dough onto lightly floured surface; gently roll in flour to coat. Knead lightly 10 times. Roll or pat ¹/₂ inch thick. Cut with floured 2-inch round cutter, or cut into diamond shapes with sharp knife. Place on ungreased cookie sheet. Brush 1 egg over dough.

Bake 10 to 12 minutes or until golden brown. Immediately remove from cookie sheet. Cool on wire rack. Split scones; spread with margarine and serve with strawberry preserves if desired. About 15 scones.

SPICY FRUIT SCONES: Omit lemon peel. Add ³/₄ teaspoon ground cinnamon and ¹/₈ teaspoon ground cloves with the salt. Substitute ¹/₂ cup diced fruits, chopped figs, currants or dates for the nuts.

Wine-and-Cheese Muffins

2 cups Bisquick® Original baking mix

2/3 cup white wine or apple juice

2 tablespoons vegetable oil

1 egg

1 cup shredded Swiss, Gruyère or Cheddar cheese (4 ounces)

2 teaspoons chopped fresh or freeze-dried chives

Heat oven to 400°. Line 12 medium muffin cups, 2½ × 1¼ inches, with paper baking cups, or grease entire cup generously. Mix baking mix, wine, oil and egg with fork in medium bowl; beat vigorously 30 strokes. Stir in cheese and chives. Divide batter evenly among cups. Bake about 20 minutes or until golden brown. Immediately remove from pan. Serve warm. 1 dozen muffins.

BEER-AND-CHEDDAR MUFFINS: Substitute beer for the wine and use Cheddar cheese.

🔔 Buy shredded cheese, or cut a 4-ounce chunk of cheese. You can then shred without having to stop and measure.

Spicy Pecan Muffins

2 cups Bisquick® Original baking mix

1/2 cup chopped pecans

1/4 cup sugar

2/3 cup cold water or milk

1 teaspoon ground allspice

1 teaspoon ground cinnamon

1 egg

2 teaspoons sugar

Heat oven to 400°. Grease 12 medium muffin cups, 2½ × 1¼ inches. Mix all ingredients except 2 teaspoons sugar; beat vigorously 30 seconds. Divide batter evenly among cups (about two-thirds full). Sprinkle with 2 teaspoons sugar. Bake about 15 minutes or until golden brown. Immediately remove from pan. Serve warm. 1 dozen muffins.

Pumpkin Muffins

These muffins are also wonderful made with sweet potatoes or yams. Substitue ½ cup mashed yams or sweet potato for the pumpkin and omit the raisins. If you like, add ½ cup chopped pecans or walnuts.

1½ cups all-purpose flour

1/2 cup sugar

1/2 cup raisins

1/4 cup (1/2 stick) margarine or butter, melted

1/2 cup milk

1/2 cup canned pumpkin

2 teaspoons baking powder

1/2 teaspoon salt

1/2 teaspoon ground cinnamon

1/2 teaspoon ground nutmeg

1 egg

Heat oven to 400°. Grease bottoms only of 12 medium muffin cups, 2½ × 1¼ inches. Mix all ingredients just until flour is moistened (batter will be lumpy). Divide batter evenly among cups (about two-thirds full). Sprinkle ¼ teaspoon sugar over batter in each cup if desired. Bake 18 to 20 minutes or until golden brown. Immediately remove from pan. 1 dozen muffins.

Christmas Brioche

*1 package regular or quick-acting active
 dry yeast*

½ cup warm water (105° to 115°)

2 tablespoons sugar

½ teaspoon salt

5 eggs

1 egg white

*¾ cup (1½ sticks) margarine or butter,
 softened*

3½ cups all-purpose flour

½ cup chopped nuts

1 cup mixed chopped candied fruit

1 egg yolk

1 tablespoon water

2 tablespoons apricot jam

2 teaspoons water

Dissolve yeast in warm water in large bowl. Add sugar, salt, 5 eggs, the egg white, margarine and 2 cups of the flour. Beat on low speed 30 seconds, scraping bowl constantly. Beat on medium speed 10 minutes, scraping bowl occasionally. Stir in remaining flour, the nuts and candied fruit until batter is smooth. Scrape dough from side of bowl. Cover with plastic wrap and let rise in warm place about 1 hour or until double. (Dough is ready if indentation remains when touched.)

Stir down dough by beating about 25 strokes. Cover bowl tightly with plastic wrap and refrigerate at least 8 hours.

Grease two 4-cup brioche pans or two 1½-quart ovenproof bowls. Stir down dough. (Dough will be very soft and slightly sticky.) Divide dough in half; refrigerate one half. Shape one-fourth of the remaining dough into a cone shape, using lightly floured hands. Shape remaining three-fourths dough into flattened round, about 3½ inches in diameter.

Place flattened round in 1 pan, patting to fit. Make indentation, about 2 inches in diameter and 1½ inches deep, in center of dough. Place cone-shaped dough, pointed side down, in indentation. Repeat with refrigerated dough. Cover and let rise in warm place about 1½ hours or until double.

Heat oven to 375°. Beat egg yolk and 1 tablespoon water slightly; brush over top of dough. (Do not allow egg yolk mixture to accumulate around edges of pans.) Bake 35 to 40 minutes or until golden brown. Immediately remove from pans. Mix apricot jam and 2 teaspoons water; brush over hot loaves. 2 loaves (12 slices each).

CLASSIC BRIOCHE: Omit nuts, candied fruit, apricot jam and 2 teaspoons water.

INDIVIDUAL BRIOCHES: Grease 24 brioche pans or medium muffin cups, 2½ × 1¼ inches. After stirring down chilled dough, divide in half; refrigerate one half. Shape remaining half dough into roll, about 7½ inches long. Cut into 15 slices, each about ½ inch thick.

Working quickly with floured hands (dough will be very soft and slightly sticky), shape 12 of the slices into balls; place in pans or muffin cups. Flatten and make a deep indentation in center of each ball with thumb. Cut each of the remaining 3 slices into 4 equal parts; shape each part into ball. Place 1 ball in each indentation. Repeat with refrigerated dough. Cover and let rise in warm place about 40 minutes or until double.

Heat oven to 375°. Beat egg yolk and 1 tablespoon water slightly; brush over top of dough. (Do not allow egg yolk mixture to accumulate around edges of pans.) Bake 15 to 20 minutes or until golden brown. Immediately remove from pans. 2 dozen individual brioches.

Christmas Brioche; Saint Lucia Crown (page 127)

Holiday Almond Braid

5 to 5¹/₂ cups all-purpose flour

¹/₂ cup sugar

1 teaspoon salt

2 packages regular or quick-acting active dry yeast

¹/₃ cup margarine or butter

³/₄ cup milk

¹/₂ cup water

2 eggs

1 cup slivered almonds, toasted

2¹/₂ teaspoons grated lemon peel

¹/₄ to ¹/₂ teaspoon ground mace or nutmeg

Glaze (right)

Mix 1¹/₂ cups of the flour, the sugar, salt and undissolved yeast in large bowl. Cut margarine into small pieces. Heat margarine, milk and water until warm (105° to 115°); stir into yeast mixture. Stir in eggs, almonds, lemon peel, mace and enough remaining flour to make a soft dough. Grease top of dough. Cover tightly with plastic wrap and refrigerate at least 2 hours but no longer than 24 hours.

Lightly grease cookie sheet. Punch down dough. Divide into 4 equal parts. Roll 3 parts into 14-inch ropes. Place ropes close together on cookie sheet. Braid ropes loosely. Pinch ends together to seal. Divide remaining dough into 3 pieces. Roll each piece into 12-inch rope. Place ropes close together. Braid ropes; place on top large braid. Cover and let rise in warm place 30 to 50 minutes or until double. (Dough is ready if indentation remains when touched.)

Heat oven to 350°. Bake 40 to 50 minutes or until deep golden brown. Remove from cookie sheet to wire rack. Brush Glaze over warm braid. 1 loaf (32 slices).

GLAZE

¹/₂ cup powdered sugar

Dash of ground mace or nutmeg

3 to 4 teaspoons lemon juice

Mix all ingredients until smooth.

🔔 Toast 2 or 3 times the amount of nuts needed for this recipe, and freeze to use later. To toast, heat oven to 350°. Place nuts in ungreased shallow baking pan, and bake, stirring occasionally, about 10 minutes or until golden brown. Nuts will continue to darken slightly after they are removed from the oven.

Julekake

1 package regular or quick-acting active dry yeast

¹/₄ cup warm water (105° to 115°)

³/₄ cup lukewarm milk

¹/₂ cup sugar

¹/₂ teaspoon salt

¹/₂ teaspoon ground cardamom

1 egg

2 tablespoons shortening

¹/₂ cup raisins

¹/₃ cup chopped citron

3¹/₄ to 3³/₄ cups all-purpose flour

1 egg yolk

2 tablespoons water

Dissolve yeast in ¹/₄ cup warm water in large bowl. Beat in lukewarm milk, sugar, salt, cardamom, egg, shortening, raisins, citron and 1¹/₂ cups of the flour. Beat until smooth. Stir in enough flour to make dough easy to handle.

Turn dough onto lightly floured surface; gently roll in flour to coat. Knead about 5 minutes or until smooth and elastic. Place in greased bowl; turn greased side up. Cover and let rise about 1½ hours or until double. (Dough is ready if indentation remains when touched.)

Grease round pan, 9 × 1½ inches. Punch down dough. Shape into round loaf. Place in pan. Cover and let rise about 45 minutes or until double.

Heat oven to 350°. Beat egg yolk and 2 tablespoons water; brush over dough. Bake 30 to 40 minutes or until golden brown. 1 loaf (16 slices).

Saint Lucia Crown

¹/₁₆ to ¹/₈ teaspoon crushed saffron*

½ cup lukewarm milk

2 packages regular or quick-acting active dry yeast

½ cup warm water (105° to 115°)

½ cup sugar

1 teaspoon salt

2 eggs, beaten

¼ cup (½ stick) margarine or butter, softened

4½ to 5 cups all-purpose flour

½ cup chopped citron

¼ cup chopped blanched almonds

1 tablespoon grated lemon peel

Powdered Sugar Glaze (right)

Candied cherries

Stir saffron into lukewarm milk. Dissolve yeast in warm water in large bowl. Stir in saffron-milk, sugar, salt, eggs, margarine and 2½ cups of the flour. Beat until smooth. Stir in citron, almonds, lemon peel and enough remaining flour to make dough easy to handle.

* 2 or 3 drops yellow food color can be substituted for the saffron.

Turn dough onto lightly floured surface; gently roll in flour to coat. Knead about 10 minutes or until smooth and elastic. Place in greased bowl; turn greased side up. Cover and let rise in warm place about 1½ hours or until double. (Dough is ready if indentation remains when touched.)

Grease 2 cookie sheets. Punch down dough; cut off one-third of dough for top braid and reserve. Divide remaining dough into 3 equal parts; roll each part into 25-inch rope. Place ropes close together on cookie sheet. Braid ropes; shape into circle and pinch ends to seal.

Divide reserved dough into 3 equal parts; roll each part into 16-inch rope. Place ropes close together on second cookie sheet. Braid ropes; shape into circle and pinch ends to seal. Cover both braids and let rise about 45 minutes or until double.

Heat oven to 375°. Bake braids 20 to 25 minutes or until golden brown. Remove from cookie sheets. Cool on wire rack. When cool, make holes for 5 candles in small braid. Drizzle both braids with Powdered Sugar Glaze. Garnish with candied cherries. Insert candles. Place small braid on large braid. 1 large loaf (32 slices).

POWDERED SUGAR GLAZE

1 cup powdered sugar

3 to 4 teaspoons water

Mix ingredients until smooth and of drizzling consistency.

LUCIA BUNS: When ready to shape dough, cut into pieces about 2½ inches in diameter. Roll each piece into 12-inch rope; form into tightly coiled S shape. Place a raisin in center of each coil. Place on greased cookie sheet. Brush tops lightly with margarine or butter. Cover and let rise about 45 minutes or until double. Bake about 15 minutes or until golden brown. About 1½ dozen buns.

Antipasto Pull-Apart

This bread makes a wonderful centerpiece—then, it can be served with a hearty soup and crisp salad.

4 to 5 cups all-purpose flour

1 tablespoon sugar

2 teaspoons salt

¹/₄ cup olive oil or ¹/₄ cup (¹/₂ stick) margarine or butter, melted

2 packages regular or quick-acting active dry yeast

2¹/₄ cups very warm water (120° to 130°)

³/₄ cup finely chopped salami (about 4 ounces)

2 cloves garlic, finely chopped

1³/₄ cups whole wheat flour

¹/₄ cup grated Romano or Parmesan cheese

2 tablespoons chopped fresh or 2 teaspoons dried basil leaves

1 egg white

1 tablespoon cold water

Mix 3 cups of the all-purpose flour, the sugar, salt, oil and yeast in large bowl. Add warm water. Beat on low speed 1 minute, scraping bowl frequently. Beat on medium speed 1 minute, scraping bowl frequently. Divide dough between 2 medium or large bowls.

Stir salami, garlic and whole wheat flour into dough in 1 bowl. If necessary, stir in enough all-purpose flour to make dough easy to handle. Turn dough onto lightly floured surface; gently roll in flour to coat. Knead about 10 minutes or until smooth and elastic. Place in greased bowl; turn greased side up. Cover and let rise in warm place 40 to 60 minutes or until double. (Dough is ready if indentation remains when touched.)

Stir cheese and basil into dough in other bowl. Stir in enough remaining all-purpose flour to make dough easy to handle. Turn dough onto lightly floured surface; gently roll in flour to coat. Knead about 10 minutes or until smooth and elastic. Place in greased bowl; turn greased side up. Cover and let rise in warm place 30 to 50 minutes or until double.

Grease large cookie sheet. Punch down whole wheat dough and let rest 5 minutes. Punch down white dough and let rest 5 minutes. Gently pat each dough into 7¹/₂-inch square. Cut each square into twenty-five 1¹/₂-inch squares. Randomly arrange white and whole wheat squares in 2 round mounds, about 6 inches across. Cover and let rise in warm place 35 to 50 minutes or until double. Beat egg white and cold water; brush over loaves.

Heat oven to 375°. Bake 35 to 40 minutes or until loaves are golden brown and sound hollow when tapped. Remove from cookie sheet. Cool on wire rack. Pull apart to serve. 2 loaves (about 25 pieces each).

ANTIPASTO SPIRAL BREAD: Grease 2 loaf pans, 9 × 5 × 3 or 8¹/₂ × 4¹/₂ × 2¹/₂ inches. Prepare dough as directed—except pat or roll each half dough into rectangle, 30 × 9 inches. Place whole wheat dough rectangle carefully on white dough rectangle. Cut crosswise in half. Roll up each half tightly, beginning at 9-inch side. Place in pans. Cover and let rise in warm place 35 to 50 minutes or until double. Mix egg white and cold water; brush over loaves. Bake 35 to 40 minutes or until loaves are deep golden brown and sound hollow when tapped; remove from pans. Cool on wire rack. 2 loaves (about 16 slices each).

Pesto Pine Bread (page 131); Savory Cheese Swirl (page 132); Poinsettia Puffs (page 133)

Shapely Breads from Refrigerator Dough

You can serve interesting fresh breads any time when you have this dough on hand ready to shape and bake. A rich dough, it's quick to mix and handles extremely well. Note that the water temperature is at the low end of the typical yeast bread water range of 105°–130°. The lower temperature slows the rising of the yeast, allowing the dough to be refrigerated up to 3 days with excellent baking results.

Holiday time usually means the refrigerator is extra full. To save space, divide the dough in half and place greased dough in tightly closed plastic bags so it's ready for use at any time. You can use this easy dough for the attractive delicious bread recipes that follow, or create your own special shape with a favorite filling.

Easy Refrigerator Dough

5 cups all-purpose or unbleached flour

1/3 cup granulated or packed brown sugar

2 packages regular or quick-acting active dry yeast

1 teaspoon salt

2/3 cup milk

2/3 cup water

1/3 cup margarine or butter

2 eggs

Mix 1½ cups of the flour, the sugar, yeast and salt in large bowl. Heat milk, water and margarine until warm (105° to 115°)—margarine need not be melted; gradually stir into flour mixture. Beat on medium speed 2 minutes, scraping bowl occasionally. Add eggs and ½ cup of the flour. Beat on high speed 2 minutes. Stir in remaining flour until stiff dough forms. Grease top of dough. Cover tightly with plastic wrap and refrigerate at least 2 hours but no longer than 3 days. Punch down dough and continue as directed in one of the recipes below. 2 loaves.

Pesto-Pine Bread

The bread takes on the green of the pesto with which it is prepared, so we recommend using Spinach Pesto made with pine nuts, for a fresh green color.

> *¹/₂ recipe Easy Refrigerator Dough (page 130)*
> *¹/₂ cup Spinach Pesto (page 245) or prepared pesto*
> *1 tablespoon pine nuts*
> *Grated Parmesan cheese*

Grease large cookie sheet. Roll dough into rectangle, 15 × 10 inches, on lightly floured surface. Reserve 2 tablespoons of the Spinach Pesto. Spread remaining pesto over dough to within ¹/₂ inch of edges. Roll up tightly, beginning at 15-inch side. Pinch edge of dough into roll to seal. Stretch and shape until even.

Cut and shape dough on cookie sheet as shown in diagram. Spread reserved pesto over top of dough. Sprinkle with pine nuts. Cover and let rise in warm place about 25 minutes or until double. (Dough is ready if indentation remains when touched.)

Heat oven to 350°. Bake 20 to 25 minutes or until golden brown. Immediately sprinkle with cheese. Remove from cookie sheet to wire rack. Serve warm or cool. 1 loaf (16 slices).

2. Assemble the tree as shown.

1. Cut corner of dough at a 45° angle to make a triangle. Measure 5 inches at the top and cut another 45° angle in the opposite direction. Continue measuring and cutting as shown.

Savory Cheese Swirl

You can substitute chopped, well-drained pimiento if red peppers are not available, and you'll have the same cheerful effect.

> *½ recipe Easy Refrigerator Dough (page 138)*
>
> *1 cup shredded Swiss or mozzarella cheese (4 ounces)*
>
> *¼ cup finely chopped red or green bell pepper*
>
> *2 tablespoons finely chopped onion*
>
> *2 tablespoons mayonnaise or salad dressing*
>
> *1 tablespoon chopped fresh or 1 teaspoon dried cilantro leaves*
>
> *½ teaspoon ground cumin*

Grease large cookie sheet. Roll dough into rectangle, 15 × 10 inches, on lightly floured surface. Mix ½ cup of the cheese and the remaining ingredients. Spread cheese mixture over dough to within ½ inch of edges. Roll up tightly, beginning at 15-inch side. Pinch edge of dough into roll to seal. Stretch and shape until even.

1. Cut roll lengthwise in half. Place strips, filling sides up and side by side, on cookie sheet.

2. Twist together gently and loosely, keeping cut sides up.

Cut roll lengthwise in half, using kitchen scissors. Place end of one strip, cut side up, in center of cookie sheet; loosely coil strip. Place second strip, cut side up, end-to-end with first strip; pinch ends together. Continue coiling second strip loosely around first strip; tuck end under coil. Cover and let rise in warm place about 25 minutes or until double. (Dough is ready if indentation remains when touched.)

Heat oven to 375°. Bake 20 to 25 minutes or until golden brown. Immediately sprinkle with remaining cheese. Serve warm. 1 loaf (16 slices).

Prune-Almond Twist

When making the Prune-Almond Sauce for this bread, use chopped almonds and omit the additional apple juice. If you do add the apple juice be sure to cook the sauce until it is very thick. If the sauce is too thin, it makes the dough slip excessively when cut.

> *½ recipe Easy Refrigerator Dough (page 130)*
>
> *1 cup Prune-Almond Sauce (page 248)*
>
> *Powdered sugar or White Chocolate Glaze (page 127)*

Grease large cookie sheet. Roll dough into rectangle, 15 × 10 inches, on lightly floured surface. Spread Prune-Almond Sauce over dough to within ½ inch of edge. Roll up tightly, begin-

ning at 15-inch side. Pinch edge of dough into roll to seal. Stretch and shape until even.

Place roll diagonally across cookie sheet. Cut roll lengthwise in half, using kitchen scissors. Arrange strips cut sides up, so cut surfaces show even stripes of prune filling (some parts of dough may be stuck together from cutting). Gently and loosely twist strips together, making 5 or 6 twists and keeping cut sides up. Cover and let rise in warm place about 25 minutes or until double. (Dough is ready if indentation remains when touched.)

Heat oven to 375°. Bake 20 to 25 minutes or until golden brown. Remove from cookie sheet to wire rack; cool slightly. Dust with powdered sugar, or drizzle with White Chocolate Glaze. Serve warm or cool. 1 loaf (16 slices).

🔔 **One can (8 ounces) prune filling can be substituted for the Prune-Almond Sauce. Stir in ½ cup slivered almonds and 1 teaspoon brandy extract.**

Poinsettia Puffs

To make the centers for these pretty "poinsettias," place ¼ of a dried apricot or maraschino cherry in the center of each puff after glazing.

> *½ recipe Easy Refrigerator Dough (page 130)*
> *¼ cup apricot preserves or jam*
> *¼ teaspoon almond extract*
> *½ cup chopped drained maraschino cherries*
> *Almond Glaze (right)*

Grease 12 medium muffin cups, 2½ × 1¼ inches. Roll dough into rectangle, 15 × 10 inches, on lightly floured surface. Heat preserves and almond extract; spread evenly over dough, using

back of spoon. Sprinkle with cherries. Roll up tightly, beginning at 15-inch side. Pinch edge of dough into roll to seal. Stretch and shape until even.

Cut roll into 12 equal slices. Place slices, cut sides up, in muffin cups. Snip through each slice 3 times, using kitchen scissors, to make 6 wedges. Gently spread pieces open. Cover and let rise in warm place about 25 minutes or until double. (Dough is ready if indentation remains when touched.)

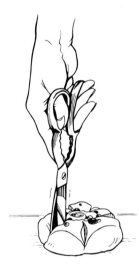

Heat oven to 375°. Bake about 15 minutes or until golden brown. Remove from pan to wire rack. Drizzle Almond Glaze over warm rolls. Serve warm or cool. 1 dozen rolls.

ALMOND GLAZE

> *½ cup powdered sugar*
> *⅛ teaspoon almond extract*
> *2 to 3 teaspoons milk*

Mix all ingredients until smooth and of drizzling consistency.

Stollen

This rich, classic Christmas bread originated in Germany, where it is called Weihnachts-stollen. Each province in the country has its own recipe and shape for the bread.

3¹/₂ cups all-purpose flour

¹/₂ cup sugar

¹/₂ teaspoon salt

1 package regular or quick-acting active dry yeast

³/₄ cup warm water (105° to 115°)

¹/₂ cup (1 stick) margarine or butter, softened

3 eggs

1 egg, separated

¹/₂ cup chopped blanched almonds

¹/₄ cup chopped citron

¹/₄ cup chopped candied cherries, if desired

¹/₄ cup raisins

1 tablespoon grated lemon peel

Margarine or butter, softened

1 tablespoon water

Creamy Frosting (right)

Mix 1³/₄ cups of the flour, the sugar, salt and yeast in large bowl. Add water, ¹/₂ cup margarine, the eggs and egg yolk. Beat on low speed 1 minute, scraping bowl frequently. Beat on medium speed 10 minutes, scraping bowl frequently. Stir in remaining flour, the almonds, citron, candied cherries, raisins and lemon peel. Scrape batter from side of bowl. Cover and let rise in warm place 1¹/₂ to 2 hours or until double. (Dough is ready if indentation remains when touched.)

Stir down batter by beating about 25 strokes. Cover tightly and refrigerate at least 8 hours.

Grease cookie sheet. Turn dough onto well-floured surface; gently roll in flour to coat. Divide in half. Press each half into oval, 10 × 7 inches. Spread with margarine. Fold lengthwise in half; press only folded edge firmly. Place on cookie sheet. Beat egg white and 1 tablespoon water; brush over dough. Cover and let rise 45 to 60 minutes or until double.

Heat oven to 375°. Bake 20 to 25 minutes or until golden brown. Cool 15 minutes. Drizzle Creamy Frosting over warm coffee cakes. If desired, decorate with almond halves, pieces of citron and candied cherry halves to resemble poinsettias, or dust frosting with powdered sugar. Serve warm or cool. 2 coffee cakes (12 slices each).

CREAMY FROSTING

1¹/₂ cups powdered sugar

¹/₂ teaspoon vanilla

2 to 3 tablespoons water

Mix all ingredients until of drizzling consistency.

△ **Measure all the ingredients before you begin, and place them on a tray in order of use.**

Cardamom-Walnut Rolls

1 package regular or quick-acting active
  dry yeast
¼ cup warm water (105° to 115°)
1¼ cups lukewarm milk
¾ cup sugar
½ cup (1 stick) margarine or butter, melted
1 teaspoon salt
9 cardamom seeds, crushed, or ½
  teaspoon ground cardamom
1 egg
4¾ cups all-purpose flour
1 egg, beaten
½ cup finely chopped walnuts
¼ cup sugar

Dissolve yeast in warm water in large bowl. Stir in lukewarm milk, ³/₄ cup sugar, the margarine, salt, cardamom, 1 egg and 2¼ cups of the flour. Beat until smooth. Stir in remaining flour. Cover and let rise in warm place about 1½ hours or until double. (Dough is ready if indentation remains when touched.)

Lightly grease rectangular pan, 13 × 9 × 2 inches. Turn dough onto lightly floured surface; gently roll in flour to coat. (If necessary, work in additional flour to make dough easy to handle.) Divide dough into 15 equal parts. Roll each part into pencil-like rope, 12 inches long. Twist each into pretzel shape. Place in pan. Cover and let rise about 40 minutes or until double.

Heat oven to 375°. Brush rolls with beaten egg. Sprinkle with walnuts and ¼ cup sugar. Bake 30 to 35 minutes or until golden brown. 15 rolls.

Note: For smaller rolls, divide dough into 24 equal parts. Roll each part into pencil-like rope, 8 inches long. Twist each into figure-eight shape. Place in greased jelly roll pan, 15¹/₂ × 10¹/₂ × 1 inch. Continue as directed—except increase walnuts to ³/₄ cup and ¼ cup sugar to ¹/₃ cup. Bake 25 to 30 minutes. 2 dozen rolls.

Panettone

2 packages regular or quick-acting active
  dry yeast
1 cup warm water (105° to 115°)
½ cup sugar
½ cup (1 stick) margarine or butter,
  softened
3 eggs
1 teaspoon salt
1 teaspoon grated lemon peel
1 teaspoon vanilla
5 to 5½ cups all-purpose flour
½ cup golden raisins
½ cup chopped citron
2 tablespoons pine nuts or walnuts
Margarine or butter, softened

Dissolve yeast in warm water in large bowl. Stir in sugar, ¹/₂ cup margarine, the eggs, salt, lemon peel, vanilla and 2¹/₂ cups of the flour. Beat until smooth. Stir in raisins, citron, pine nuts and enough flour to make dough easy to handle.

Turn dough onto lightly floured surface; gently roll in flour to coat. Knead about 5 minutes or until smooth and elastic. Place in greased bowl; turn greased side up. Cover and let rise in warm place 1¹/₂ to 2 hours or until double. (Dough is ready if indentation remains when touched.)

Punch down dough; divide in half. Shape each half into round loaf, about 6 inches in diameter. Place each loaf in ungreased round pan, 8 × 1¹/₂ inches. Cut an X ¹/₂ inch deep on top of each loaf. Generously grease one side of a strip of heavy brown paper, about 25 × 4 inches.

Fit and coil paper around inside of pan, greased side toward center, forming a collar; fasten with paper clip. Repeat for second loaf. Cover and let rise about 1 hour or until double.

Heat oven to 350°. Bake 35 to 45 minutes or until golden brown. Remove loaves from pans to wire rack; remove paper. Brush margarine on tops of loaves; cool. 2 loaves (16 slices each).

*Snowman Buns (**right**) and Snowflake Buns (**right**)*

Squash Rolls

1 cup milk

¹/₂ cup sugar

2 tablespoons margarine or butter

1 teaspoon salt

1 package regular or quick-acting active dry yeast

¹/₄ cup warm water (105° to 115°)

1 cup mashed cooked winter squash*

4¹/₂ to 5 cups all-purpose flour

Heat milk, sugar, margarine and salt until margarine is melted; cool to lukewarm. Dissolve yeast in warm water in large bowl. Stir in milk mixture, squash and 2 cups of the flour. Beat until smooth.

Stir in enough remaining flour to make dough easy to handle.

Turn dough onto lightly floured surface; gently roll in flour to coat. Knead about 5 minutes or until smooth and elastic. Place in greased bowl; turn greased side up. Cover and let rise in warm place about 1¹/₂ hours or until double. (Dough is ready if indentation remains when touched.)

Grease 24 medium muffin cups, 2¹/₂ × 1¹/₄ inches. Punch down dough. Shape into 1-inch balls. Place 3 balls in each muffin cup. Let rise 30 to 45 minutes or until double.

Heat oven to 400°. Bake 15 to 20 minutes or until golden brown. 2 dozen rolls.

* 1 cup frozen squash, thawed and brought to room temperature, can be substituted for the fresh squash.

Snowman Buns

These buns are as fun to give as they are to make. Try tying a ribbon around the center for an easy package look. They are also especially nice for one- or two-person households.

> *1 package regular or quick-acting active*
>   *dry yeast*
>
> *³/₄ cup warm water (105° to 115°)*
>
> *¹/₃ cup sugar*
>
> *¹/₄ cup shortening*
>
> *2 teaspoons ground nutmeg, if desired*
>
> *1 teaspoon salt*
>
> *2 eggs*
>
> *3¹/₂ cups all-purpose flour*
>
> *60 currants (about 1 rounded tablespoon)*
>
> *1 egg, slightly beaten*

Dissolve yeast in warm water in large bowl. Beat in sugar, shortening, nutmeg, salt, 2 eggs and 2 cups of the flour. Beat on low speed 30 seconds, scraping bowl constantly. Beat on medium speed 2 minutes, scraping bowl occasionally. Stir in remaining flour until smooth. Cover and let rise in warm place about 45 minutes or until double. (Dough is ready if indentation remains when touched.)

Stir down dough by beating 25 strokes. Turn onto well-floured surface. Gently roll in flour to coat. Cut into 12 equal parts (each part will make 1 snowman). Shape one-half of each part into 4-inch oval for the body. Shape one-half of the remaining dough into a ball and attach for the head. Press in tiny piece of dough for nose. Shape remaining dough into 4-inch roll; cut in half and attach for arms.

Grease cookie sheet. Arrange snowmen about 3 inches apart on cookie sheet. Cover and let rise about 45 minutes or until double.

Heat oven to 350°. Press in 2 currants for eyes and 3 currants for buttons. Brush buns with beaten egg. Bake about 15 minutes or until golden brown. Serve warm. 1 dozen buns.

SNOWFLAKE BUNS: Cut dough into 16 equal parts. Shape into balls. Place 4 balls with sides touching in shape of square on greased cookie sheet. Repeat with remaining balls to make 4 squares. Cover and let rise about 45 minutes or until double. Prepare Baked-on Decorator's Frosting (page 5). Outline snowflake designs on each roll with frosting. Bake 12 to 15 minutes. 16 buns.

Parmesan-Pepper Rolls

> *2¹/₄ cups all-purpose flour*
>
> *2 tablespoons sugar*
>
> *2 tablespoons grated Parmesan cheese*
>
> *1 teaspoon salt*
>
> *¹/₄ teaspoon coarsely ground pepper*
>
> *1 package regular or quick-acting active*
>   *dry yeast*
>
> *1 cup very warm water (120° to 130°)*
>
> *1 egg*
>
> *2 tablespoons vegetable oil*

Mix 1¹/₄ cups of the flour, the sugar, cheese, salt, pepper and yeast in large bowl. Beat in warm water, egg and oil until smooth. Stir in remaining flour until smooth. Scrape batter from side of bowl. Cover and let rise in warm place about 30 minutes or until double.

Grease 12 medium muffin cups, 2¹/₂ × 1¹/₄ inches. Stir down batter, beating about 25 strokes. Divide among muffin cups. Let rise uncovered 20 to 30 minutes or until batter rounds over tops of cups.

Heat oven to 400°. Bake 15 to 20 minutes or until golden brown. 1 dozen rolls.

Refrigerator Roll Dough

1 package regular or quick-acting active
  dry yeast

1½ cups warm water (105° to 115°)

1 cup unseasoned lukewarm mashed
  potatoes

⅔ cup sugar

⅔ cup shortening

1½ teaspoons salt

2 eggs

6 to 7 cups all-purpose flour

Dissolve yeast in warm water in large bowl. Stir in potatoes, sugar, shortening, salt, eggs and 3 cups of the flour. Beat until smooth. Mix in enough remaining flour to make dough easy to handle.

Turn dough onto lightly floured surface; gently roll in flour to coat. Knead about 5 minutes or until smooth and elastic. Place in greased bowl; turn greased side up. Cover bowl tightly; refrigerate at least 8 hours but no longer than 5 days.

Punch down dough; divide into 4 equal parts. Use one-fourth of the dough for any Dinner Roll recipe below.

WHOLE WHEAT REFRIGERATOR ROLL DOUGH: Substitute 3 to 4 cups whole wheat flour for the second addition of all-purpose flour.

DINNER ROLLS

BROWN-AND-SERVE ROLLS: Shape Refrigerator Roll Dough as directed in any roll recipe (right). Cover and let rise in warm place 1 hour. Heat oven to 275°. Bake 20 minutes (do not allow to brown). Remove from pans; cool to room temperature. Wrap in aluminum foil. Store in refrigerator up to 8 days or in freezer up to 2 months. At serving time, heat oven to 400°. Bake 8 to 12 minutes or until brown.

CRESCENT ROLLS: Grease cookie sheet. Roll one-fourth of Refrigerator Roll Dough into 12-inch circle about ¼ inch thick on well-floured surface. Spread with margarine or butter, softened. Cut into 16 wedges. Roll wedges up tightly, beginning at rounded edge, stretching dough as it is rolled. Place rolls with points underneath on cookie sheet. Curve slightly. Brush with margarine or butter, softened. Cover and let rise in warm place 1 hour. Heat oven to 400°. Bake 15 minutes. 16 rolls.

FOUR-LEAF CLOVERS: Grease 8 to 10 medium muffin cups, 2½ × 1¼ inches. Shape one-fourth of Refrigerator Roll dough into 2-inch balls. Place 1 ball in each muffin cup. Snip each ball completely in half, then into fourths, using scissors. Brush with margarine or butter, softened. Cover and let rise in warm place 1 hour. Heat oven to 400°. Bake 15 to 20 minutes. 8 to 10 rolls.

COCKTAIL BUNS

½ recipe Refrigerator Roll Dough (left)

1 egg yolk

1 tablespoon water

Poppy seed or sesame seed

Grease cookie sheet. Shape Refrigerator Roll Dough into 1-inch balls. Place 1 inch apart on cookie sheet. Beat egg yolk and water; brush tops of balls with egg mixture. Sprinkle with poppy seed. Cover and let rise in warm place about 1 hour or until double. Heat oven to 400°. Bake about 15 minutes or until golden brown. 4 dozen buns.

Hot Cross Buns

1/2 recipe Refrigerator Roll Dough (page 138)

3/4 cup raisins

1/3 cup chopped citron

1/4 teaspoon ground nutmeg

1 egg white, slightly beaten

Quick Frosting (below)

Grease cookie sheet. Turn Refrigerator Roll Dough onto generously floured surface. Squeeze raisins, citron and nutmeg into dough until well distributed. Cut dough into 24 equal pieces. Shape each piece into ball. Place about 2 inches apart on cookie sheet. Snip X shape on top of each bun, using scissors. Cover and let rise in warm place about 1 hour or until double. Heat oven to 375°. Brush tops of buns with egg white. Bake about 20 minutes or until golden brown; cool. Frost X shapes on tops of buns with Quick Frosting. 2 dozen buns.

QUICK FROSTING

3/4 cup powdered sugar

2 teaspoons water or milk

1/4 teaspoon vanilla

Mix all ingredients until smooth and of spreading consistency.

Anise Rolls

5 3/4 to 6 cups all-purpose flour

3/4 cup packed brown sugar

1/2 cup (1 stick) margarine or butter, softened

1 1/2 teaspoons salt

1 teaspoon anise seed, crushed

2 packages regular or quick-acting active dry yeast

3/4 cup very warm water (120° to 130°)

5 eggs

1 egg

1 tablespoon anise seed

Mix 2 cups of the flour, the brown sugar, margarine, salt, crushed anise seed and yeast in large bowl. Stir in warm water and 5 eggs. Beat on low speed 1 minute, scraping bowl frequently. Beat on medium speed 1 minute, scraping bowl frequently. Stir in enough remaining flour, 1 cup at a time, to make dough easy to handle.

Turn dough onto lightly floured surface; gently roll in flour to coat. Knead about 10 minutes or until smooth and elastic. Place in greased bowl; turn greased side up. Cover and let rise in warm place about 1 hour or until double. (Dough is ready if indentation remains when touched.)

Grease cookie sheets. Punch down dough. Turn onto lightly floured surface; knead until smooth. Divide dough into 18 equal pieces. Shape each piece into a smooth oval, 3 to 4 inches long; flatten slightly. Place 2 inches apart on cookie sheets. Cover and let rise about 45 minutes or until double.

Heat oven to 350°. Beat 1 egg; brush on rolls. Sprinkle with 1 tablespoon anise seed. Bake about 20 minutes or until golden brown. Cool on wire rack. 1 1/2 dozen rolls.

Cheese Straw Twists

These easy bread sticks are welcome additions to your bread basket—the crisp-tender morsels will melt in your mouth! For a peppery twist, mix 2 teaspoons cracked black pepper with the parmesan cheese mixture. To serve as appetizers, cut the twists in half before baking.

²/₃ cup grated Parmesan cheese

1 tablespoon paprika

1 package (17¹/₄ ounces) frozen puff pastry, thawed

1 egg, slightly beaten

Heat oven to 425°. Line 2 cookie sheets with cooking parchment paper or heavy brown paper. Mix cheese and paprika. Roll 1 sheet of pastry into rectangle, 12 × 10 inches, on lightly floured surface with floured cloth-covered rolling pin.

Brush pastry with egg. Sprinkle with 3 tablespoons of the cheese mixture. Press cheese mixture gently into pastry. Turn pastry over. Repeat with egg and cheese mixture. Fold pastry lengthwise in half.

Cut pastry crosswise into ¹/₂-inch strips. Unfold strips and roll each end in opposite directions to twist. Place twists on cookie sheet. Bake 7 to 8 minutes or until puffed and golden brown. Repeat with remaining sheet of pastry, egg and cheese mixture. Remove from cookie sheet to wire rack. Serve warm or cool. About 4 dozen twists.

Cheese Straw Twists; Antipasto Pull-Apart (page 128)

Italian Flatbread

2¹/₂ to 3 cups all-purpose or unbleached flour

2 teaspoons sugar

¹/₄ teaspoon salt

1 package regular or quick-acting active dry yeast

¹/₄ cup olive or vegetable oil

1 cup very warm water (120° to 130°)

Olive or vegetable oil

2 tablespoons chopped fresh herbs (such as basil, oregano or rosemary)

2 tablespoons grated Parmesan cheese

Mix 1 cup of the flour, the sugar, salt and yeast in large bowl. Add ¹/₄ cup oil and the warm water. Beat on medium speed 3 minutes, scraping bowl occasionally. Stir in enough remaining flour until dough is soft and leaves side of bowl.

Turn dough onto lightly floured surface; gently roll in flour to coat. Knead 5 to 10 minutes or until dough is smooth and elastic. Place in greased bowl; turn greased side up. Cover and let rise in warm place 1 to 1¹/₂ hours or until double. (Dough is ready if indentation remains when touched.)

Heat oven to 425°. Grease 2 cookie sheets. Punch down dough, and divide in half. Shape each half into flattened 12-inch round on cookie sheet. Cover and let rise in warm place 20 minutes. Prick centers and 1 inch in from edge thoroughly with fork. Brush with oil. Sprinkle each with 1 tablespoon herbs and cheese. Bake 12 to 15 minutes or until golden brown. Serve warm. 2 flatbreads (12 slices each).

RED PEPPER FLATBREAD: For each flatbread, cook 1 medium red bell pepper, cut into ¹/₄-inch rings, and 1 small onion, sliced, in 1 tablespoon olive or vegetable oil in 10-inch skillet over medium heat, stirring frequently, until softened. Arrange on each oil-brushed flatbread and sprinkle with herbs and cheese before baking.

Delectable Drinks

*P*arties and family gatherings call for plenty of thirst-quenching beverages. You'll love our Holiday Eggnog and Hot Buttered Rum, delicious with or without rum. Or try some of our enticing sparkling punches, such as Five Fruit Punch, for your next party.

Holiday Eggnog

Soft Custard (below)

1 cup whipping (heavy) cream

2 tablespoons powdered sugar

1/2 teaspoon vanilla

1/2 cup rum

1 or 2 drops yellow food color, if desired

Ground nutmeg

Prepare Soft Custard. Just before serving, beat whipping cream, powdered sugar and vanilla in chilled small bowl until stiff. Stir rum and food color into chilled custard. Gently stir 1 cup of the whipped cream into custard.

Pour eggnog into small punch bowl. Drop remaining whipped cream in 4 or 5 mounds onto eggnog. Sprinkle nutmeg on whipped cream mounds. Serve immediately. Immediately refrigerate any remaining eggnog. 10 servings.

SOFT CUSTARD

3 eggs, slightly beaten

1/3 cup sugar

Dash of salt

2 1/2 cups milk

1 teaspoon vanilla

Mix eggs, sugar and salt in heavy 2-quart sauce-
pan. Gradually stir in milk. Cook over low heat 15 to 20 minutes, stirring constantly, just until mixture coats a metal spoon; remove from heat. Stir in vanilla. Place saucepan in cold water until custard is cool. (If custard curdles, beat vigorously with hand beater until smooth.) Cover and refrigerate at least 2 hours but no longer than 24 hours.

Magical Yogurt Drink

1 container (1/2 gallon) vanilla frozen yogurt

5 cups white grape juice, chilled

5 cups red-colored fruit drink (such as wild berry or punch), chilled

Divide frozen yogurt evenly between 2 large pitchers. Pour grape juice over yogurt in 1 pitcher. Pour fruit drink over yogurt in second pitcher. Let stand about 10 minutes or until yogurt is partially melted.

Beat contents of each pitcher with wire whisk until smooth. To serve, divide grape juice mixture among 20 glasses. Carefully pour fruit drink mixture into filled glasses along inside edge to form marbled-looking beverage. Serve immediately. Immediately refrigerate any remaining beverages. 20 servings.

Pumpkin Milk Shakes

1 cup vanilla ice cream
³/₄ cup milk
¹/₄ cup mashed cooked or canned
  pumpkin
Dash of ground cinnamon
Dash of ground nutmeg

Place all ingredients in blender. Cover and blend on high speed about 15 seconds or until smooth. 2 servings (about 1 cup each).

Wine Snowball

²/₃ cup dry red wine
1¹/₃ cups ginger ale or club soda
2 sticks cinnamon

Mix wine and ginger ale in freezer tray or square pan, $8 \times 8 \times 2$ or $9 \times 9 \times 2$ inches. Freeze about 2 hours or until mushy. Spoon into 2 champagne or sherbet glasses. Garnish each with cinnamon stick. 2 servings (about 1 cup each).

Quick Cranberry Punch

1 can (6 ounces) frozen lemonade
  concentrate
1 bottle (32 ounces) cranberry juice
  cocktail, chilled
2 cans (12 ounces each) ginger ale,
  chilled

Prepare lemonade as directed on can in large pitcher. Stir in cranberry juice cocktail and enough ice to chill. Just before serving, stir in ginger ale. 12 servings (about ³/₄ cup each).

Frosty Citrus Punch

2 cans (6 ounces each) frozen limeade or
  lemonade concentrate, thawed
3 cups cold water
2 cans (12 ounces each) lemon-lime
  carbonated beverage, chilled (3 cups)
1 cup lime or lemon sherbet, softened (¹/₂
  pint)

Mix limeade concentrate and cold water; refrigerate until chilled. Just before serving, stir in carbonated beverage. Pour into small punch bowl. Float scoops of sherbet on top. 15 servings.

Fruit Glow Punch

1 can (6 ounces) frozen orange juice
  concentrate, thawed
1 can (6 ounces) frozen lemonade
  concentrate, thawed
1 bottle (32 ounces) apple juice, chilled
1 bottle (2 liters) ginger ale, chilled
1 pint lemon or orange sherbet

Mix orange juice concentrate, lemonade concentrate and apple juice in large punch bowl. Stir in ginger ale. Spoon sherbet into punch bowl. Float ice ring or ice cubes in punch bowl if desired. Serve immediately. 28 servings (about ¹/₂ cup each).

Strawberry-Grapefruit Drink

1 package (10 ounces) frozen sweetened strawberries, partially thawed
3 cups chilled grapefruit juice

Break up strawberries. Place strawberries and 1 cup of the grapefruit juice in blender. Cover and blend on high speed about 30 seconds or until smooth. Add remaining grapefruit juice. Cover and blend until mixed. Serve over ice. 4 servings.

Sparkling Pineapple Punch

½ cup sugar
½ cup water
2 three-inch sticks cinnamon
¼ cup lime juice
1 can (46 ounces) pineapple juice, chilled
1 bottle (1 liter) sparkling water, chilled
1 bottle (750 milliliters) champagne or sparkling white wine, chilled*

Heat sugar, water and cinnamon to boiling; reduce heat. Cover and simmer 15 minutes. Cover and refrigerate at least 2 hours or until chilled.

Remove cinnamon from syrup. Just before serving, mix syrup and remaining ingredients in large punch bowl. 26 servings.

* 1 bottle (1 liter) ginger ale can be substituted for the champagne.

Cranberry-Orange Slush Cocktail

The perfect drink to have on hand for drop-in guests! The slush freezes quickly when packaged in 1-pint containers and can be used directly from the freezer. If you'd like to freeze in large quantities for punch, freeze for one or two days, until firm.

2 cups brandy
1 bottle (32 ounces) cranberry juice cocktail
1 can (12 ounces) frozen orange juice concentrate, thawed
1 can (12 ounces) frozen cranberry juice concentrate, thawed
2 bottles (1 liter each) lemon-lime carbonated beverage or sparkling water

Mix all ingredients except carbonated beverage in nonmetal container. Divide among pint containers. Cover and freeze at least 8 hours until slushy.

For each serving, mix equal amounts of slush mixture and carbonated beverage in glass. 30 servings.

CRANBERRY-ORANGE PUNCH: Place slush mixture in small punch bowl. Add carbonated beverage; stir.

△ **You can make this drink up to 2 months ahead of time. Covered tightly, it keeps in the freezer very well.**

Cranberry-Orange Slush Cocktail; Holiday Eggnog (page 142); Stollen (page 134)

Cranberry-Lemon Punch

To serve a smaller group, this punch can easily be cut in half.

> *3 quarts water*
> *1½ cups sugar*
> *2 cups chilled orange juice*
> *2 cups chilled strong tea*
> *1 bottle (64 ounces) cranberry juice cocktail, chilled*
> *1 bottle (32 ounces) apple juice, chilled*
> *2 cans (6 ounces each) frozen lemonade concentrate, thawed*

Heat water and sugar to boiling, stirring constantly, until sugar is dissolved; cool.

Just before serving, mix syrup and remaining ingredients in large punch bowl. 60 servings.

🔔 **Use 3 tablespoons instant tea and cold water in place of chilled strong tea.**

Five Fruit Punch

> *Fruit Ice Cubes (below)*
> *1 bottle (48 ounces) cranberry-raspberry drink*
> *1 can (12 ounces) frozen pineapple-orange-guava juice concentrate, thawed*
> *1 bottle (1 liter) ginger ale, chilled*
> *1 bottle (750 milliliters) catawba grape juice or champagne, chilled*

Prepare Fruit Ice Cubes. Mix cranberry-raspberry drink and juice concentrate; refrigerate until chilled. Just before serving, pour juice mixture into large punch bowl. Stir in ginger ale and catawba juice. Add Fruit Ice Cubes. 28 servings.

FRUIT ICE CUBES

Fill ice-cube trays with water or fruit juice. Add a raspberry, pineapple chunk, small orange slice or star fruit slice and, if desired, a mint leaf to each cube section; freeze.

Wassail

You can make a glass punch bowl safer for hot beverages by filling with hot water and letting it stand about 30 minutes. Pour out the water and slowly add the hot punch.

> *1 gallon apple cider*
> *²/₃ cup sugar*
> *2 teaspoons whole allspice*
> *2 teaspoons whole cloves*
> *2 three-inch sticks cinnamon*
> *2 oranges, studded with cloves*

Heat all ingredients except oranges to boiling in Dutch oven; reduce heat. Cover and simmer 20 minutes, strain. Pour into small punch bowl. Float oranges in bowl. Serve hot. 32 servings.

Hot Cinnamon-Orange Cider

> *1 bottle (64 ounces) apple cider*
> *1 quart orange juice*
> *¹/₃ cup red cinnamon candies*
> *1 tablespoon whole allspice*
> *3 tablespoons honey*

Heat apple cider, orange juice, candies and allspice to boiling; reduce heat. Cover and simmer 5 minutes. Remove allspice. Stir in honey. Serve hot. 12 servings.

Cranberry-Lemon Punch (left); Frosty Citrus Punch (page 143)

Royal Cranberry Punch

¹/₂ cup packed brown sugar

1 teaspoon pumpkin pie spice

7 cups water

2 cans (16 ounces each) jellied cranberry sauce

¹/₄ cup lemon juice

1 can (12 ounces) frozen orange juice concentrate, thawed

Mix brown sugar, pumpkin pie spice and 1 cup of the water in Dutch oven. Heat to boiling over high heat, stirring constantly. Boil and stir until sugar is dissolved; remove from heat. Stir in cranberry sauce until well blended. Stir in remaining water, the lemon juice and orange juice concentrate. Heat to boiling; reduce heat. Simmer uncovered 5 minutes. Serve hot. 24 servings.

Warming Tomato Drink

Keep a pitcher of this drink in your refrigerator ready to heat up, to warm you when you come in after playing in the snow.

2 cans (10¹/₂ ounces each) condensed beef broth (about 2¹/₂ cups)

1 cup tomato juice

1 cup water

1¹/₂ teaspoons prepared horseradish

¹/₂ teaspoon dried dill weed

Heat all ingredients to simmering. Serve hot or cold. 6 servings.

TO MICROWAVE: Mix all ingredients in 8-cup microwavable measure. Microwave uncovered on high about 4 minutes or until hot.

Hot Cappuccino Nog

3 eggs, slightly beaten
1/3 cup granulated sugar
Dash of salt
2 1/2 cups milk
1 teaspoon vanilla
1 cup hot espresso coffee
1/2 cup coffee liqueur or brandy, if desired
1 cup whipping (heavy) cream
1 tablespoon packed brown sugar
Ground cinnamon

Mix eggs, granulated sugar and salt in heavy 2-quart saucepan. Gradually stir in milk. Cook over low heat 15 to 20 minutes, stirring constantly, just until mixture coats a metal spoon; remove from heat. Stir in vanilla. Mix coffee and liqueur. Gradually stir coffee mixture into custard mixture; keep warm. Just before serving, beat whipping cream and brown sugar in chilled small bowl until stiff. Gently stir 1 cup of the whipped cream into custard.

Pour eggnog into small heatproof punch bowl. Drop remaining whipped cream in 4 or 5 mounds onto eggnog. Sprinkle cinnamon on whipped cream mounds. Serve immediately. Immediately refrigerate any remaining eggnog. 8 servings.

Hot Buttered Rum

Once you have the rich, buttery mix prepared, you can offer warm cheer any time you wish. It's also a satisfying, warming drink when made without the rum.

1 cup (2 sticks) margarine or butter
1 cup plus 2 tablespoons packed brown sugar
1 cup whipping (heavy) cream
2 cups powdered sugar
1/8 teaspoon ground cloves
1/8 teaspoon ground cinnamon
1/4 teaspoon ground nutmeg

Have ready for each serving:

1 ounce rum (2 tablespoons)
1/2 cup boiling water
Ground nutmeg

Beat margarine and brown sugar in medium bowl on medium speed about 5 minutes or until fluffy. Beat in whipping cream and powdered sugar alternately on low speed until smooth. Stir in cloves, cinnamon and nutmeg. Spoon into 1-quart freezer container. Cover, label and freeze up to 3 months.

For each serving, place rum and 2 tablespoons Hot Buttered Rum batter in mug. Stir in boiling water. Sprinkle with nutmeg. About 3 cups batter. 24 servings.

Mulled Wine

2 cups pineapple juice

1 cup water

¹/₂ cup orange juice

1 cup packed brown sugar

¹/₂ teaspoon salt

1 four-inch stick cinnamon

6 whole cloves

3 whole allspice

Peel of 2 oranges, cut into ¹/₄-inch strips

1 bottle (750 milliliters) dry red wine

Heat all ingredients except wine to boiling in Dutch oven, stirring occasionally; reduce heat. Simmer uncovered 15 minutes. Remove spices and orange peel. Stir in wine. Heat just until hot (do not boil). Serve hot in mugs or heatproof glasses garnished with orange slice and cinnamon stick if desired. 10 servings.

Mulled Wine can be covered and refrigerated up to 1 week. Right before serving, heat just until hot—do not boil.

Hot Cappuccino Nog (left); Wassail (page 146); Pumpkin Muffins (page 123)

CHAPTER

2

Holiday Menus for Family and Friends

Roast Turkey (page 153)

A Traditional Christmas Dinner for 8

Holiday Eggnog (page 142)
Hot Apple Cider or Sparkling Cider*
Roast Turkey with Old-fashioned Stuffing
Giblet Gravy
Velvet Mashed Potatoes
Steamed Peas and Carrots with Herbs*
Deluxe Creamed Onions
Fresh Cranberry Salad
Pickles and Relishes*
Squash Rolls (page 136)
Christmas Coconut Cake (page 63)
OR
Classic Pumpkin Pie (page 88)

* Recipes not included.

Planning Guide

One or Two Days Before
- Thaw turkey if frozen.
- Prepare dessert.
- Prepare Squash Rolls.

Early in the Day
- Prepare Fresh Cranberry Salad.
- Prepare Roast Turkey with Old-fashioned Stuffing.

Several Hours Before
- Prepare Velvet Mashed Potatoes.
- Prepare Deluxe Creamed Onions.
- Prepare peas and carrots.

20 Minutes Before
- Warm rolls in warm oven from roast and prepare Giblet Gravy while turkey is standing.

Roast Turkey

When buying turkeys under 12 pounds, allow ³/₄ pound per serving. For heavier turkeys (12 pounds and over), allow about ¹/₂ pound per serving.

Rub cavity of turkey lightly with salt if desired. Do not salt cavity if turkey is to be stuffed. Stuff turkey just before roasting—not ahead of time. (See Old-fashioned Stuffing, page 154.) Fill wishbone area with stuffing first. Fasten neck skin to back with skewer. Fold wings across back with tips touching. Fill body cavity lightly. (Do not pack—stuffing will expand while cooking.) Tuck drumsticks under band of skin at tail or tie together with heavy string, then tie to tail.

Place turkey, breast side up, on rack in shallow roasting pan. Brush with melted margarine or butter. Insert meat thermometer so tip is in thickest part of inside thigh muscle and does not touch bone. Do not add water.

Roast uncovered in 325° oven. Follow Timetable (right) for approximate total cooking time. Place a tent of aluminum foil loosely over turkey when it begins to turn golden. When two-thirds done, cut band of skin or string holding legs.

This Timetable is based on chilled or completely thawed turkeys at a temperature of about 40° and placed in preheated ovens. Differences in the shape and tenderness of individual turkeys can also necessitate increasing or decreasing the cooking time slightly. For prestuffed turkeys, follow package directions very carefully; do not use Timetable. Whole birds should reach an internal temperature of 180° when done.

There is no substitute for a meat thermometer for determining the doneness of a turkey. Placed in the thigh muscle, it should register 180° when the turkey is done, and the drumstick should move

Timetable for Roasting Turkey

READY-TO-COOK WEIGHT	APPROXIMATE TOTAL ROASTING TIME* (HOURS)
Whole Turkey (unstuffed)	
6 to 8 pounds	2¹/₄ to 3¹/₄
8 to 12 pounds	3 to 4
12 to 16 pounds	4 to 5
16 to 20 pounds	4¹/₂ to 5¹/₂
20 to 24 pounds	5 to 6¹/₂
Whole Turkey (stuffed)	
6 to 8	3 to 3¹/₂
8 to 12	3¹/₂ to 4¹/₂
12 to 16	4 to 5
16 to 20	4¹/₂ to 5¹/₂
20 to 24	5 to 6¹/₂
Turkey Breast	
2 to 4	1¹/₂ to 2
3 to 5	1¹/₂ to 2¹/₂
5 to 7	2 to 2¹/₂

easily when lifted or twisted. Roast until juices run clear (no pink should remain). If the turkey is stuffed, the point of the thermometer can be placed in the center of the stuffing and will register 165° when done.

When turkey is done, remove from oven and allow to stand about 20 minutes for easiest carving. As soon as possible after serving, remove every bit of stuffing from turkey. Cool stuffing, turkey meat and any gravy promptly; refrigerate separately. Use gravy or stuffing within 1 or 2 days; heat them thoroughly before serving. Serve cooked turkey meat within 2 or 3 days after roasting. If frozen, it can be kept up to 3 weeks.

🔔 **For faster preparation and easier carving, try roasting a turkey breast.**

Old-fashioned Stuffing

Make your favorite stuffing, or try a new one, and maybe even begin a family tradition.

1½ cups chopped celery (stalks and
leaves)

¾ cup finely chopped onion

1 cup (2 sticks) margarine or butter

9 cups soft bread cubes (about 15 slices
bread)

2 tablespoons chopped fresh or 1½
teaspoons dried sage leaves

1 tablespoon fresh chopped or 1 teaspoon
dried thyme leaves

1½ teaspoons salt

½ teaspoon pepper

Cook celery and onion in margarine in 10-inch skillet, stirring frequently, until onion is tender. Stir in about one-third of the bread cubes. Place in deep bowl. Add remaining bread cubes and ingredients; toss. Stuff turkey just before roasting. 9 cups stuffing (enough for a 12-pound turkey).

Note: To bake stuffing separately, place in greased 3-quart casserole or baking dish, 13 × 9 × 2 inches. Cover and bake in 325° oven 30 minutes. Uncover and bake 15 minutes longer.

CHESTNUT STUFFING: Decrease bread cubes to 7 cups and add 1 pound chestnuts, cooked and chopped, with the remaining ingredients. To prepare chestnuts, cut an X on rounded side of each chestnut. Heat chestnuts and enough water to cover to boiling. Boil uncovered 10 minutes; drain. Remove shells and skins. Heat chestnuts and enough water to cover to boiling. Boil uncovered 10 minutes; drain and chop.

CORN BREAD STUFFING: Substitute corn bread cubes for the soft bread cubes.

OYSTER STUFFING: Decrease bread cubes to 8 cups and add 2 cans (8 ounces each) oysters, drained and chopped, with the remaining ingredients.

SAUSAGE STUFFING: Decrease bread cubes to 8 cups and omit salt. Cook 1 pound bulk pork sausage until brown; drain, reserving fat. Substitute fat for part of the margarine. Crumble sausage and add with the remaining ingredients.

Giblet Gravy

Turkey giblets
4 cups water, salted if desired
½ cup all-purpose flour
Salt and pepper

Cook gizzard, heart and neck in water 1 to 2 hours or until tender. Add liver the last 10 minutes. Drain; reserve liquid for gravy. Remove meat from neck; finely chop giblets. Refrigerate liquid and giblets until ready to use.

Place roasted turkey on warm platter; keep warm while preparing gravy. Pour drippings from pan into bowl, leaving brown particles in pan. Return ½ cup drippings to pan. (Measure accurately so gravy is not greasy.) Stir in flour. Cook over low heat, stirring constantly, until smooth and bubbly; remove from heat. Add enough water to reserved liquid to measure 4 cups; stir into flour mixture. Heat to boiling, stirring constantly. Boil and stir 1 minute. Stir in a few drops browning sauce if desired. Sprinkle with salt and pepper.

THIN GRAVY: Decrease drippings to 1 tablespoon and flour to 1 tablespoon.

Velvet Mashed Potatoes

For added flavor and a touch of color, stir in about 1 tablespoon fresh chopped chives or dillweed.

> *3 pounds potatoes (about 9 medium), peeled and cut into pieces*
>
> *1/2 to 3/4 cup milk*
>
> *1 package (3 ounces) cream cheese, cut into cubes and softened*
>
> *1/3 cup margarine or butter, softened*
>
> *1/2 teaspoon salt*
>
> *Dash of pepper*

Heat 1 inch water (salted if desired) to boiling in 3-quart saucepan. Add potatoes. Cover and heat to boiling. Cook 20 to 25 minutes or until tender; drain. Shake pan with potatoes over low heat to dry.

Mash potatoes until no lumps remain. Beat in milk in small amounts (amount of milk needed to make potatoes smooth and fluffy depends on kind of potatoes used). Add cream cheese, margarine, salt and pepper. Beat vigorously until potatoes are light and fluffy.

Deluxe Creamed Onions

> *2 pounds small white onions**
>
> *2 tablespoons margarine or butter*
>
> *2 tablespoons all-purpose flour*
>
> *1/2 teaspoon salt*
>
> *1/8 teaspoon pepper*
>
> *1 1/2 cups half-and-half*
>
> *3 large carrots, shredded (about 1 1/2 cups)*

Heat 1 inch water (salted if desired) to boiling in 3-quart saucepan. Peel onions; add to water. Cover and heat to boiling. Cook until tender, small onions 15 to 20 minutes, large onions 30 to 35 minutes; drain.

Heat margarine in same saucepan over low heat until melted. Stir in flour, salt and pepper. Cook over low heat, stirring constantly, until smooth and bubbly; remove from heat. Stir in half-and-half. Heat to boiling, stirring constantly. Boil and stir 1 minute. Stir in carrots. Cook about 5 minutes or until carrots are hot. Pour sauce over hot onions.

* 2 cans (16 ounces each) whole onions, heated and drained, can be substituted for the cooked fresh onions.

Fresh Cranberry Salad

> *2 cups water*
>
> *3/4 cup sugar*
>
> *3 cups cranberries*
>
> *1 package (6 ounces) orange-flavored gelatin*
>
> *1 can (8 1/4 ounces) crushed pineapple in syrup, undrained*
>
> *1/2 cup chopped celery or walnuts*
>
> *Salad greens*

Heat water and sugar to boiling in 2-quart saucepan, stirring occasionally. Boil 1 minute. Stir in cranberries. Heat to boiling; boil 5 minutes, stirring occasionally. Stir in gelatin until dissolved. Stir in pineapple and celery. Pour into ungreased 6-cup mold or 8 individual molds. Refrigerate at least 6 hours until firm. Unmold onto salad greens. Garnish with sour cream and pineapple chunks if desired.

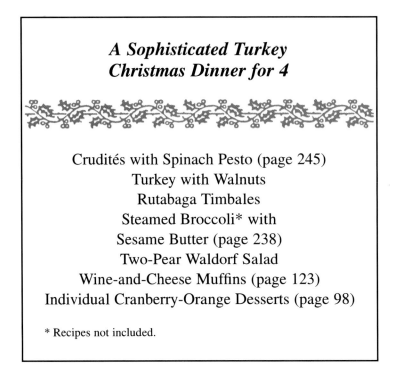

A Sophisticated Turkey Christmas Dinner for 4

Crudités with Spinach Pesto (page 245)
Turkey with Walnuts
Rutabaga Timbales
Steamed Broccoli* with
Sesame Butter (page 238)
Two-Pear Waldorf Salad
Wine-and-Cheese Muffins (page 123)
Individual Cranberry-Orange Desserts (page 98)

* Recipes not included.

Planning Guide

Several Days Before
- Prepare crudités, Spinach Pesto and Sesame Butter. Cover and refrigerate.

One Day Before
- Prepare and bake Individual Cranberry-Orange Desserts; cover and refrigerate.
- Bake Wine-Cheese Muffins; cover loosely.
- Prepare Rutabaga Timbales for baking; cover and refrigerate.

Several Hours Before
- Prepare Two-Pear Waldorf Salad.

About 45 Minutes Before
- Bake Rutabaga Timbales.
- Cook broccoli.
- Prepare Turkey Slices with Walnuts.

About 15 Minutes Before
- Reheat muffins in 300° oven 10 minutes.

Turkey with Walnuts

2 tablespoons margarine or butter

1 package (about 16 ounces) uncooked turkey breast slices

¼ teaspoon salt

1 tablespoon margarine or butter

⅓ cup walnut pieces

2 green onions, sliced

1 teaspoon cornstarch

½ cup dry white wine or chicken broth

1 teaspoon sugar

Heat 2 tablespoons margarine in 12-inch skillet over medium-high heat until melted. Cook turkey slices in margarine about 4 minutes or until brown on both sides, sprinkling with salt after turning. Remove turkey from skillet; keep warm.

Add 1 tablespoon margarine to skillet. Cook walnuts and onions in margarine over medium heat 2 to 3 minutes or until onions are tender. Stir cornstarch into wine; pour into skillet. Stir in sugar. Heat to boiling; boil and stir 1 minute. Pour over turkey.

Rutabaga Timbales

1 pound rutabaga (about 1 large), cut into 2-inch pieces

2 cloves garlic, cut in half

1 teaspoon salt

¼ teaspoon pepper

4 eggs

½ cup half-and-half

Heat 1 inch water (salted if desired) to boiling. Add rutabagas and garlic. Cover and heat to boiling; reduce heat. Simmer 30 to 40 minutes or until tender; drain.

Heat oven to 350°. Grease six 6-ounce custard cups or individual ramekins. Place rutabagas, garlic, salt and pepper in blender or food processor. Cover and blend, or process, stopping occasionally to scrape sides, until smooth.

Beat eggs in large bowl. Mix in half-and-half and rutabaga mixture. Pour into custard cups. Place cups in rectangular pan, $13 \times 9 \times 2$ inches, on oven rack. Pour very hot water into pan to within ½ inch of tops of cups. Bake 30 to 35 minutes or until knife inserted halfway between center and edge comes out clean. Remove timbales from cups. Serve warm.

🔔 **Prepare timbales up to one day ahead; cover and refrigerate. Increase the baking time by 5 to 10 minutes.**

Two-Pear Waldorf Salad

Depending on the variety of pears at your grocery store, you can try other tempting pear combinations.

⅓ cup plain yogurt

1 tablespoon mayonnaise or salad dressing

½ teaspoon finely grated lime peel

1 teaspoon lime juice

½ cup seedless red grape halves

2 tablespoons chopped walnuts

1 Bosc or Anjou pear, coarsely chopped

1 Asian pear, coarsely chopped

1 medium stalk celery, sliced (about ½ cup)

Mix yogurt, mayonnaise, lime peel and lime juice in medium bowl. Add remaining ingredients; toss.

A Romantic Christmas Dinner for 2

Champagne or Sparkling Apple Juice*
Camembert Cheese with
Sliced Fresh Fruit*
Peachy Cornish Game Hens
Orange Rice
Sautéed Julienne Zucchini and Carrots*
Tossed Green Salad* with Fresh Herb
Viniagrette (page 260)
Croissants* with Date Butter (page 238)
Christmas Tortoni (page 110)

* Recipes not included.

Planning Guide

Up to Two Weeks Before
- Prepare Christmas Tortoni.
- Mix Date Butter.
- Prepare Fresh Herb Viniagrette.

One Day Before
- Tear greens for salad; cover tightly and refrigerate.
- Cut up zucchini and carrots.

Several Hours Before
- Prepare cornish game hens for baking Peachy Cornish Game Hens.

About 1 Hour Before
- Bake Peachy Cornish Game Hens.
- Prepare Orange Rice; add to oven with game hens 35 minutes before hens are done.

About 15 Minutes Before
- Cook vegetables.
- Warm croissants uncovered in 300° oven about 10 minutes.
- Toss salad.

Peachy Cornish Game Hens

2 Rock Cornish hens (³/₄ to 1 pound each)

Salt

Margarine or butter, melted

¹/₄ cup peach jam or orange marmalade

1 teaspoon soy sauce

1 clove garlic, finely chopped

Orange Rice (right)

Heat oven to 350°. Sprinkle cavities of hens with salt. Place breast sides up, on rack in shallow pan. Brush with margarine. Roast uncovered 45 minutes, brushing with margarine 3 or 4 times.

While hens are roasting prepare Orange Rice. Add to oven with hens 35 minutes before hens are done. Mix jam, soy sauce and garlic. Brush hens with jam mixture. Roast uncovered about 15 minutes longer, brushing once with jam mixture, until juices run clear. Serve with Orange Rice.

Orange Rice

When grating orange peel, be sure not to grate in the white section—it will give you a bitter flavor.

¹/₂ cup uncooked regular long grain rice

1 teaspoon grated orange peel

¹/₄ teaspoon ground nutmeg

2 medium carrots, sliced (about 1 cup)

1 cup hot chicken broth

2 tablespoons orange juice

1 tablespoon chopped fresh parsley

Heat oven to 350°. Mix rice, orange peel and nutmeg in ungreased 1-quart casserole. Stir in carrots and broth. Cover and bake 30 to 35 minutes or until liquid is absorbed. Sprinkle with orange juice. Add parsley; toss until well mixed. Let stand 5 minutes before serving.

🔔 **Use 1 cup frozen sliced carrots instead of preparing fresh carrots.**

Peachy Cornish Game Hens

*A Christmas
Roast Goose Dinner for 6*

Roast Goose with Browned Potatoes
Apple-Raisin Dressing
Asparagus with Gruyère
Orange-Avocado Salad
Parmesan Bubble Loaf
Christmas Steamed Pudding (page 102)

Planning Guide

Several Weeks Before
- Check oven to be sure the dishes for the goose, dressing and vegetable will fit. Two racks are needed—one in the lowest position and the second in the upper third of the oven. The asparagus can be steamed on top of the stove if necessary.
- Prepare Parmesan Bubble Loaf; cover tightly and freeze.

One Day Before
- Prepare ingredients for Orange-Avocado Salad.
- Prepare Christmas Steamed Pudding; cover tightly.
- Prepare asparagus for Asparagus with Gruyère

About 4 Hours Before
- Adjust oven racks.
- Prepare Roast Goose; roast on lowest oven rack.

Roast Goose with Browned Potatoes (page 162)

- Prepare Apple-Raisin Dressing for baking; add to oven on upper rack 15 minutes before goose is done (standing time for goose will allow for the longer baking).
- Remove Parmesan Bubble Loaf from freezer.
- Prepare Asparagus with Gruyère; add to oven along with dressing.
- Cook Christmas Steamed Pudding.

About 15 Minutes Before Serving
- Complete Orange-Avocado Salad.
- Heat Parmesan Bubble Loaf loosely covered with aluminum foil in 350° oven.

At Serving Time
- Cover steamed pudding tightly with aluminum foil and heat in 300° oven for about 20 minutes during the main course.

Apple-Raisin Dressing

3 medium stalks celery (with leaves),
*   chopped (about 1½ cups)*
1 medium onion, chopped (about ½ cup)
1 cup (2 sticks) margarine or butter
8 cups soft bread cubes (about 13 slices
*   bread)*
½ cup raisins
1½ teaspoons salt
1½ teaspoons dried sage leaves
¼ teaspoon pepper
3 medium tart apples, chopped (about 3
*   cups)*

Heat oven to 350°. Grease rectangular pan, 13 × 9 × 2 inches, or 3-quart casserole. Cook celery and onion in margarine in 10-inch skillet, stirring frequently, until onion is tender. Stir in about one-third of the bread cubes. Place in deep bowl. Add remaining bread cubes and ingredients; toss. Place in pan. Cover and bake 15 minutes. Uncover and bake about 15 minutes longer or until hot and slightly crisp.

Roast Goose with Browned Potatoes

1 goose (9 to 11 pounds)
4 to 6 large potatoes, peeled and cut in
*   half*
Salt and freshly ground pepper
Paprika

Heat oven to 350°. Trim excess fat from goose. Rub cavity of goose lightly with salt. Fasten neck skin of goose to back with skewer. Fold wings across back with tips touching. Tie drumsticks to tail. Prick skin all over with fork. Place goose, breast side up, on rack in shallow roasting pan.

Insert meat thermometer so tip is in thigh muscle and does not touch bone.

Roast uncovered 3 to 3½ hours, removing excess fat from pan occasionally, until thermometer registers 180° or drumstick moves easily and juices run clear. If necessary, place a tent of aluminum foil loosely over goose to prevent excessive browning.

One hour and 15 minutes before goose is done, place potatoes in roasting pan around goose. Brush potatoes with goose fat; sprinkle with salt, pepper and paprika. When done, place goose and potatoes on heated platter. Cover and let stand 15 minutes for easier carving. Garnish with kumquats and parsley if desired.

Asparagus with Gruyère

1½ pounds asparagus*
½ teaspoon salt
¼ cup (½ stick) margarine or butter
½ cup grated Gruyère or Parmesan
*   cheese*

Heat oven to 350°. Break off tough ends of asparagus as far down as stalks snap easily. Arrange in single layer in ungreased rectangular baking dish, 11 × 7 × 1½ inches. Sprinkle with salt. Cover with aluminum foil and bake about 25 minutes or until tender.

Heat margarine over low heat until light brown; drizzle over asparagus. Sprinkle with cheese. Bake uncovered 5 to 8 minutes or just until cheese softens. 6 servings.

* 2 packages (10 ounces each) frozen asparagus spears can be substituted for the fresh asparagus. Rinse asparagus with cold water to separate; drain. Increase first bake time to about 35 minutes.

Orange-Avocado Salad

For a fresh, bright orange color, peel the oranges with a sharp knife, cutting away the skin and the membrane completely.

3 oranges, peeled and sliced

2 avocados, peeled and sliced

6 thin slices red onion, separated into rings

Salad greens

Orange Dressing (below)

Arrange oranges, avocados and onion on salad greens on 6 salad plates. Serve with Orange Dressing. 6 servings.

ORANGE DRESSING

1/3 cup vegetable oil

1/4 cup orange juice

2 tablespoons sugar

2 tablespoons lemon juice

1 teaspoon grated orange peel

1/2 teaspoon dry mustard

1/4 teaspoon salt

Shake all ingredients in tightly covered container.

Parmesan Bubble Loaf

1 package regular or quick-acting active dry yeast

1/4 cup warm water (105° to 115°)

3/4 cup lukewarm milk

1/4 cup sugar

1 teaspoon salt

1 egg

1/4 cup (1/2 stick) margarine or butter, softened

3 1/2 to 3 3/4 cups all-purpose flour

1/2 cup (1 stick) margarine or butter, melted

1 1/4 cups grated Parmesan cheese (about 5 ounces)

Dissolve yeast in warm water in large bowl. Stir in lukewarm milk, sugar, salt, egg, 1/4 cup margarine and 2 cups of the flour. Beat until smooth. Mix in enough remaining flour to make dough easy to handle.

Turn dough onto lightly floured surface; gently roll in flour to coat. Knead about 5 minutes or until smooth and elastic. Place in greased bowl; turn greased side up. Cover and let rise in warm place about 2 hours or until double. (Dough is ready if indentation remains when touched.)

Line tube pan, 10 × 4 inches, with aluminum foil; grease. Punch down dough. Turn onto lightly floured surface; divide into 24 equal pieces. Dip each piece into melted margarine; roll in cheese. Place 12 pieces in pan in single layer. Arrange second layer of 12 pieces on top of first. Cover and let rise in warm place until double.

Heat oven to 375°. Bake about 35 minutes or until golden brown. Remove from pan. Serve warm. To serve, pull apart or slice.

The Magical Touch

Christmas is a time to pull out the stops and make the food you serve look extra-special. The serving ideas below will give foods that magical touch, whether you spent all day in the kitchen preparing it from scratch or purchased it from a favorite deli or restaurant.

We've divided the tips into food categories so you can easily find ideas for the items you are serving:

The Table

❅ For holiday placemats, cut heavy, plain-colored foil giftwrap into placemats, 12×18 inches. Glue 10-inch doilies to the center, if desired.

❅ Use a roll of holiday giftwrap to make a tablerunner 12 inches wide for the center of your table. Geometric patterns and/or stripes work particularly well.

❅ Tie holiday ribbons with jingle bells around napkins to make napkin rings.

❅ Decorate the base of water or wine glasses with ribbons or metallic cord. Add a tiny package or ornament.

❅ Place votive candle holders in the center of squares of iridescent, metallic or holiday cellophane wrap. Bring the edges up and ruffle evenly; tie ribbon or cord midway around the candleholder, then flare the ruffled edges outward. The candle will look larger and have more reflection when burning.

Appetizers

❅ Use hollowed out vegetables as edible containers for dips. Try red, yellow or green bell peppers, cutting off the tip where it's widest so there's ample room for dipping. Cut a zig-zag or curved scalloped edge for more interest. Small heads of red or green cabbage or iceberg lettuce with the center removed also makes an attractive bowl. Surround the dip with cut-up vegetables or dippers of your choice.

❅ Cut vegetable slices for dipping diagonally, to create more interest. Carrots, zucchini, yel-

low squash, celery and cucumbers are all attractive cut this way. Use a rippled cutter if desired.

❅ Cut miniature squash (pattypan, zucchini or yellow) in half right through the stem and cut large mushrooms in half.

❅ Blanch broccoli and green beans for the brightest color when using as vegetable dippers that will sit out for a while.

❅ Place a bowl of dip in the center of a round plate and arrange vegetable dippers in the shape

of a wreath around it. Make a "ribbon bow" out of red bell pepper pieces. The plate size can be easily adjusted to the number to be served. Or, arrange vegetable sticks in a tree shape, and use cherry tomatoes or other colorful vegetables for the "ornaments."

❉ Shape spreads in free-form holiday shapes such as stars, bells, wreaths and so forth to make them look more festive.

❉ Serve snack mixes, such as Reindeer Snack, page 268 in carafes or pitchers with wide spouts for easy pouring.

Meats, Main Dishes and Side Dishes

❉ Bowls for soups and stews needn't only be china! Use hollowed-out large hard rolls or small bread loaves (leaving at least a 1-inch wall), baked acorn squash halves (cut crosswise) or fried tortilla bowls. Bread from the center of rolls or loaves can be used to make croutons or bread pudding (see page 102).

❉ Use sprigs of fresh rosemary as a garnish and dust with powdered sugar to look like snowy evergreen branches.

❉ Use holiday-shaped pastas for a festive twist to your pasta dishes.

❉ Cut vegetables into holiday shapes to use as garnishes.

❉ Use green onion tops or chives to make bows around bundles of hot vegetable sticks or whole green beans. This is also fun to use for cold appetizer vegetable dippers.

❉ Cut oranges, lemons or limes in half with a zig-zag cut and remove the pulp. Fill the "shells" with cranberry relish or sauce, Corn Salsa (page 254) or Black Bean Relish (page 256). Make one "shell" per serving and use to garnish your holiday meat platter.

❉ Cut citrus peel into short, thin pieces and sprinkle on foods. Or cut long pieces of peel and tie knots in them to use for garnishing serving platters or individual plates.

❉ For vegetable fans, cut four or five lengthwise slits almost to end of pickles, chilies (use gloves so the acid doesn't burn your fingers!), baby carrots or other small vegetables. Spread apart to form fans. Use as part of a relish tray or to garnish serving platters or individual plates.

Breads

❉ Form butter into holiday shapes. Soften butter and swirl freehand, or cut Christmas shapes with cookie cutters (cutting a 1-pound block of butter lengthwise into fourths is easiest).

❉ Serve flavored butters with savory or sweet breads (page 238). Fill attractive small containers or pipe into rosettes and refrigerate until used.

❉ Before baking plain yeast breads or rolls,

brush with beaten egg white and decorate with Baked-on Decorator's Frosting (page 5).

❉ Brush hot nut breads with corn syrup for a shiny appearance.

❉ If you're making breadsticks, curve one end to look like a candy cane (see Cheese Straw Twists, page 141).

Desserts

❄ Use a small brush to paint sauce designs on individual plates before adding the dessert. Or, drizzle sauce with a spoon or place it in a heavy plastic bag, cut off a tiny corner and pipe a snowflake or other attractive design.

❄ Before adding dessert, sprinkle center and/or edges of plates with powdered sugar, ground cinnamon or edible glitter. Place dessert on top; add sauce if desired.

❄ Place desserts on a mirror or mirror square for extra reflection and sparkle.

❄ Decorations from chocolate are easy to make.

—For chocolate leaves:
Wash and dry 12 to 18 fresh leaves (such as lemon, grape or rose leaves) or pliable plastic leaves. Heat ½ cup (3 ounces) semisweet chocolate chips or 2 squares (1 ounce each) semisweet chocolate and 1 teaspoon shortening over low heat until melted. Brush chocolate about ⅛ inch thick over backs of leaves. Refrigerate until firm, at least 1 hour. Peel off leaves. Refrigerate chocolate leaves until ready to use.

—For chocolate twigs:
Heat vanilla- or chocolate-flavored candy-coating in small saucepan over low heat, stirring constantly, just until melted. Pour chocolate mixture into small plastic bag, a large envelope, a squeeze bottle or a pastry bag fitted with small writing tip. (Snip a tiny corner from bottom of bag or envelope.) Squeeze melted coating into twig shapes; sprinkle with granulated or coarse sugar, if desired. Let dry. Peel twigs from waxed paper; arrange on dessert. Use twigs with chocolate leaves, to decorate Bûche de Noël (page 68) or with poinsettias to decorate the Raspberry-White Chocolate Cream Cake (page 64).

—For white chocolate poinsettias (shown on page 64):
Heat vanilla-flavored candy coating in small saucepan over low heat, stirring constantly, until melted. Stir in a tiny amount of red paste food color until desired shade is reached. Paint coating mixture on back side of fresh mint leaves or washable artificial leaves which resemble poinsettia leaves; let dry. Peel coating from leaves; arrange on cake.

Beverages

❄ Add a cinnamon stick, candy cane or peppermint stick to cups of hot beverages. Of course the flavors should be compatible.

❄ Make fruit ice cubes for cold beverages. Fill ice-cube trays with water or fruit juice. Submerge a raspberry, cranberry, pineapple chunk, small quartered orange slice, slice of star fruit, lemon peel cut into holiday shapes such as stars and, if desired, a mint leaf, in each ice-cube compartment; freeze. Add to individual beverages or punch.

❄ Dip the rims of glasses or mugs in a shallow dish of water or fruit juice, then into cinnamon-sugar, flavored gelatin or coarse colored sugar. Make them ahead so they're ready to be filled with your special holiday beverages.

Smart Tips for Easy Entertaining

The first thing to do in planning for holiday entertaining is to relax and let yourself off the hook. Don't expect to be able to work outside the home, volunteer in the community, raise a family, decorate and entertain lavishly. There are a number of ways to plan a wonderful party and not be overwhelmed:

❀ Choose a menu that fits your kitchen facilities, time constraints and cooking experience. When planning to entertain, try not to create a party that will exhaust you.

❀ If this is a family event, have a meeting and plan for everyone to help out in some way, establishing deadlines as to when duties should be completed. Keep the list handy on the refrigerator or bulletin board.

❀ Concentrate on one or two impressive food or decorating ideas, then relax and enjoy your guests.

❀ Decide on which part of the meal you want to spend your time, and then pick the rest up from the deli, bakery or a favorite restaurant.

❀ Plan a mix of do-ahead dishes with some that can easily be whipped together at the last minute, so you don't make all of the food at one time.

❀ Serve foods buffet-style (see Bountiful Buffets, page 198–199) for easiest serving.

❀ Supplement your top-of-the-stove cooking with microwave cooking.

❀ Cohost the event with one or two family members or friends so you can share the preparation. Or provide the main dish and beverages, then ask guests to bring accompanying dishes. Or consider a potluck—it's always fun.

❀ Set up drinks and snacks in a self-serve center.

❀ Hire a teenage family member or neighbor to help clean up throughout the party so there won't be so much to do at the end. Make a list of your expectations so things run smoothly.

❀ If you run out of refrigerator space, store food on ice in a cooler, borrow a shelf in a neighbor's refrigerator or in cold-weather climates, cover and store in an unheated garage (40° or cooler).

❀ Try something other than the usual open house as an alternative. Invite guests to a morning coffee or afternoon tea. An unusual assortment of international coffees and teas would go well with a variety of cookies, breads and desserts.

❀ Invite guests to help out in the kitchen and participate in any food preparation. It makes them feel useful and can break the ice with new acquaintances. This is a perfect time to visit and catch up on news.

❀ Plan to serve in the easiest way you can. A stack of plates set out for a buffet takes less time and effort than setting a table; paper plates keep cleanup a snap.

A Roast Beef Christmas Dinner for 6

Basil Brie in Pastry
Standing Beef Rib Roast with
Yorkshire Pudding
Three-Cheese Tortellini
Steamed Green Beans with Garlic Butter
(page 238)
Cinnamon Squash Rings
Roquefort and Toasted Walnut Salad
Christmas Brioche (page 125)
Pear-Fig Strudel with Eggnog Sauce (page 99)

Planning Guide

Several Weeks Before
• Prepare Christmas Brioche; cover tightly and freeze.

One or Two Days Before
• Bake Pear-Fig Strudel with Eggnog Sauce; cover and refrigerate.
• Mix Garlic Butter.
• Prepare ingredients for Roquefort and Toasted Walnut Salad; do not toss; cover and refrigerate.

Several Hours Before
• Remove Christmas Brioche from freezer.
• Prepare Basil Brie in Pastry for baking; cover and refrigerate. Bake just before roasting beef.

About 3 Hours Before
• Prepare Standing Beef Rib Roast with Yorkshire Pudding.
• Prepare Cinnamon-Squash Rings for baking; cover and refrigerate.

About 40 Minutes Before
• Bake Cinnamon Squash Rings.
• Prepare Three-Cheese Tortellini.
• Toss salad.
• Cook green beans; drain and add ¼ cup Garlic Butter.

At Serving Time
• Warm Streudel uncovered in 300° oven for 20 minutes during the main course if desired.

Standing Rib Roast with Yorkshire Pudding (page 170); Basil Brie in Pastry (page 170)

Basil Brie in Pastry

2 tablespoons grated Parmesan cheese

2 tablespoons finely chopped fresh or 2 teaspoons dried basil leaves

1 round Brie cheese (14 ounces)

½ package (17¼-ounce size) frozen puff pastry, thawed

Heat oven to 400°. Grease cookie sheet. Mix Parmesan cheese and basil. Cut cheese round horizontally into 2 layers. Sprinkle basil mixture evenly over cut surface. Reassemble cheese round.

Roll pastry into rectangle, 12 × 10 inches, on lightly floured surface. Cut out one 10-inch circle. Place 8½-inch circle on cookie sheet. Place cheese in center. Bring pastry up and over cheese. Press to make smooth and even. Brush pastry lightly with water and press gently to seal. Place pastry-wrapped cheese, seam side down, on cookie sheet. Cut decorations from remaining pastry if desired; moisten pastry with water to attach.

Bake about 25 minutes or until golden brown. Cool on cookie sheet on wire rack 30 minutes before serving. Serve with assorted crackers or fruit if desired.

Standing Beef Rib Roast with Yorkshire Pudding

Yorkshire Pudding is an English classic, similar to a popover. However, instead of baking in individual cups, Yorkshire Pudding is baked in a pan, nestled with the roast beef drippings. When puffed and golden, it is cut into squares and served with the roast beef.

4- to 6-pound beef rib roast
Salt and pepper
Yorkshire Pudding Batter (right)

Heat oven to 325°. Place beef roast, fat side up, on rack in shallow roasting pan. Sprinkle with salt and pepper. Insert meat thermometer so tip is in center of thickest part of beef and does not touch bone or rest in fat. Do not add water.

Roast uncovered to desired degree of doneness: 135° for rare, 23 to 25 minutes per pound; 155° for medium, 27 to 30 minutes per pound. About 30 minutes before roast reaches desired temperature, prepare Yorkshire Pudding Batter. Heat square pan, 9 × 9 × 2 inches, or rectangular baking dish, 11 × 7 × 1½ inches, in oven.

When roast reaches desired temperature, remove from oven. Increase oven temperature to 425°. Transfer roast to warm platter; cover with aluminum foil. Pour ¼ cup drippings from roasting pan; place drippings in heated square pan. Pour in pudding batter. Bake about 25 minutes or until puffed and golden brown. Cut into squares; serve with beef.

YORKSHIRE PUDDING BATTER

1 cup all-purpose flour
1 cup milk
½ teaspoon salt
2 eggs

Mix all ingredients with hand beater just until smooth.

Roquefort and Toasted Walnut Salad

Toasted Walnut Dressing (page 171)
½ cup crumbled Roquefort or blue

cheese (about 2 ounces)

½ cup ½-inch pieces fresh chives

⅓ cup coarsely chopped walnuts, toasted

1 small head radicchio, torn into bite-size pieces (about 4 cups)

1 head Bibb lettuce, torn into bite-size pieces (about 4 cups)

Prepare Toasted Walnut Dressing. Toss with remaining ingredients. 6 servings.

TOASTED WALNUT DRESSING

⅓ cup olive or vegetable oil

¼ cup coarsely chopped walnuts, toasted

2 tablespoons lemon juice

⅛ teaspoon salt

Dash of pepper

1 clove garlic

Place all ingredients in blender or food processor. Cover and blend on high speed about 1 minute, or process, until smooth.

Three-Cheese Tortellini

1 package (7 ounces) dried cheese-filled tortellini

¼ cup (½ stick) margarine or butter

1 small green bell pepper, chopped (about ½ cup)

2 shallots, finely chopped

1 clove garlic, finely chopped

¼ cup all-purpose flour

¼ teaspoon pepper

1¾ cups milk

½ cup shredded mozzarella cheese (2 ounces)

½ cup shredded Swiss cheese (2 ounces)

¼ cup grated Parmesan or Romano cheese

Cook tortellini as directed on package; drain. Heat margarine in 3-quart saucepan over medium-high heat. Cook bell pepper, shallots and garlic in margarine about 3 minutes, stirring occasionally. Stir in flour and pepper. Cook over medium heat, stirring constantly, until mixture is bubbly; remove from heat. Stir in milk. Heat to boiling, stirring constantly. Boil and stir 1 minute; remove from heat. Stir in mozzarella and Swiss cheeses until melted. Add tortellini; stir until coated. Sprinkle with Parmesan cheese.

Cinnamon Squash Rings

For a prettier center, use a scalloped-edge round cookie cutter to cut out the center of the squash rings.

2 tablespoons packed brown sugar

2 tablespoons milk

1 egg

¾ cup soft bread crumbs (about 2½ slices bread)

¼ cup yellow or white cornmeal

2 teaspoons ground cinnamon

1 large acorn squash (about 1½ pounds), cut crosswise into ½-inch slices and seeded

⅓ cup margarine or butter, melted

Heat oven to 400°. Mix brown sugar, milk and egg. Mix bread crumbs, cornmeal and cinnamon. Dip squash slices into egg mixture, then coat with bread crumb mixture; repeat.

Place in ungreased rectangular pan, 13 × 9 × 2 inches. Drizzle with margarine. Bake uncovered 30 to 35 minutes or until squash is tender.

🔔 **You can cut and seed squash up to 2 days ahead of time. Cover and refrigerate.**

*Festive Pork
Christmas Dinner for 12*

Hot Buttered Rum (page 148)
Nutty Fruit Spread
OR
Savory Stuffed Mushrooms
Crown Roast of Pork with Mushroom Stuffing
OR
Apricot-Pistachio Rolled Pork
Duchess Potatoes
Red Cabbage with Apples and Prunes
Mixed Greens with Parmesan Walnuts
Cardamom-Walnut Rolls (page 135)
Pumpkin-Pecan Cheesecake (page 81)

Planning Guide

Several Weeks Before
- Prepare Pumpkin-Pecan Cheesecake; cover tightly and freeze.
- Prepare Cardamom-Walnut Rolls; cover tightly and freeze.

One or Two Days Before
- Prepare Nutty Fruit Spread. Or, prepare Savory Stuffed Mushrooms for baking; cover and refrigerate.
- Prepare ingredients for Red Cabbage with Apples and Prunes; do not cook.

Several Hours Before
- Remove rolls from freezer and thaw loosely covered at room temperature.
- Remove cheesecake from freezer and thaw covered cheesecake in refrigerator.

- Tear greens and prepare walnuts for Mixed Greens with Parmesan Walnuts; do not toss.
- Prepare Duchess Potatoes for baking.
- Prepare and roast meat.

About 30 minutes Before
- Cook Red Cabbage with Apples and Prunes.

About 15 Minutes Before
- Microwave or bake Savory Stuffed Mushrooms.
- Bake Duchess Potatoes while roast is standing.
- Toss salad.

Crown Roast of Pork with Mushroom Stuffing (page 175); Red Cabbage with Apples and Prunes (page 177)

Nutty Fruit Spread

½ cup diced dried fruit and raisin
mixture

¼ cup chopped honey-roasted nuts

2 tablespoons orange-flavored liqueur or
orange juice

1 tablespoon honey

1 package (8 ounces) cream cheese,
softened

Mix all ingredients. Spoon into serving dish. Cover and refrigerate about 1 hour or until firm. Serve with sliced fruit or assorted crackers if desired. About 1½ cups spread.

Savory Stuffed Mushrooms

36 medium mushrooms (about 1 pound)

1 small onion, chopped (about ¼ cup)

¼ cup chopped green bell pepper

2 tablespoons margarine or butter

1½ cups soft bread crumbs (about 2½
slices bread)

1½ teaspoons chopped fresh or ½
teaspoon dried thyme leaves

½ teaspoon salt

¼ teaspoon ground turmeric

¼ teaspoon pepper

Remove stems from mushrooms; reserve caps. Finely chop enough stems to measure ⅓ cup. Cook mushroom stems, onion and bell pepper in margarine in 10-inch skillet about 5 minutes, stirring occasionally, until tender; remove from heat. Stir in remaining ingredients.

Heat oven to 350°. Lightly grease shallow baking dish, 12 × 7 × 1½ inches, with nonstick cooking spray. Fill mushroom caps with bread crumb mixture. Place mushrooms, filled sides up, in baking dish.

Bake uncovered 15 minutes. Set oven control to broil. Broil with tops 3 to 4 inches from heat about 2 minutes or until light brown. 36 appetizers.

TO MICROWAVE: Remove stems from mushrooms; reserve caps. Finely chop enough stems to measure ⅓ cup. Place mushroom stems, onion, bell pepper and margarine in 1-quart microwavable casserole. Cover tightly and microwave on high 2 to 3 minutes, stirring after 1 minute, until tender. Stir in remaining ingredients. Fill mushroom caps with bread crumb mixture. Arrange mushroom caps, filled sides up (smallest mushrooms in center), on two 10-inch microwavable plates. Microwave one plate at a time uncovered on high 1½ to 2 minutes, rotating plate ½ turn after 1 minute, until hot.

Mixed Greens with Parmesan Walnuts

Savory, toasted cheese and nuts add a special touch to this salad.

Parmesan Walnuts (below)

1 medium head lettuce

1 medium bunch leaf lettuce

½ small bunch curly endive

6 ounces spinach

⅓ to ½ cup oil-and-vinegar dressing

Prepare Parmesan Walnuts. Tear greens into bite-size pieces (about 18 cups). Toss with dressing until greens are well coated. Toss with Parmesan Walnuts. 12 servings.

PARMESAN WALNUTS

2 tablespoons margarine or butter

¼ teaspoon hickory smoked salt or
seasoned salt

1½ cups broken walnuts

3 tablespoons grated Parmesan cheese

Heat oven to 350°. Heat margarine and hickory salt in square pan, 9 × 9 × 2 inches, in oven 2 to 3 minutes or until margarine is bubbly. Stir in walnuts; bake 5 minutes. Sprinkle with cheese; toss until walnuts are evenly coated. Bake 3 to 5 minutes longer or until cheese is light brown; cool. Store tightly covered in refrigerator.

Crown Roast of Pork with Mushroom Stuffing

7½- to 8-pound pork crown roast (about 20 ribs)

2 teaspoons salt

1 teaspoon pepper

Mushroom Stuffing (right)

Heat oven to 325°. Sprinkle pork roast with salt and pepper. Place pork, bone ends up, in roasting pan on rack in shallow roasting pan. Wrap bone ends in aluminum foil to prevent excessive browning. Insert meat thermometer so tip is in thickest part of meat and does not touch bone. Place a small heatproof bowl or crumpled aluminum foil in crown to hold shape of roast evenly. Roast uncovered until thermometer registers 160° (medium), 20 to 25 minutes per pound; or 170° (well), 26 to 31 minutes per pound. Prepare Mushroom Stuffing.

One hour before pork is done, remove bowl and fill center of crown with Mushroom Stuffing. Cover only stuffing with aluminum foil during first 30 minutes. When pork is done, place on large warm platter and allow to stand about 20 minutes for easiest carving. Remove foil wrapping; place paper frills on bone ends if desired. Remove stuffing to another bowl. To carve, cut roast between ribs. 12 servings.

MUSHROOM STUFFING

1 medium onion, finely chopped (about ½ cup)

⅔ cup margarine or butter

8 cups unseasoned croutons

1 tablespoon chopped fresh or 1 teaspoon dried sage, thyme or marjoram leaves

1 teaspoon poultry seasoning

1 teaspoon salt

½ teaspoon pepper

1 pound fresh mushrooms, sliced, or 1 can (6 ounces) sliced mushrooms, drained

2 medium stalks celery, chopped (about 1 cup)

Cook onion in margarine in Dutch oven over medium heat about 3 minutes, stirring frequently, until tender. Stir in half of the croutons. Cook, stirring frequently, until evenly mixed and croutons are softened. Mix in remaining croutons and ingredients.

CROWN ROAST OF PORK WITH ORANGE AND APPLE STUFFING: Substitute Orange and Apple Stuffing for the Mushroom Stuffing. For Orange and Apple Stuffing, prepare Mushroom Stuffing—except increase salt and sage to 2 teaspoons. Omit mushrooms. Mix in 1 cup chopped apple, 1 cup diced orange sections or mandarin orange segments and 2 teaspoons grated orange peel with the remaining croutons.

Buy fresh mushrooms already sliced in the produce or deli section of your supermarket.

Apricot-Pistachio Rolled Pork

An elegant, impressive pork dish that slices beautifully, as well as being delicious.

> *4-pound pork boneless top loin roast (single uncut roast)*
>
> *½ cup chopped dried apricots*
>
> *½ cup chopped pistachio nuts*
>
> *2 cloves garlic, finely chopped*
>
> *¼ teaspoon salt*
>
> *¼ teaspoon pepper*
>
> *¼ cup apricot brandy or apricot nectar*
>
> *¼ cup apricot preserves*
>
> *Crunchy Topping (right)*

To cut pork roast into a large rectangle that can be filled and rolled, cut lengthwise about ½ inch from top of pork to within ½ inch of opposite edge; open flat. Repeat with other side of pork, cutting from the inside edge to the outer edge; open flat to form rectangle (see diagram).

Cut lengthwise about ½ inch from top of pork to within ½ inch of opposite edge; open flat. Repeat with other side of pork, cutting loose from inside edge; open flat to form rectangle.

Sprinkle apricots, nuts, garlic, salt and pepper over pork to within 1 inch of edge. Tightly roll up pork, beginning with short side. Secure with toothpicks or tie with string. Pierce pork all over with metal skewer. Brush entire surface with brandy. Let stand 15 minutes. Brush again with brandy. Cover and refrigerate at least 2 hours.

Heat oven to 325°. Place pork, fat side up, on rack in shallow roasting pan. Insert meat thermometer so tip is in thickest part of pork. Roast uncovered 1½ hours. Brush preserves over pork. Sprinkle with Crunchy Topping. Roast uncovered 30 to 60 minutes longer or until meat thermometer registers 160°. Cover and let stand 15 minutes before serving for easier carving.

CRUNCHY TOPPING

> *1 tablespoon margarine or butter*
>
> *¼ cup coarsely crushed cracker crumbs*
>
> *2 tablespoons chopped pistachio nuts*
>
> *¼ teaspoon garlic salt*

Heat margarine in 2-quart saucepan over medium heat until melted. Stir in remaining ingredients. Cook and stir 1 minute; cool.

Duchess Potatoes

For a different twist, use sweet potatoes or yams, and sprinkle with nutmeg or cinnamon after baking.

4 pounds potatoes (about 12 medium),
*   peeled and cut into pieces*

2/3 to 1 cup milk

1/2 cup margarine or butter, softened

1/2 teaspoon salt

Dash of pepper

4 eggs, beaten

Margarine or butter, melted

Heat 1 inch water (salted if desired) in 3-quart saucepan to boiling. Add potatoes. Cover and heat to boiling. Cook whole potatoes 30 to 35 minutes, pieces 20 to 25 minutes or until tender; drain. Shake pan with potatoes over low heat to dry.

Heat oven to 425°. Grease cookie sheet. Mash potatoes until no lumps remain. Beat in milk in small amounts (amount of milk needed to make potatoes smooth and fluffy depends on kind of potatoes used). Add 1/2 cup margarine, the salt and pepper. Beat vigorously until potatoes are light and fluffy. Add eggs; beat until blended.

Drop potato mixture by spoonfuls into mounds onto cookie sheet. Or place in decorating bag with star tip and form rosettes or pipe a border around meat. Brush with melted margarine. Bake about 15 minutes or until light brown.

♤ **Cover the cookie sheet with aluminum foil or parchment paper to cut down on cleanup. You can also prepare the potatoes, then cover and refrigerate until about 25 minutes before serving. Increase baking time by 5 to 10 minutes.**

Red Cabbage with Apples and Prunes

3 tablespoons margarine or butter

3 medium apples, coarsely chopped
*   (about 3 cups)*

2 small onions, thinly sliced

1/2 head red cabbage, coarsely shredded
*   (about 9 cups)*

1/3 cup apple jelly

3/4 cup dry red wine or apple juice

1/3 cup red wine vinegar

1/4 teaspoon ground cloves

1 cup pitted prunes, cut in half

1 tablespoon plus 2 teaspoons cornstarch

Heat margarine in Dutch oven over medium heat until melted. Cook apples and onions in margarine about 5 minutes, stirring frequently, just until apples are softened. Stir in cabbage, jelly, wine, vinegar and cloves. Heat to boiling; reduce heat. Cover and simmer about 15 minutes. Stir in prunes. Cover and simmer about 10 minutes, stirring occasionally, until cabbage is crisp-tender; drain, reserving liquid.

Mix 2 tablespoons reserved liquid into cornstarch; gradually stir in remaining reserved liquid. Stir until smooth; pour into Dutch oven. Heat to boiling, stirring constantly. Boil and stir 1 minute. Pour over cabbage mixture.

♤ **Use a food processor with the slicing blade to shred the cabbage.**

Company's Coming
Holiday Dinner for 6

Stuffed Mussels
OR
Seafood Coquille
Peppered Pork Chops
Artichoke Hearts with Olives and Potatoes
Honey-Mint Carrots
Pickled Beets and Onions (page 259) served
with Sliced Oranges
Crescent Rolls (page 138)
Della Robbia Apple Pie (page 87)

Planning Guide

Several Weeks Before
- Bake Crescent Rolls; cover and freeze tightly.

One or Two Days Before
- Prepare Pickled Beets one day ahead.
- Bake Della Robbia Apple Pie.

Several Hours Before
- Cook potatoes for Artichoke Hearts with Olives and Potatoes.
- Prepare ingredients for Honey-Mint Carrots; do not cook.

- Prepare Stuffed Mussels or Seafood Coquille for cooking; cover and refrigerate.
- Remove rolls from freezer and thaw loosely covered at room temperature.

About 30 Minutes Before
- Bake appetizer.
- Prepare Peppered Pork Chops.
- Cook Artichoke Hearts with Olives and Potatoes.
- Cook Honey-Mint Carrots.

Peppered Pork Chops (page 181); Stuffed Mussels (page 180); Crescent Rolls (page 138)

Stuffed Mussels

24 fresh large mussels (about 2 pounds)

2 tablespoons olive or vegetable oil

2 tablespoons chopped fresh parsley

4 large cloves garlic, finely chopped

1/2 cup dry white wine, white grape juice
or chicken broth

1/2 cup Italian-style dry bread crumbs

1 tablespoon grated Parmesan cheese

1 teaspoon finely chopped imported
Italian black olives or black olives

1/4 teaspoon salt

1/4 teaspoon pepper

Heat oven to 375°. Discard any broken-shell or open (dead) mussels. Scrub remaining mussels in cold water, removing any barnacles with a dull paring knife. Remove beards by tugging them away from shells. Place mussels in container. Cover with cool water. Agitate water with hand, then drain and discard water. Repeat several times until water runs clear; drain.

Heat oil in 12-inch skillet over medium-high heat. Cook parsley and garlic in oil, stirring frequently, until garlic is golden. Add mussels and wine. Heat to boiling; reduce heat. Cover and simmer 5 minutes or until mussels open, removing mussels as they open. (Discard unopened mussels.)

Mix remaining ingredients. Remove top shell from each mussel and discard. Place mussels in half-shells in ungreased rectangular baking dish, 13 × 9 × 2 inches. Sprinkle about 1 teaspoon bread crumb mixture over each mussel. Bake uncovered about 20 minutes or until golden brown.

🔔 **Clean the mussels a day before serving, then cover and refrigerate.**

Seafood Coquille

You can fill the baking shells early in the day, then cover and refrigerate. When you're ready to serve, broil about 5 minutes or until mixture is heated through.

1/3 cup finely chopped onion

1 clove garlic, crushed

1/3 cup margarine or butter

1/4 cup all-purpose flour

1/4 teaspoon salt

1/4 teaspoon pepper

1 1/3 cups milk

2/3 cup sauterne wine or apple juice

1 can (6 1/2 ounces) crabmeat, drained and
cartilage removed

1 cup cooked peeled medium or small
shrimp

6 tablespoons shredded Swiss cheese or 6
teaspoons grated Parmesan cheese

Cook onion and garlic in margarine in 1 1/2-quart saucepan, stirring occasionally, until onion is tender. Stir in flour, salt and pepper. Cook over low heat, stirring constantly, until bubbly; remove from heat. Stir in milk and wine. Heat to boiling, stirring constantly. Boil and stir 1 minute. Stir in crabmeat and shrimp.

Divide mixture among 6 baking shells or 6-ounce ramekins. Top each with 1 tablespoon Swiss cheese or 1 teaspoon Parmesan cheese.

Set oven control to broil. Broil with tops 4 to 5 inches from heat 3 to 4 minutes or until cheese is golden. 6 servings.

Peppered Pork Chops

1 tablespoon whole black peppercorns, coarsely crushed

6 pork loin chops, 1/2 inch thick

1/4 cup (1/2 stick) margarine or butter

2 tablespoons olive or vegetable oil

4 cloves garlic, cut in half

1 cup sliced mushrooms (about 8 ounces)

1/2 teaspoon salt

1/2 cup Marsala, dry red wine or apple juice

Sprinkle half of the crushed peppercorns over one side of pork chops; gently press into pork. Turn pork; repeat with remaining peppercorns.

Heat margarine and oil in 12-inch skillet over medium-high heat. Cook garlic in margarine and oil, stirring frequently, until golden. Add pork. Cook uncovered 5 minutes. Turn pork. Add mushrooms, salt and wine. Cover and simmer about 5 minutes longer or until pork is done.

Honey-Mint Carrots

Mint adds a fresh taste of summer to these tasty carrots.

6 medium carrots, cut into 1/4-inch diagonal slices (about 3 cups)*

1 tablespoon honey

1 tablespoon chopped fresh or 1 teaspoon dried mint leaves

Heat 1 inch water to boiling. Add carrots. Heat to boiling; reduce heat. Cover and simmer about 10 minutes or until crisp-tender; drain. Toss with honey and mint.

* 1 package (16 ounces) frozen sliced carrots, cooked and drained, can be substituted for the cooked fresh carrots.

Artichoke Hearts with Olives and Potatoes

2 pounds small red potatoes, cut in half

2 cups chicken broth

1/4 cup olive or vegetable oil

1 small onion, thinly sliced

2 packages (9 ounces each) frozen artichoke hearts, thawed

1 cup sliced pitted green olives

1 tablespoon lemon juice

2 teaspoons capers, drained

3/4 teaspoon salt

1/4 teaspoon pepper

Grated Parmesan cheese

Place potatoes in 3-quart saucepan; add broth. Heat to boiling; reduce heat. Cover and simmer about 10 minutes or until tender; drain.

Heat oil in 12-inch skillet over medium-high heat. Cook onion in oil about 2 minutes, stirring frequently, until onion is tender; reduce heat to medium. Stir in potatoes and remaining ingredients except cheese. Cook uncovered about 5 minutes, stirring frequently, until hot. Sprinkle with cheese.

⌂ **Buy sliced olives to save on preparation time.**

*Holiday Ham
Dinner for 12*

Spinach Dip
Glazed Baked Ham
Pine Nut and Green Onion Pilaf
Carrots with Rum Raisins
Christmas Eve Salad
Savory Cheese Swirl (page 132)
Cheesecake Squares (page 84) with Cranberries
Jubilee (page 105)

Planning Guide

Several Weeks Before
- Bake Cheesecake Squares; cover tightly and freeze.

One or Two Days Before
- Prepare Refrigerator Dough and filling for Savory Cheese Swirl; refrigerate.
- Prepare Cranberries Jubilee.
- Measure ingredients for Pine Nut and Green Onion Pilaf; do not cook.
- Prepare fruits and vegetables for Christmas Eve Salad; do not add liquid. Cover and refrigerate.
- Prepare Carrots with Rum Raisins for cooking.
- Prepare ingredients for Spinach Dip; do not microwave. Cover and refrigerate.

Several Hours Before
- Remove Cheesecake from freezer and thaw in refrigerator.
- Shape and bake Savory Cheese Swirl.

About 3 Hours Before
- Prepare Glazed Baked Ham.
- Prepare Carrots with Rum Raisins.
- Cook Pine Nut and Green Onion Pilaf.
- Complete Christmas Eve Salad.

Just Before Serving
- Microwave Spinach Dip.

At Dessert Time
- Reheat Cranberries Jubilee and serve on or under Cheesecake Squares.

Glazed Baked Ham (page 184)

Spinach Dip

This classic dip is fun served in hollowed-out round bread or individual loaves. When dip is finished, you can eat your bowl!

2 cups shredded Cheddar cheese (8 ounces)

4 green onions, sliced

2 medium tomatoes, chopped (about 1½ cups)

1 package (10 ounces) frozen chopped spinach, thawed and well drained

1 package (8 ounces) cream cheese, softened

Bagel chips or crackers, if desired

Mix all ingredients except bagel chips in medium microwavable bowl. Cover tightly and microwave on medium (50%) 9 to 12 minutes, stirring every 3 minutes, until Cheddar cheese is melted and mixture is warm. Serve warm with bagel chips. About 4 cups dip.

Glazed Baked Ham

6- to 8-pound fully cooked smoked bone-in ham

Whole cloves, if desired

¼ cup honey

½ teaspoon dry mustard

¼ teaspoon ground cloves

Heat oven to 325°. Place ham, fat side up, on rack in shallow roasting pan. Insert meat thermometer so tip is in thickest part of ham and does not touch bone or rest in fat. Cover ham and bake until thermometer registers 135°, 13 to 17 minutes per pound.

About 20 minutes before ham is done, remove from oven. Pour drippings from pan. Remove any skin from ham. Cut uniform diamond shapes on fat surface of ham. Insert clove in each diamond. Mix honey, mustard and cloves; brush on ham. Bake uncovered 20 minutes.

Cover ham and let stand about 10 minutes or until thermometer registers 140°. Garnish with orange slices and maraschino cherries if desired.

Pine Nut and Green Onion Pilaf

2 cups uncooked regular long grain rice

1 cup sliced green onions

1 cup pine nuts

¼ cup (½ stick) margarine or butter

5 cups chicken broth

2 teaspoons grated lemon peel

½ teaspoon salt

½ cup sliced green onion tops

Cook rice, 1 cup onions and the pine nuts in margarine in 3-quart saucepan about 5 minutes, stirring frequently, until nuts are light brown. Stir in broth, lemon peel and salt.

Heat to boiling, stirring once or twice; reduce heat. Cover and simmer 14 minutes. (Do not lift cover or stir.) Remove from heat. Fluff rice lightly with fork. Cover and let steam 5 to 10 minutes. Sprinkle with onion tops.

Carrots with Rum Raisins

The mellow flavors of rum and raisins give sparkle to an old favorite.

²/₃ cup rum or ¹/₂ cup water mixed with 1 teaspoon rum extract

²/₃ cup raisins

12 pearl onions, peeled and cut in half

¹/₄ cup (¹/₂ stick) margarine or butter

3 pounds small whole carrots

¹/₂ cup dry white wine or apple juice

1 teaspoon finely chopped fresh dill weed

1 teaspoon salt

¹/₂ teaspoon crushed red pepper

1 cup whipping (heavy) cream

Pour rum over raisins. Let stand 30 minutes.

Cook onions in margarine in 3-quart saucepan over low heat 5 minutes, stirring occasionally, until onions begin to soften. Stir in carrots, raisins and rum. Cook, stirring occasionally, until rum has evaporated. Stir in wine, dill weed, salt and red pepper. Cover and cook over medium heat 25 minutes, stirring occasionally, until carrots are tender. Stir in whipping cream. Heat to boiling. Boil uncovered 5 minutes, stirring occasionally.

Use small whole carrots, found in the produce section, that come already peeled and packaged.

Christmas Eve Salad

This unusual and colorful salad is a Mexican tradition.

3 medium oranges, peeled and sectioned

3 bananas, sliced

1 can (8¹/₄ ounces) sliced beets, drained and liquid reserved

1 can (15¹/₄ ounces) pineapple chunks in juice, drained and juice reserved

¹/₂ jicama, peeled and sliced, or 1 can (8 ounces) sliced water chestnuts, drained

3 tablespoons lemon juice

3 tablespoons sugar

¹/₂ teaspoon salt

4 cups shredded lettuce

1 lime, cut into wedges

¹/₃ cup chopped peanuts

¹/₂ cup pomegranate seeds or sliced radishes

1 tablespoon anise seed

1 tablespoon sugar

Place oranges, bananas, beets, pineapple and jicama in large glass or plastic bowl. Mix reserved beet liquid and pineapple juice, the lemon juice, 3 tablespoons sugar and the salt; pour over fruit. Let stand 10 minutes; drain. Arrange fruit on lettuce. Garnish with lime, peanuts and pomegranate seeds. Mix anise seed and 1 tablespoon sugar; sprinkle over salad.

A Roast Lamb
Christmas Dinner for 8

Mushroom Pita Bites
Roast Leg of Lamb
Cinnamon Sweet Potatoes
Hot Minted Fruit
Cherry Tomato–Brussels Sprouts Salad
Pesto-Pine Bread (page 131)
Champagne Cream Torte (page 106)

Planning Guide

One or Two Days Before

- Prepare Refrigerator Dough and filling for Pesto-Pine Bread.
- Prepare Champagne Cream and bake Cream Puff Dough for Champagne-Cream Torte. Cover and refrigerate filling; store pastry loosely covered at room temperature.
- Prepare and marinate Brussels sprouts for Cherry Tomato–Brussels Sprouts Salad. Cut up tomatoes.
- Cook sweet potatoes for Cinnamon-Sweet Potatoes; slip off skins and cut up.

Several Hours Before

- Cut up fruit and measure ingredients for Hot Minted Fruit.

About 3 Hours Before

- Prepare Roast Leg of Lamb.

About 20 Minutes Before

- Bake Mushroom Pita Bites.
- Prepare Hot Minted Fruit.
- Prepare Cinnamon-Sweet Potatoes.
- Toss salad.

At Dessert Time

- Assemble Champagne-Cream Torte.

Roast Leg of Lamb (page 188); Cinnamon Sweet Potatoes (page 188); Cherry Tomato-Brussels Sprouts Salad (page 189)

Roast Leg of Lamb

The garlic and herbs here complement the lamb nicely. If you like, you can serve with a dollop of mint jelly, and mirror the flavors found in the Hot Minted Fruit.

5- to 7-pound leg of lamb

3 cloves garlic, cut into slivers

3 teaspoons dried dill weed

1½ teaspoons salt

1 tablespoon fresh or 1 teaspoon crushed dried rosemary leaves

½ teaspoon pepper

Heat oven to 325°. Do not remove fell (paperlike covering) from lamb. Make 10 or 12 small slits in lamb with tip of knife. Insert slivers of garlic into slits. Mix remaining ingredients; rub over surface of lamb. Place lamb, fat side up, on rack in shallow roasting pan. Insert meat thermometer so tip is in center of thickest part of lamb and does not touch bone or rest in fat. Do not add water.

Roast uncovered until thermometer registers desired doneness: 140° (rare), 20 to 25 minutes per pound; 160° (medium), 25 to 30 minutes per pound; 170° (well), 25 to 30 minutes per pound. Remove roast from oven when thermometer registers 5° lower than desired doneness. Cover roast with aluminum foil tent and let stand 15 to 20 minutes. Temperature will rise about 5° and roast will be easier to carve.

Cinnamon Sweet Potatoes

2½ pounds sweet potatoes or yams (about 8 medium)*

½ cup packed brown sugar

¼ cup (½ stick) margarine or butter

3 tablespoons water

½ teaspoon ground cinnamon

½ teaspoons salt

Heat enough water to cover sweet potatoes (salted if desired) to boiling. Add potatoes. Cover and heat to boiling. Cook 30 to 35 minutes or until tender; drain. Slip off skins. Cut potatoes into ½-inch slices.

Heat remaining ingredients in 8-inch skillet over medium heat, stirring constantly, until smooth and bubbly. Add potatoes. Stir gently until potatoes are glazed and hot. 8 servings.

ORANGE SWEET POTATOES: Substitute 3 tablespoons orange juice for the water and add 1 tablespoon grated orange peel.

* 2 cans (18 ounces each) vacuum-pack sweet potatoes, cut into ½-inch slices, can be substituted for the cooked fresh sweet potatoes.

Cherry Tomato–Brussels Sprouts Salad

2 package (10 ounces each) frozen Brussels sprouts

³/4 cup oil-and-vinegar dressing

¹/2 pint cherry tomatoes, cut in half

Lettuce leaves

Cook Brussels sprouts as directed on package; drain. Pour dressing over hot Brussels sprouts, turning each until well coated. Cover and refrigerate at least 3 hours.

Add tomatoes to Brussels sprouts; toss. Serve on lettuce leaves.

Mushroom Pita Bites

2 pita breads (6 inches in diameter)

2 cups sliced mushrooms (about 5 ounces)*

1 small red onion, thinly sliced

¹/4 cup chopped green bell pepper

2 tablespoons chopped fresh or 2 teaspoons dried basil leaves

1 cup finely shredded mozzarella cheese (4 ounces)

1 tablespoon grated Parmesan cheese

Heat oven to 425°. Split each pita bread around edge in half, using knife. Place pita rounds, cut sides up, on ungreased cookie sheet. Arrange mushrooms on pita rounds. Top with onion and bell pepper. Sprinkle with basil and cheeses. Bake 8 to 10 minutes or until cheese is melted. Cut each pita round into 8 pieces. 8 servings.

* 1 can (4 ounces) mushroom stems and pieces, drained, can be substituted for fresh mushrooms.

Hot Minted Fruit

Leftover fruit? Try serving it over pound cake or angel food cake.

²/3 cup mint-flavored apple jelly

2 tablespoons margarine or butter

2 tablespoons lemon juice

4 cups peeled fresh pears, cut into chunks, or 2 cans (16 ounces each) pear halves, drained and cut into fourths

4 cups fresh pineapple chunks (1 medium pineapple) or 2 cans (15¹/4 ounces each) pineapple chunks, drained

Cook jelly, margarine and lemon juice in 2-quart saucepan, stirring frequently, until jelly is melted. Stir in pears and pineapple. Heat over low heat about 10 minutes or until fruit is hot. 8 servings.

TO MICROWAVE: Place jelly, margarine and lemon juice in 2-quart microwavable casserole. Microwave uncovered on high 3 to 4 minutes, stirring every minute, until jelly is melted. Stir in pears and pineapple. Cover tightly and microwave 3 to 4 minutes or until fruit is hot.

🔔 **Buy fresh pineapple that is already cut up or peeled and cored.**

*A Holiday Luncheon
for 4*

Mushroom Ravioli
OR
Fruit-stuffed Trout
OR
Salmon Steaks with Orange Bearnaise Sauce
Almond Pilaf
Warm Greens with Balsamic Vinegar
Popovers with Herb Butter (page 238)
Pear Tart Tatin (page 97)

Planning Guide

One or Two Days Before
- Mix Herb Butter.

Several Hours Before
- Assemble Ravioli for Mushroom Ravioli; cover and refrigerate; do not cook.
- Prepare popovers. Pierce with knife to let steam out; let stand on wire rack.
- Prepare Almond Pilaf for baking.
- Prepare Warm Greens with Balsamic Vinegar; do not cook dressing or toss.
- Cook pears for Pear Tart Tatin; do not cover with pastry and bake.
- Prepare ingredients for main dish; do not cook.

About One Hour Before Serving
- Bake Almond Pilaf and Cheese Triangles at the same time. Let Pilaf stand, covered, while cooking main dish.

About 40 Minutes Before
- Cook and complete Ravioli for Mushroom Ravioli.
- Cook main dish.
- Toss salad.
- Reheat popovers in preheated 300° oven 5 to 10 minutes if desired.
- Reheat cooked pears; cover and bake Pear Tart Tatin just before serving main course.

Mushroom Ravioli; Salmon Steaks with Orange Bearnaise Sauce (page 192); Almond Pilaf (page 193)

Mushroom Ravioli

Ravioli (right)
²/₃ cup whipping (heavy) cream
2 tablespoons grated Parmesan cheese
¹/₄ teaspoon chicken bouillon granules
2 tablespoons chopped walnuts, toasted

Prepare Ravioli; reserve. Heat 6 cups water to boiling in Dutch oven. Meanwhile, heat whipping cream, cheese and bouillon granules to boiling in 1¹/₂-quart saucepan; reduce heat. Simmer uncovered about 10 minutes, stirring occasionally, until thickened. Stir in walnuts.

Add 4 ravioli to boiling water. Boil uncovered about 2 minutes or just until ravioli are tender. Remove with slotted spoon to wire rack to drain. Repeat with remaining ravioli. Serve ravioli with sauce. Sprinkle with additional grated Parmesan cheese if desired.

RAVIOLI

1 tablespoon margarine or butter
4 ounces mushrooms, chopped
¹/₄ cup ricotta cheese
1 tablespoon finely chopped walnuts, toasted
¹/₂ teaspoon chopped fresh or ¹/₄ teaspoon dried tarragon leaves
¹/₄ teaspoon salt
Dash of pepper
12 wonton skins (about 3 inches square)

Heat margarine in 10-inch skillet over medium-high heat. Cook mushrooms in margarine, stirring frequently, until brown; drain. Mix mushrooms and remaining ingredients except wonton skins. Place about 1 tablespoon filling on center of each wonton skin. Brush edges with water; fold diagonally in half over filling to form triangle. Press edges to seal.

Fruit-stuffed Trout

Fruit Stuffing (below)

4 pan-dressed rainbow trout (6 to 8 ounces each) or drawn trout (about 12 ounces each)

2 tablespoons margarine or butter, melted

1 tablespoon lemon juice

Heat oven to 425°. Grease jelly roll pan, 15½ × 10½ × 1 inch. Prepare Fruit Stuffing. Stuff fish with Fruit Stuffing. Close openings with skewers or toothpicks if necessary. Place fish in pan. Mix margarine and lemon juice; drizzle over fish. Bake uncovered 15 to 18 minutes or until fish flakes easily with fork. 4 servings.

FRUIT STUFFING

1 cup unseasoned croutons

⅓ cup diced dried fruit and raisin mixture

2 tablespoons margarine or butter, melted

2 tablespoons dry white wine or chicken broth

¼ teaspoon salt

⅛ teaspoon ground allspice

1 green onion, chopped

Mix all ingredients until liquid is absorbed.

TO GRILL: Grease wire grill. Place stuffed fish on grill. Cover and grill about 4 inches from medium coals 12 to 15 minutes, turning fish once and brushing occasionally with margarine mixture, until fish flakes easily with fork.

Salmon Steaks with Orange Bearnaise Sauce

4 salmon steaks, about 1 inch thick (about 1½ pounds)

Salt and pepper, if desired

2 tablespoons margarine or butter, melted

Orange Bearnaise Sauce (below)

Set oven control to broil. Sprinkle both sides of fish steaks with salt and pepper; brush with half of the margarine. Place fish on rack in broiler pan. Broil with tops about 4 inches from heat about 6 minutes or until light brown; brush fish with margarine. Turn carefully; brush with margarine. Broil 4 to 6 minutes longer or until fish flakes very easily with fork.

While fish is broiling, prepare Orange Bearnaise Sauce. Serve sauce over fish.

ORANGE BEARNAISE SAUCE

½ cup cold water

1 tablespoon cornstarch

¼ cup (½ stick) margarine or butter

1 tablespoon finely chopped onion

1 tablespoon orange juice

1 teaspoon chopped fresh or ¼ teaspoon dried chervil leaves

1 teaspoon chopped fresh or ¼ teaspoon dried tarragon leaves

½ teaspoon grated orange peel

⅛ teaspoon salt

1 or 2 drops yellow food color if desired

⅓ cup plain yogurt

Gradually stir cold water into cornstarch in 1-quart saucepan. Stir in remaining ingredients except yogurt. Heat over medium heat, stirring constantly, until mixture thickens and boils. Boil and stir 1 minute; remove from heat. Place yogurt in small bowl; beat vigorously with fork until smooth. Pour hot mixture into yogurt, beating constantly with fork.

TO MICROWAVE: Decrease water by 1 tablespoon. Gradually stir water into cornstarch in 2-cup microwavable measure. Stir in remaining ingredients except yogurt. Microwave uncovered on high 2½ to 3½ minutes, stirring every minute, until thickened. Place yogurt in small bowl; beat vigorously with fork until smooth. Pour hot mixture into yogurt, beating constantly with fork.

🔔 **Prepare the bearnaise sauce ahead; cover and refrigerate in microwavable container. Just before serving, microwave uncovered on medium (50%), stirring every minute, 2 to 3 minutes, or until hot. Or, heat over low heat, stirring frequently, until hot.**

Almond Pilaf

1½ cups uncooked regular long grain rice

1 medium onion, chopped (about ½ cup)

¼ cup (½ stick) margarine or butter

½ teaspoon ground allspice

½ teaspoon ground turmeric

¼ teaspoon salt

¼ teaspoon curry powder

⅛ teaspoon pepper

3 cups hot chicken broth

¼ cup slivered blanched almonds

Heat oven to 350°. Cook rice and onion in margarine in 10-inch skillet, stirring frequently, until onion is tender. Stir in allspice, turmeric, salt, curry powder and pepper. Place in ungreased 2-quart casserole. Stir in broth. Cover and bake about 40 minutes or until liquid is absorbed and rice is tender. Stir in almonds. 8 servings.

BROWN RICE–ALMOND PILAF: Substitute brown rice for the regular rice. Bake 60 to 70 minutes.

Warm Greens with Balsamic Viniagrette

½ cup Balsamic Vinaigrette (below)

8 ounces mushrooms, sliced (about 3 cups)

4 cups 2-inch bite-size pieces leaf lettuce

4 cups 2-inch bite-size pieces spinach

3 cups 2-inch bite-size pieces radicchio

¼ cup pine nuts, toasted

Heat Balsamic Vinaigrette in 10-inch skillet over medium heat. Cook mushrooms in vinaigrette 3 minutes; remove from heat. Add remaining ingredients. Toss 1 to 2 minutes or until greens begin to wilt. Serve immediately. Sprinkle with freshly ground pepper if desired.

BALSAMIC VINAIGRETTE

⅓ cup water

¼ cup balsamic or cider vinegar

¼ cup olive or vegetable oil

1 teaspoon honey

¼ teaspoon salt

¼ teaspoon paprika

1 clove garlic, crushed

Shake all ingredients in tightly covered container. Refrigerate at least 1 hour. Shake before using.

Meatless
South-of-the-Border Dinner for 6

Cowboy Caviar
Vegetable Burritos
Green Rice
Orange and Jicama Salad
Date-Pecan Upside-down Cake (page 78)
Cinnamon Ice Cream*
Mexican Chocolate

* Recipes not included.

Planning Guide

One or Two Days Before
- Prepare bean mixture for Cowboy Caviar.
- Prepare Pumpkin Seed Sauce. Measure remaining ingredients for Vegetable Burritos; do not cook.
- Prepare sauce for Green Rice; measure remaining ingredients but do not cook.
- Cook syrup for Mexican Chocolate.

Several Hours Before
- Prepare Date-Pecan Upside-down Cake.
- Prepare Orange and Jicama Salad; refrigerate until serving.

About 30 Minutes Before
- Cook Green Rice.

About 15 Minutes Before
- Complete Vegetable Burritos.
- Complete Mexican Chocolate.

Cowboy Caviar

This isn't really caviar—instead it's a zesty twist on appetizers that everyone will enjoy.

2 tablespoons vegetable oil

2 tablespoons lime juice

1/4 teaspoon salt

1/4 teaspoon crushed red pepper

1/4 teaspoon ground cumin

1/8 teaspoon pepper

1 small onion, finely chopped (about 1/4 cup)

1 clove garlic, finely chopped

1 can (15 ounces) black beans, rinsed and drained

1 can (4 ounces) chopped ripe olives, drained

1 package (8 ounces) cream cheese, softened

2 hard-cooked eggs, chopped

1 green onion, sliced

Mix all ingredients except cream cheese, eggs and onion. Cover and refrigerate at least 2 hours.

Spread cream cheese on serving plate. Spoon bean mixture evenly over cream cheese. Arrange eggs on bean mixture in ring around edge of plate. Sprinkle with onion. Serve with tortilla chips or assorted crackers if desired.

Vegetable Burritos

Pumpkin Seed Sauce (page 244)

1 cup chopped broccoli

1 medium onion, finely chopped (about 1/2 cup)

2 cloves garlic, finely chopped

2 tablespoons vegetable oil

1 cup 2 × 1/4-inch julienne strips yellow squash

1 cup 2 × 1/4-inch julienne strips zucchini

1/4 cup shelled pumpkin seeds, toasted

1 tablespoon lemon juice

1 teaspoon ground red chiles

1/4 teaspoon salt

1/4 teaspoon ground cumin

1 small red bell pepper, finely chopped (about 1/2 cup)

6 flour tortillas (10 inches in diameter), warmed

Prepare Pumpkin Seed Sauce. Cook broccoli, onion and garlic in oil in 10-inch skillet, stirring frequently, until onion is tender. Stir in remaining ingredients except tortillas. Cook about 2 minutes, stirring occasionally, until squash is crisp-tender.

Spoon about 1/2 cup of the vegetable mixture onto center of each tortilla. Fold one end of tortilla up about 1 inch over mixture; fold right and left sides over folded end, overlapping. Fold remaining end down. Serve with Pumpkin Seed Sauce.

Orange and Jicama Salad

3 tablespoons vegetable oil

2 tablespoons white vinegar

1/2 teaspoon salt

3 medium oranges, peeled and sectioned

1 medium green, red or yellow bell pepper, cut into 1-inch pieces

1 small red onion, thinly sliced and separated into rings

8 ounces jicama, peeled and cut into 1 1/2 × 1/2-inch julienne strips

Chili powder or paprika

Mix oil, vinegar and salt in large bowl. Add remaining ingredients except chili powder; toss. Sprinkle lightly with chili powder. Serve on lettuce leaves if desired.

Mexican Chocolate

1/2 cup sugar

3 tablespoons freeze-dried or powdered instant coffee (dry)

1 teaspoon ground cinnamon

1/2 teaspoon ground nutmeg

1/4 teaspoon salt

3 ounces unsweetened chocolate

1 1/2 cups water

4 cups milk

Whipped cream

Heat all ingredients except milk and whipped cream in 2-quart saucepan over low heat, stirring constantly, until chocolate is melted and mixture is smooth. Heat to boiling; reduce heat. Simmer 4 minutes, stirring constantly. Stir in milk. Heat over low heat. Just before serving, beat with hand beater until foamy. Top each serving with whipped cream.

Green Rice

2 cups water

1/2 cup chopped fresh parsley

1/2 cup chopped fresh cilantro

1 teaspoon salt

Dash of pepper

2 poblano chiles, seeded and coarsely chopped

2 cloves garlic, cut into fourths

1 small onion, cut into fourths

1 cup uncooked regular long grain rice

2 tablespoons vegetable oil

Place all ingredients except rice and oil in blender. Cover and blend on medium-high speed about 30 seconds or until smooth. Strain; reserve liquid.

Cook rice in oil in 2-quart saucepan over medium heat about 1 minute, stirring frequently, until rice is well coated with oil. Pour reserved liquid over rice. Heat rice mixture to boiling, stirring once or twice; reduce heat. Cover and simmer 14 minutes. (Do not lift cover or stir.) Remove from heat. Fluff rice lightly with fork. Cover and let steam 5 to 10 minutes. Garnish with sliced pimiento if desired.

Cowboy Caviar (page 195); Vegetable Burritos (page 195); Orange and Jicama Salad; Mexican Chocolate

Bountiful Buffets

Christmas is the perfect time to simplify entertaining by serving food buffet-style. Whether all of your foods are made from scratch, or picked up from the deli or catered, the buffet is the easiest way to serve any size group. It also lends itself well to open houses, so popular at this time of year.

❄ Have the house in order well before the party so you can focus on food and decorations. Plan enough food and beverages so you won't run out (see charts below and at right). Be sure to have nonalcoholic beverages available.

❄ Choose a variety of foods that offer contrasts in flavor, color, texture and temperature. Prepare as much ahead as possible so you won't have to spend the evening in the kitchen.

❄ Common sense and convenience are the watchwords of a good buffet. To avoid congestion in a small room, start the line so guests finish at the door and can easily leave the room.

❄ Begin at one end of the table with plates, then move on in order to the main dish, vegetables, salad, breads, condiments, flatware and napkins. Placing flatware and napkins at the end of the line allows guests free hands to serve themselves.

Planning a large get-together where food is involved can be a little tricky if you're not used to serving a crowd. Our handy chart takes the guesswork out of how much food you will need. Keep in mind that the number of servings does not necessarily mean the number of guests served. So consider the appetites and eating habits of your guests when figuring the number of servings needed. Also consider the time of day, weather conditions and the types and numbers of foods served. Plan on one drink per hour per guest, unless the room is very hot, then plan on two.

Fruit and Vegetable Yields

Fruits	Approximate Yield	Vegetables	Approximate Yield
Cantaloupe, 4-pound	36 chunks	Celery, 4 medium stalks	33 sticks, 4 × 1/2″
Grapes, 1 pound seedless	12 to 15 clusters	Cucumbers, 2 large	45 sticks, 4 × 3/4″
Honeydew, 2-pound	36 chunks	Mushrooms, 1 pound	20 medium
Pineapple, 3- to 4-pound	40 chunks	Pea pods, 4 ounces	30 pea pods
Strawberries, 1 pound large	20 to 25 berries	Zucchini, 3 medium	35 slices, 1/2″

Vegetables	Approximate Yield	Salad Greens	Approximate Yield
Asparagus, 1 pound	30 to 45 spears	Boston lettuce, 1/2-pound head	6 cups bite-size pieces
Bell pepper, 1 large	24 strips, 3 1/2 × 1/2″	Iceberg lettuce, 1 1/2-pound head	12 cups bite-size pieces
Broccoli or cauliflower, 2 pounds	32 flowerets, 1 1/4″	Leaf lettuce, 1-pound bunch	8 cups bite-size pieces
Carrots, 1 pound	65 sticks 3 × 1/2″	Romaine, 1 1/2-pound bunch	12 cups bite-size pieces
		Spinach, 3/4-pound bunch	8 cups bite-size pieces

Number of Servings Chart

Food Item	Serving Size	12 Servings	24 Servings	48 Servings
Meats and Shellfish, bone-in and unshelled	³/₄ pound	9 pounds	18 pounds	36 pounds
Meats and Fish, boneless	¹/₄ pound	3 pounds	6 pounds	12 pounds
Side Dishes such as Potato Salad, Baked Beans or Coleslaw	¹/₂ cup	1¹/₂ quarts	3 quarts	1¹/₂ gallons
Meat Cold Cuts	2¹/₂ ounces	2 pounds	4 pounds	8 pounds
Cheese Slices	1 ounce	1 pound	2 pounds	4 pounds
Rolls	1¹/₂ rolls	2 dozen	3 dozen	6 dozen
Crackers	4 crackers	8 ounces	1 pound	2 pounds
Tossed Salad	1¹/₂ cups	4¹/₂ quarts	9 quarts	4¹/₂ gallons
Salad Dressing	2 tablespoons	1¹/₂ cups	3 cups	1¹/₂ quarts
Dip	2 tablespoons	1¹/₂ cups	3 cups	6 cups
Chips	1 ounce	12 ounces	1¹/₂ pounds	3 pounds
Fruit or Vegetable Dippers	4 pieces	4 dozen	8 dozen	16 dozen
Cakes 13 × 9″, 12-cup Ring or 9″ Layer	¹/₁₆ cake	1 cake	2 cakes	3 cakes
Cookies	2 cookies	2 dozen	4 dozen	8 dozen
Ice Cream	¹/₂ cup	2 quarts	1 gallon	2 gallons
Coffee, Brewed	³/₄ cup	9 cups water	18 cups water	36 cups water
Ground Coffee		1¹/₂ cups	3 cups	5 cups
Tea, Brewed	³/₄ cup	9 cups water	18 cups water	36 cups water
Loose Tea	1 tablespoon	¹/₄ cup	¹/₂ cup	1 cup
Teabags	1 teabag	12 bags	24 bags	48 bags
Iced Tea	1 cup	3 quarts	1¹/₂ gallons	3 gallons
Punch	¹/₂ cup	1¹/₂ quarts	3 quarts	1¹/₂ gallons
Mineral Water	8 ounces	3 quarts	6 quarts	12 quarts
Ice	4 ounces	3 pounds	6 pounds	12 pounds

*International Holiday
Buffet for 12*

Meatballs in Chipotle Sauce
Burgundy Meatballs
Swedish Meatballs
Hot Buttered Noodles* • Hot Cooked Rice*
Herbed Vegetable Bake
Molded Salad*
Assorted Relishes*
Antipasto Pull-Apart (page 128) • Bread Sticks*
Triple Ginger Pound Cake (page 76)
OR
Chocolate Nesselrode Cake (page 71)

*Recipes not included.

Planning Guide

Several Weeks Before

- Prepare meatballs for all recipes; cover tightly and freeze.
- Prepare Antipasto Pull-Apart; cover tightly and freeze.

One or Two Days Before

- Prepare Chipotle Sauce; cover and refrigerate.
- Prepare Burgundy Sauce; cover and refrigerate.
- Prepare sauce for Swedish Meatballs except—do not add sour cream; cover and refrigerate.
- Prepare dessert.
- Place all meatballs in refrigerator to thaw.

Early in the Day

- Prepare molded salad of your choice.
- Prepare Assorted Relishes of your choice.
- Prepare ingredients for Herbed Vegetable Bake; do not bake.

Just Before Serving

- Bake Herbed Vegetable Bake 30 minutes before serving.
- Prepare hot-cooked rice (baking in oven with vegetables will dovetail and save a burner.
- Boil water for noodles; cook noodles.
- Reheat all kinds of meatballs; add sour cream to Swedish meatballs.

Meatballs in Chipotle Sauce

Chipotle Sauce (below)

1 pound ground beef

1 pound ground pork

1/2 cup dry bread crumbs

1/2 cup milk

2 tablespoons finely chopped onion

2 tablespoons chopped fresh cilantro

2 teaspoons salt

1/2 teaspoon pepper

2 eggs

Prepare Chipotle Sauce. Mix remaining ingredients; shape into 1½-inch balls. Heat sauce and meatballs to boiling; reduce heat. Cover and simmer about 20 minutes or until meatballs are done.

CHIPOTLE SAUCE

2 to 4 dried chipotle chilies

2 slices bacon, finely cut up

1 small onion, finely chopped (about 1/4 cup)

1 cup beef broth

1/4 cup finely chopped carrot

1/4 cup finely chopped celery

1/4 cup chopped fresh cilantro

1/2 teaspoon salt

1/4 teaspoon pepper

4 medium tomatoes, finely chopped (about 3 cups)

Cover chilies with warm water. Let stand about 1 hour or until softened. Drain and finely chop chilies. Cook bacon and onion in 2-quart saucepan, stirring frequently, until bacon is crisp. Stir in chilies and remaining ingredients.

Burgundy Meatballs

2 pounds ground beef

1 cup dry bread crumbs

1/2 cup water chestnuts, finely chopped

1/2 cup milk

1 teaspoon salt

1 teaspoon Worcestershire sauce

1/8 teaspoon pepper

2 eggs

1 medium onion, chopped (about 1/2 cup)

Burgundy Sauce (below)

Chopped fresh parsley

Heat oven to 400°. Mix all ingredients except Burgundy Sauce and parsley. Shape mixture into 1-inch balls. Place in ungreased jelly roll pan, 15½ × 10½ × 1 inch. Bake uncovered about 10 minutes or until done.

Prepare Burgundy Sauce. Stir meatballs into Burgundy Sauce. Meatball mixture can be covered and refrigerated up to 24 hours at this point. Heat meatball mixture to boiling; reduce heat. Cover and simmer about 10 minutes or just until meatballs are hot. Garnish with parsley.

BURGUNDY SAUCE

1/3 cup cornstarch

1/2 cup cold water

1 cup burgundy, dry red wine or beef broth

1 clove garlic, crushed

2 cans (10½ ounces each) condensed beef broth

Mix cornstarch and cold water in 3-quart saucepan. Gradually stir in remaining ingredients. Heat to boiling, stirring constantly. Boil and stir 1 minute.

Swedish Meatballs

Meatballs (below)
1 can (10³/4 ounces) condensed cream of chicken soup
¹/2 cup half-and-half
¹/8 teaspoon ground nutmeg
¹/2 cup sour cream

Cook Meatballs; drain. Stir in soup, half-and-half and nutmeg. Heat to boiling, stirring occasionally; reduce heat. Cover and simmer 15 minutes. Stir in sour cream; heat through. Sprinkle with parsley if desired. 4 servings.

MEATBALLS

¹/2 pound ground beef
¹/2 pound ground pork
¹/2 cup dry bread crumbs
¹/4 cup half-and half
2 tablespoons finely chopped onion
1 teaspoon salt
¹/2 teaspoon ground allspice
¹/2 teaspoon Worcestershire sauce
Dash of pepper
1 egg

Mix all ingredients. Shape mixture into thirty 1-inch balls. Cook in 10-inch skillet over medium heat about 20 minutes, turning occasionally, until brown.

TO MICROWAVE: Prepare Meatballs—except do not cook. Place in square microwavable dish, 8 × 8 × 2 inches. Cover and microwave on high about 6 minutes, stirring after 3 minutes, until almost done; drain. Mix soup, half-and-half, nutmeg and sour cream; stir into meatballs. Cover and microwave about 5 minutes or until bubbly.

Herbed Vegetable Bake

This casserole can be prepared the day before. Cover and refrigerate, but plan to add 5 to 10 minutes to the cooking time.

1 small bunch broccoli (about 1 pound), cut into flowerets and 1-inch pieces
1 small head cauliflower (about 1¹/4 pounds), cut into flowerets
5 or 6 carrots (about 1 pound), cut diagonally into ¹/4-inch slices
¹/3 cup margarine or butter, melted
Salt and pepper
1 tablespoon chopped fresh or 1 teaspoon dried basil leaves
1 tablespoon chopped fresh or 1 teaspoon dried tarragon leaves
2 cloves garlic, finely chopped
2 small onions, thinly sliced and separated into rings

Heat oven to 400°. Arrange broccoli along 1 long side of ungreased rectangular baking dish, 13 × 9 × 2 inches. Arrange cauliflower along other side of dish. Arrange carrots down center between broccoli and cauliflower. Drizzle with margarine. Sprinkle with salt, pepper, basil, tarragon and garlic. Arrange onions evenly over top. Cover with aluminum foil and bake about 30 minutes or until vegetables are crisp-tender.

Tree-Trimming Treats for 24

Appetizers

Wassail (page 146)
Sparkling Pineapple Punch (page 144)
Nutty Cereal Snack
Assorted Cheeses and Crackers*
Italian Deviled Eggs
Southwest Riblets

* Recipes not included.

Mexican Cheese Puffs
Frosty Smoked Salmon Spread (page 240)
Liptauer Cheese Spread
Liver Pâté
Shrimp and Pistachio Spread
Corn and Walnut Dip
Crudités* • Tortilla Chips*

Desserts

Gingered Pineapple
Assorted Christmas Cookies,* Candies* and/or Fruitcake*
Fudge-Pecan Torte (page 74)
Raspberry Trifle (page 101)

Planning Guide

Several Weeks Before
- Prepare Christmas Cookies, Candies and/or Fruitcake days or weeks ahead. Cover tightly.
- Prepare Fudge-Pecan Torte; cover tightly and freeze.

One or Two Days Ahead
- Prepare Nutty Cereal Snack; Italian Deviled Eggs; Frosty Smoked Salmon Spread; Liptauer Cheese Spread; Liver Pâté; Shrimp and Pistachio Spread; Corn and Walnut Dip.
- Prepare Gingered Pineapple. Cover and refrigerate.
- Prepare Raspberry Trifle. Cover and refrigerate.

- Remove desserts from freezer and thaw at room temperature. Arrange cookies and candy on serving plates; cover.
- Prepare syrup for Sparkling Pineapple Punch.

Several Hours Before
- Thaw desserts.
- Mix ingredients for Wassail; do not heat.
- Measure ingredients for Mexican Cheese Puffs; do not bake.
- Prepare sauce for Southwest Riblets; do not bake.

About 1 Hour Before
- Bake Southwest Riblets.
- Bake Mexican Cheese Puffs.
- Heat Wassail.
- Mix Sparkling Pineapple Punch.

Nutty Cereal Snack

3 cups crispy corn puff cereal

2 cups tiny duck- or fish-shaped cheese-flavored crackers

2 cups pretzel sticks

2 cups cashews, peanuts or mixed nuts

¹/₂ cup (1 stick) margarine or butter

1 teaspoon Worcestershire sauce

¹/₂ teaspoon garlic salt

¹/₂ teaspoon celery salt

Heat oven to 300°. Mix cereal, crackers, pretzels and cashews in ungreased rectangular pan, 13 × 9 × 2 inches. Heat margarine in 1-quart saucepan until melted; remove from heat. Stir in remaining ingredients. Pour over cereal mixture, tossing until well coated. Bake uncovered 25 minutes, stirring occasionally. Serve warm or cool. About 9 cups snack.

Italian Deviled Eggs

Prosciutto and anchovies add an Italian flair to deviled eggs.

6 hard-cooked eggs

2 ounces prosciutto or fully cooked Virginia ham

2 tablespoons mayonnaise or salad dressing

1 teaspoon dry mustard

¹/₂ teaspoon white pepper

3 flat fillets of anchovy in oil

1 can (3¹/₄ ounces) tuna in oil, drained

1 green onion, finely chopped, or 2 tablespoons chopped chives

Cut peeled eggs lengthwise in half. Slip out yolks. Place yolks and remaining ingredients except prosciutto and onion in food processor or blender. Cover and process, or blend, until smooth. Stir in prosciutto and onion. Fill whites with egg yolk mixture, mounding it lightly. Sprinkle with chives if desired. Cover and refrigerate up to 24 hours. 12 appetizers.

Liptauer Cheese Spread

¹/₂ cup (1 stick) margarine or butter, softened

¹/₂ cup sour cream

2 tablespoons chopped fresh chives

1 tablespoon caraway seed

1 tablespoon paprika

2 tablespoons anchovy paste

2 teaspoons capers

¹/₂ teaspoon dry mustard

1 package (8 ounces) cream cheese, softened

Place all ingredients in blender. Cover and blend on high speed about 2 minutes, stopping blender occasionally to scrape sides, until smooth. Spoon mixture into crock or serving container. Cover tightly and refrigerate until well chilled, at least 4 hours but no longer than 1 week. Let stand uncovered at room temperature about 1 hour before serving. Serve with assorted crackers if desired. Refrigerate any remaining spread. About 2 cups spread.

Liver Pâté

This recipe can easily be doubled or tripled. However, do not increase the reserved liquid; the 1/4 cup will work for all amounts.

1 package (8 ounces) frozen chicken livers, thawed

1/2 cup chicken broth

1 small onion, chopped (about 1/4 cup)

1 clove garlic, finely chopped

1 teaspoon chopped fresh or 1/4 teaspoon dried thyme leaves

1/4 cup (1/2 stick) margarine or butter, softened

1/4 teaspoon dry mustard

1/8 teaspoon salt

Dash of pepper

3 slices bacon, crisply cooked and crumbled

Mix chicken livers, broth, onion, garlic and thyme in 2-quart saucepan. Heat to boiling; reduce heat. Cover and simmer 12 to 15 minutes or until livers are tender when pierced with fork. Cool mixture; drain, reserving liquid.

Place liver mixture, 1/4 cup of the reserved liquid and the remaining ingredients in blender or food processor. Cover and blend on high speed about 1 minute, stopping blender occasionally to scrape sides, or process 30 seconds, until smooth. Pack mixture in 1 1/2-cup mold or bowl. Cover and refrigerate at least 4 hours. At serving time, unmold pâté onto serving plate. Garnish with fresh thyme if desired. Serve with apple slices or crackers if desired. About 1 cup spread.

Southwest Riblets

1 medium onion, chopped (about 1/2 cup)

2 tablespoons vegetable oil

1 tablespoon ground red chiles

6 dried juniper berries, crushed, if desired

3 cloves garlic, finely chopped

1/2 teaspoon salt

1/2 ounce unsweetened chocolate, grated

1 cup water

2 tablespoons cider vinegar

1 can (6 ounces) tomato paste

2 tablespoons sugar

3-pound rack fresh pork back ribs, cut lengthwise across bones in half

Cook onion in oil in 2-quart saucepan 2 minutes, stirring frequently. Stir in ground red chiles, juniper berries, garlic and salt. Cover and cook 5 minutes, stirring occasionally. Stir in chocolate until melted.

Pour water, vinegar and tomato paste into food processor or blender. Add onion mixture and sugar. Cover and process, or blend, until well blended.

Heat oven to 375°. Cut between pork back ribs to separate. Place in single layer in roasting pan. Pour sauce evenly over pork. Bake uncovered 30 minutes; turn pork. Bake about 30 minutes longer or until done. About 28 appetizers.

Corn and Walnut Dip

2 packages (8 ounces each) cream cheese, softened

¼ cup vegetable oil

¼ cup lime juice

1 tablespoon ground red chilies

1 tablespoon ground cumin

½ teaspoon salt

Dash of pepper

1 can (8¾ ounces) whole kernel corn, drained

1 cup chopped walnuts

1 small onion, chopped (about ¼ cup)

Beat all ingredients except corn, walnuts and onion in large bowl on medium speed until smooth. Stir in corn, walnuts and onion. Serve with tortilla chips if desired. About 4 cups dip.

Shrimp and Pistachio Spread

1 cup creamed cottage cheese

2 tablespoons lemon juice

½ teaspoon onion powder

1 cup chopped cooked shrimp*

½ cup chopped pistachio nuts

Place cottage cheese, lemon juice and onion powder in blender or food processor. Cover and blend on high speed about 2 minutes, stopping blender occasionally to scrape sides, or process 30 sec-

Italian Deviled Eggs (page 204); Southwestern Riblets (page 205); Sparkling Pineapple Punch (page 144); Shrimp and Pistachio Spread; Mexican Cheese Puffs; Liver Pâté (page 205)

onds, until smooth. Pour into small bowl. Stir in shrimp and nuts. Cover and refrigerate at least 1 hour. Serve with assorted crackers or ruffled potato chips if desired. About 2 cups dip.

* 1 can (4¼ ounces) tiny shrimp, rinsed and drained, can be substituted for the cooked shrimp.

Mexican Cheese Puffs

1 cup Bisquick® Original baking mix

3 tablespoons margarine or butter, softened

3 tablespoons chopped green chilies

1 egg

1 cup shredded Cheddar cheese (4 ounces)

Heat oven to 400°. Grease cookie sheet. Mix baking mix, margarine, chilies and egg in medium bowl. Stir in cheese. Drop dough by rounded teaspoonfuls about 1 inch apart onto cookie sheet. Bake 10 to 12 minutes or until golden brown.

Gingered Pineapple

1 medium pineapple, peeled and cut into chunks*

1 teaspoon finely chopped gingerroot or ½ teaspoon ground ginger

1 medium orange

Place pineapple in glass or plastic dish. Sprinkle with gingerroot. Grate 2 teaspoons orange peel; sprinkle over pineapple. Cut orange in half and remove seeds. Squeeze juice (about ¼ cup) over pineapple. Stir gently. Cover and refrigerate at least 1 hour, stirring once, to blend flavors.

* 3 cans (8 ounces each) pineapple chunks in juice, drained, can be substituted for the fresh pineapple.

Appetizer Open House for 20

Eggplant Dip
Easy Crab Dip
Hot Artichoke Dip
Crudités*
Pickled Herring* and Smoked Oysters*

* Recipes not included.

Assorted Cheeses* and Crackers*
Chicken Kabobs with Peanut Sauce
Curried Meatballs with Chutney Sauce
Shrimp with Prosciutto
Stuffed Prunes with Bacon
Pesto Pinwheels
Frosty Citrus Punch (page 143)
Royal Cranberry Punch (page 147)
Assorted Christmas Cookies and Candy*
(pages 1 to 62)

Planning Guide

Several Weeks Before
- Cook meatballs for Curried Meatballs with Chutney Sauce. Cover and freeze.
- Bake cookies and make candy. Cover tightly and freeze.

Several Days Before
- Prepare Easy Crab Dip

Two Days Before
- Prepare Eggplant Dip; cover and refrigerate.

Prepare One Day Before
- Bake Pesto Pinwheels
- Prepare chicken for Chicken Kabobs with Peanut Sauce; cover and refrigerate.
- Prepare Hot Artichoke Dip for baking: cover and refrigerate.
- Remove meatballs from freezer and place in refrigerator to thaw.
- Mix Chutney Sauce for meatballs.
- Peel shrimp and prepare Shrimp with Prosciutto for baking; cover and refrigerate.
- Stuff prunes and let stand in port for Stuffed Prunes with Bacon; cover and refrigerate.

- Remove cookies and candy from freezer.

Several Hours Before
- Prepare Stuffed Prunes with Bacon for broiling; cover and refrigerate.
- Mix limeade and water for Frosty Citrus Punch; cover and refrigerate.

About 1 hour before
- Cook Peanut Sauce for Chicken Kabobs with Peanut Sauce.
- Arrange crackers, cookies and other foods not perishable.

About 30 Minutes Before
- Bake Shrimp with Prosciutto

About 20 Minutes Before
- Bake Hot Artichoke Dip and heat meatballs in a covered baking pan at the same time.
- Remove Easy Crab Dip from refrigerator.
- Heat Royal Cranberry Punch

At Serving Time
- Complete Frosty Citrus Punch
- Broil Stuffed Prunes with Bacon.

Eggplant Dip

1 medium eggplant (about 1½ pounds)

1 small onion, cut into fourths

1 clove garlic

¼ cup lemon juice

1 tablespoon olive or vegetable oil

1½ teaspoons salt

Heat oven to 400°. Prick eggplant 3 or 4 times with fork. Bake about 40 minutes or until tender; cool. Peel eggplant; cut into cubes. Place eggplant, onion, garlic, lemon juice, oil and salt in blender. Cover and blend on high speed until smooth. Serve with vegetable dippers if desired. About 2 cups dip.

Easy Crab Dip

1 package (8 ounces) cream cheese, softened

¼ cup mayonnaise or salad dressing

1 to 2 tablespoons ketchup

2 tablespoons finely chopped green onions

1 package (6 ounces) frozen crabmeat or 6 ounces imitation crabmeat, thawed, drained and cartilage removed

Beat cream cheese, mayonnaise, ketchup and onions in medium bowl on medium speed until fluffy. Beat in crabmeat on low speed. Cover and refrigerate at least 1 hour. Remove from refrigerator 15 minutes before serving. About 2 cups dip.

Hot Artichoke Dip

1 can (14 ounces) artichoke hearts, drained and chopped

½ cup mayonnaise or salad dressing

½ cup grated Parmesan cheese

4 green onions, chopped

Heat oven to 325°. Mix all ingredients except crackers in shallow 1-quart casserole. Cover and bake 10 to 15 minutes or until hot. Serve with crackers if desired. About 12 servings.

Chicken Kabobs with Peanut Sauce

4 large boneless, skinless chicken breast halves (about 1½ pounds)

¼ cup soy sauce

1 tablespoon vegetable oil

1 teaspoon packed brown sugar

¼ teaspoon ground ginger

1 clove garlic, crushed

Peanut Sauce (below)

Cut chicken into ¾-inch pieces. (For ease in cutting, partially freeze chicken.) Mix chicken, soy sauce, oil, brown sugar, ginger and garlic in medium glass or plastic bowl. Cover and refrigerate at least 2 hours, stirring occasionally.

Prepare Peanut Sauce. Remove chicken from marinade; reserve marinade. Thread 4 or 5 chicken pieces on each of fourteen to sixteen 6- or 8-inch metal skewers. Brush chicken with marinade. Set oven control to broil. Arrange kabos on rack in broiler pan.

Broil kabobs with tops about 4 inches from heat 4 to 5 minutes; turn. Brush with marinade. Broil 4 to 5 minutes longer or until chicken is white. Serve with Peanut Sauce. About 16 appetizers.

PEANUT SAUCE

1 small onion, finely chopped (about ¼ cup)

1 tablespoon vegetable oil

⅓ cup peanut butter

⅓ cup water

1 tablespoon lemon juice

¼ teaspoon ground coriander

3 to 4 drops red pepper sauce

Cook onion in oil in 1½-quart saucepan, stirring occasionally, until tender; remove from heat. Stir in remaining ingredients. Heat over low heat just until blended (sauce will separate if overcooked).

Curried Meatballs with Chutney Sauce

Chutney Sauce (below)

1 pound ground turkey

1/2 cup crushed buttery cracker crumbs

1/3 cup evaporated skimmed milk

2 tablespoons finely chopped green onions

1 1/2 to 2 teaspoons curry powder

1/4 teaspoon salt

Prepare Chutney Sauce. Heat oven to 400°. Mix remaining ingredients; shape into forty-eight 1-inch balls. Place in ungreased rectangular pan, 13 × 9 × 2 inches. Bake uncovered 10 to 15 minutes or until no longer pink in center. Serve hot with Chutney Sauce. 4 dozen appetizers.

CHUTNEY SAUCE

2/3 cup plain yogurt

1 tablespoon finely chopped chutney

1/4 teaspoons curry powder

Mix all ingredients. Cover and refrigerate 1 hour.

Pesto Pinwheels

1 package (17 1/4 ounces) frozen puff pastry, thawed

1 cup Spinach Pesto (page 245) or other prepared pesto

1 egg, beaten

Heat oven to 400°. Roll each sheet of puff pastry on a very lightly floured surface into rectangle, 14 × 10 inches. Spread 1/2 cup of the Spinach Pesto evenly over each rectangle to within 1/2 inch of long sides. Loosely roll pastry from narrow end; brush edge of roll with egg and pinch into roll to seal. Cut into 1/2-inch slices, using sharp knife. Place on ungreased cookie sheet. Bake 8 to 10 minutes or until golden brown. 40 appetizers.

Shrimp with Prosciutto

2 tablespoons margarine or butter

2 tablespoons olive or vegetable oil

2 anchovy fillets in oil, finely chopped

1 tablespoon chopped fresh parsley

2 cloves garlic, finely chopped

18 raw jumbo shrimp (in shells)

9 thin slices prosciutto or fully cooked Virginia ham, cut in half

1/2 cup dry white wine

1 to 2 tablespoons lemon juice

Heat oven to 375°. Heat margarine and oil in baking dish, 9 × 9 × 2 inches, in oven until margarine melts. Mix anchovies, parsley and garlic; spread over margarine mixture in baking dish. Peel shrimp, leaving tails intact. Make a shallow cut lengthwise down back of each shrimp; wash out vein. Wrap 1 half-slice prosciutto around each shrimp. Place shrimp on anchovy mixture. Bake uncovered 10 minutes. Pour wine and lemon juice over shrimp. Bake about 10 minutes longer or until shrimp are pink. 18 appetizers.

Stuffed Prunes with Bacon

24 pitted prunes

24 walnut halves

1/2 cup ruby port

1/4 cup water

12 slices bacon

Stuff each prune with walnut half. Mix port and water; pour over prunes in bowl. Let stand about 2 hours, stirring occasionally, until prunes are plump. Cut bacon slices in half. Wrap bacon around prunes; secure with toothpicks. Arrange on rack in broiler pan. Set oven control to broil. Broil with tops about 4 inches from heat 10 to 12 minutes, turning once, until bacon is crisp. Serve hot. 24 appetizers.

A Holiday
Brunch for a Bunch for 12

Mixed Fresh Fruit
Brunch Oven Omelet with Canadian-style
Bacon
Sour Cream Coffee Cake (page 117)
Poinsettia Puffs (page 133)

Planning Guide

Several Weeks Before
- Prepare Sour Cream Coffee Cake; cover tightly and freeze.

One or Two Days Before
- Prepare Refrigerated Dough and filling for Poinsettia Puffs.
- Cut up fruit for Mixed Fresh Fruit.
- Remove coffee cake from freezer to thaw at room temperature.

About 2 Hours Before
- Prepare and bake Poinsettia Puffs.

Just Before Serving
- Prepare Brunch Oven Omelet with Canadian-style Bacon.
- Toss Mixed Fresh Fruit.

Brunch Oven Omelet with Canadian-style Bacon

Oven Canadian-style Bacon (right)

¹/₄ cup (¹/₂ stick) margarine or butter

1¹/₂ dozen eggs

1 cup sour cream

1 cup milk

2 teaspoons salt

¹/₄ cup chopped green onions

Chopped fresh parsley

Heat oven to 325°. Prepare Oven Canadian-style Bacon; reserve. Heat margarine in rectangular baking dish, 13 × 9 × 2 inches, in oven until melted. Tilt dish to coat bottom. Beat eggs, sour cream, milk and salt in large bowl until blended. Stir in onions. Pour into dish. Bake omelet mixture and bacon about 35 minutes or until eggs are set but moist and bacon is hot. Arrange omelet on large platter with bacon. Sprinkle with parsley.

OVEN CANADIAN-STYLE BACON

1 pound Canadian-style bacon, cut into twenty-four ¹/₈-inch slices

¹/₄ cup maple-flavored syrup

Reassemble slices of bacon on aluminum foil. Pour syrup over bacon. Wrap and place in pan.

Mixed Fresh Fruit

¹/₂ cup orange-flavored liqueur or orange juice

4 cups cut-up fresh pineapple

2 cups seedless green grapes, cut in half

2 cups fresh strawberries or 1 package (16 ounces) frozen whole strawberries, partially thawed

Pour orange-flavored liqueur over pineapple and grapes; toss. Just before serving, toss with strawberries. Garnish with mint leaves if desired.

Brunch Oven Omelet with Canadian Bacon; Mixed Fresh Fruit

A Christmas Morning Brunch for 6

Hot Cappuccino Nog (page 148)
Fresh-squeezed Orange Juice*
Smoked Salmon Roulade
with
Stollen or Assorted Nut Breads (pages 111–114)
OR
Morning Glory Oven French Toast
Apple-Grapefruit Salad
Assorted Christmas Cookies (pages 1–46)

* Recipes not included.

Planning Guide

Several Weeks Before

- Prepare assorted Christmas cookies; cover tightly and freeze.
- Prepare Stollen (do not frost) or nut breads; cover tightly and freeze.

One or Two Days Before

- Remove cookies from freezer and thaw at room temperature.
- Prepare toppings for French Toast;
- Prepare ingredients for Apple-Grapefruit Salad; cover and refrigerate.

Several Hours Before

- Prepare ingredients for main dish.

About 30 Minutes Before

- Prepare Hot Cappuccino Nog; cover and refrigerate.
- Prepare main dish.

About 15 Minutes Before

- Arrange salad.
- Warm toppings for French Toast if desired.

Morning Glory Oven French Toast

To make your morning less rushed, mix egg whites, milk, granulated sugar, salt and cinnamon the night before; cover and refrigerate. You can also prepare your desired toppings, then cover and refrigerate them as well.

3 eggs or 5 egg whites

¾ cup milk

1 tablespoon granulated sugar

¼ teaspoon salt

¼ teaspoon ground cinnamon

18 slices French bread, each ½ inch thick (about ½ pound)

Powdered sugar, if desired

Cranberry-Raspberry Topping (below), Honeyed Pineapple-Papaya Topping (right) or Spiced Orange Cream Topping (right)

Heat oven to 500°. Beat egg whites, milk, granulated sugar, salt and cinnamon in small bowl with fork. Dip bread into egg white mixture; place on plate. Lightly grease cookie sheet. Heat cookie sheet in oven 1 minute; remove from oven. Place dipped bread on hot cookie sheet. Bake 5 to 8 minutes or until bottoms are golden brown. Turn bread; bake 2 to 4 minutes longer or until golden brown. Sprinkle with powdered sugar. Serve with toppings.

CRANBERRY-RASPBERRY TOPPING

1 package (10 ounces) frozen raspberries, thawed

1 cup sugar

1 cup cranberries

Drain raspberries, reserving ½ cup juice. Mix juice and sugar in 2-quart saucepan. Heat to boiling; boil 5 minutes. Stir in raspberries and cranberries; reduce heat. Simmer about 3 minutes, stirring occasionally, until cranberries are tender but do not burst. Serve warm or cool.

HONEYED PINEAPPLE-PAPAYA TOPPING

½ cup apricot all-fruit spread

2 tablespoons honey

1 papaya, peeled, seeded and cut into small pieces

1 cup cut-up pineapple

¼ cup pomegranate seeds

Mix fruit spread and honey in medium bowl. Add papaya and pineapple; toss. Add pomegranate seeds; toss. Cover and refrigerate until serving time if desired. (If refrigerated, let stand about 15 minutes before serving; toss.)

SPICED ORANGE CREAM TOPPING

¼ cup vanilla yogurt

¼ cup orange marmalade

½ teaspoon ground cinnamon

⅛ teaspoon ground nutmeg

1 cup whipped cream or frozen (thawed) whipped topping

Mix yogurt, marmalade, cinnamon and nutmeg. Fold into whipped cream. Refrigerate until serving time.

🔔 **Mix the eggs, milk, granulated sugar, salt and cinnamon the night before; cover and refrigerate.**

Morning Glory Oven French Toast with Cranberry-Raspberry Topping; Apple-Grapefruit Salad (page 216); Hot Cappuccino Nog (page 148)

Smoked Salmon Roulade

1/2 cup all-purpose flour

1 cup milk

3 tablespoons chopped green onions

1 tablespoon chopped fresh or 1 teaspoon dried dill weed

2 tablespoons margarine or butter, melted

1/4 teaspoon salt

4 eggs

1 cup flaked or finely chopped smoked salmon*

1 package (10 ounces) frozen asparagus cuts

1 1/2 cups shredded Gruyère or Emmentaler cheese (6 ounces)

Heat oven to 350°. Line jelly roll pan, 15 1/2 × 10 1/2 × 1 inch, with aluminum foil. Grease foil generously. Beat flour, milk, onions, dill weed, margarine, salt and eggs until well blended. Pour into pan. Sprinkle with salmon. Bake 15 to 18 minutes or until eggs are set.

Meanwhile, cook asparagus as directed on package; drain and keep warm. After removing roulade from oven, immediately sprinkle with cheese and asparagus. Roll up, beginning at narrow end, using foil to lift and roll roulade. Cut into slices.

HAM ROULADE: Substitute 1 cup coarsely chopped fully cooked smoked ham for the smoked salmon.

* 1 can (7 1/2 ounces) red salmon, drained and flaked, can be substituted for the smoked salmon.

Apple-Grapefruit Salad

This festive, easy salad is spiked with a tangy lime and honey dressing.

Lime-Honey Dressing (below)

3 unpeeled red or green apples, sliced

2 grapefruit, peeled and sectioned

Salad greens

1/2 cup pomegranate seeds

Prepare Lime-Honey Dressing. Arrange apple slices and grapefruit sections on salad greens. Sprinkle with pomegranate seeds. Serve with dressing. 6 servings.

LIME-HONEY DRESSING

3 tablespoons frozen (thawed) limeade or lemonade concentrate

3 tablespoons honey

3 tablespoons vegetable oil or sour cream

1/4 teaspoon poppy seed

Shake all ingredients in tightly covered container; refrigerate.

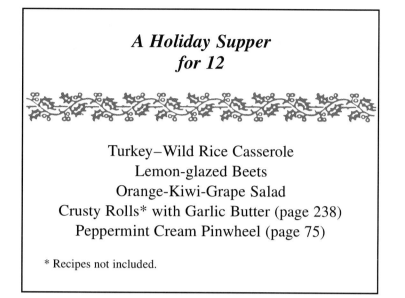

A Holiday Supper
for 12

Turkey–Wild Rice Casserole
Lemon-glazed Beets
Orange-Kiwi-Grape Salad
Crusty Rolls* with Garlic Butter (page 238)
Peppermint Cream Pinwheel (page 75)

* Recipes not included.

Planning Guide

Several Weeks Before
- Bake cake for Peppermint Cream Pinwheel; cover tightly and freeze.

One Day Before
- Mix Garlic Butter.
- Thaw cake and prepare Peppermint Cream Pinwheel.
- Prepare Turkey–Wild Rice Casserole for baking; cover and refrigerate.

Several Hours Before
- Prepare ingredients for Orange-Kiwi-Grape Salad.

About 1 Hour Before
- Bake Turkey–Wild Rice Casserole.

About 15 Minutes Before
- Prepare Lemon-glazed Beets.
- Complete Orange-Kiwi-Grape Salad.
- Heat rolls if desired.

Turkey–Wild Rice Casserole

Cooked White and Wild Rice (below)
1/2 cup (1 stick) margarine or butter
1/2 cup all-purpose flour
1 1/2 teaspoons salt
1/4 teaspoon pepper
1 1/2 cups chicken broth
2 1/4 cups milk
3 cups cubed cooked turkey or chicken
1/2 cup slivered almonds
*1 small green bell pepper, chopped (about
   1/2 cup)*
*8 ounces mushrooms, sliced (about 3
   cups)**
1 jar (2 ounces) sliced pimientos, drained

Prepare Cooked White and Wild Rice. Heat oven to 350°. Grease rectangular baking dish, 13 × 9 × 2 inches. Heat margarine in Dutch oven until melted. Stir in flour, salt and pepper. Cook over medium heat, stirring constantly, until smooth and bubbly; remove from heat. Stir in broth and milk. Heat to boiling, stirring constantly. Boil and stir 1 minute. Stir in cooked rice and remaining ingredients. Pour into baking dish. Bake 40 to 45 minutes or until center is hot. Sprinkle with chopped fresh parsley if desired.

COOKED WHITE AND WILD RICE

1/2 cup uncooked wild rice
1 1/4 cups water
1/2 teaspoon salt
1/2 cup uncooked regular long grain rice
1 cup water

Heat wild rice, 1 1/4 cups water and the salt to boiling in 2-quart saucepan; reduce heat. Cover and simmer 30 minutes. Stir in regular rice and 1 cup water. Heat to boiling; reduce heat. Cover and simmer 15 minutes. (Do not lift cover or stir.) Remove from heat. Fluff rice lightly with fork. Cover and let steam 5 minutes.

Lemon-glazed Beets

2/3 cup lemon or orange marmalade
1/4 cup white vinegar
*4 cans (16 ounces each) small whole or
   sliced beets, drained*

Heat marmalade and vinegar in 3-quart saucepan over medium heat, stirring occasionally, until hot. Stir in beets. Cover and heat about 10 minutes, stirring occasionally, until beets are hot.

* 2 jars (4 1/2 ounces each) sliced mushrooms, drained, can be substituted for the fresh mushrooms.

Orange-Kiwi-Grape Salad

6 seedless oranges, peeled and sliced
3 kiwifruit, peeled and sliced
Salad greens
2 cups seedless green grapes, cut in half
Honey-Spice Dressing (below)

Arrange oranges and kiwifruit on salad greens. Top with grapes. Serve with Honey-Spice Dressing. 12 servings.

HONEY-SPICE DRESSING

1/3 cup lemon juice
1/3 cup honey
3/4 teaspoon ground cinnamon

Mix all ingredients.

ORANGE-APPLE-GRAPE SALAD: Substitute 3 medium apples, thinly sliced, for the kiwifruit.

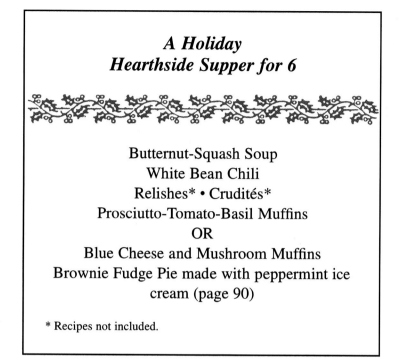

A Holiday
Hearthside Supper for 6

Butternut-Squash Soup
White Bean Chili
Relishes* • Crudités*
Prosciutto-Tomato-Basil Muffins
OR
Blue Cheese and Mushroom Muffins
Brownie Fudge Pie made with peppermint ice
cream (page 90)

* Recipes not included.

Planning Guide

Up to a Week Before
- Prepare Brownie Fudge Pie.

One or Two Days Before
- Prepare White Bean Chili; cover and refrigerate.
- Prepare Butternut-Squash Soup; cover and refrigerate.
- Measure ingredients for muffins.

In the Morning
- Prepare Relishes and Crudités.

Just Before Serving
- Mix and bake muffins.
- Reheat chili and soup.

Butternut-Squash Soup

1 medium onion, chopped (about 1/2 cup)

2 tablespoons margarine or butter

2 cups chicken broth

1-pound butternut squash, peeled, seeded and cut into 1-inch cubes

2 pears, peeled and sliced

1 teaspoon chopped fresh or 1/2 teaspoon dried thyme leaves

1/4 teaspoon salt

1/4 teaspoon white pepper

1/4 teaspoon ground coriander

1 cup whipping (heavy) cream

1 unpeeled pear, sliced

1/2 cup chopped pecans, toasted

Cook onion in margarine in Dutch oven, stirring frequently, until tender. Stir in broth, squash, 2 sliced pears, the thyme, salt, white pepper and coriander. Heat to boiling; reduce heat. Cover and simmer 10 to 15 minutes or until squash is tender.

Pour about half of the soup into food processor or blender. Cover and process, or blend, until smooth; pour into another container. Repeat with remaining soup. Return soup to Dutch oven. Stir in whipping cream. Heat, stirring frequently, until hot. (Do not boil.) Garnish with sliced pear and pecans.

White Bean Chili

Chicken and white beans make a tasty change from red beans and beef.

1 large onion, chopped (about 1 cup)

1 clove garlic, finely chopped

1/4 cup (1/2 stick) margarine or butter

4 cups 1/2-inch cubes cooked chicken

3 cups chicken broth

2 tablespoons chopped fresh cilantro

3 tablespoons chopped fresh or 1 tablespoon dried basil leaves

2 teaspoons ground red chiles

1/4 teaspoon ground cloves

2 cans (16 ounces each) great northern beans, undrained

1 medium tomato, chopped (about 3/4 cup)

Blue or yellow corn tortilla chips

Cook onion and garlic in margarine in Dutch oven, stirring frequently, until onion is tender. Stir in remaining ingredients except tomato and tortilla chips. Heat to boiling; reduce heat. Cover and simmer 1 hour, stirring occasionally. Serve with tomato and tortilla chips.

Butternut-Squash Soup; White Bean Chili; Prosciutto-Tomato-Basil Muffins (page 222)

Prosciutto-Tomato-Basil Muffins

Savory muffins such as these and the Blue Cheese and Mushroom Muffins are especially nice with soup.

1 egg

1 cup milk

¼ cup vegetable oil

2 cups all-purpose flour

¾ cup finely chopped prosciutto (about ¼ pound)

½ cup chopped sun-dried tomatoes in olive oil, rinsed and drained

2 tablespoons chopped fresh or 2 teaspoons dried basil leaves

2½ teaspoons baking powder

Heat oven to 400°. Grease 12 medium muffin cups, 2½ × 1¼ inches. Beat egg in large bowl. Stir in milk and oil. Stir in remaining ingredients just until flour is moistened. Divide batter evenly among cups (cups will be full).

Bake about 20 minutes or until golden brown. Immediately remove from pan. Serve warm. 1 dozen muffins.

SHAVED HAM AND CHEESE MUFFINS: Omit prosciutto, tomatoes and basil. Stir in ¼ pound shaved ham, chopped, ¼ cup pitted ripe olives, drained and chopped, and 2 tablespoons chopped fresh parsley with the flour. Sprinkle 2 teaspoons grated Parmesan cheese over batter in each cup.

Blue Cheese and Mushroom Muffins

½ cup coarsely chopped mushrooms

1 large clove garlic, finely chopped

2 tablespoons margarine or butter

1 egg

1¼ cups milk

3 tablespoons margarine or butter, melted

2 cups all-purpose flour

¼ cup crumbled blue cheese

2 tablespoons chopped green onions

3 teaspoons baking powder

¼ teaspoon salt

⅛ teaspoon white pepper

Heat oven to 400°. Grease 12 medium muffin cups, 2½ × 1¼ inches. Cook mushrooms and garlic in 2 tablespoons margarine in 6-inch skillet over medium heat about 3 minutes, stirring frequently, until mushrooms are tender. Remove mushrooms with slotted spoon; reserve.

Beat egg slightly with fork in large bowl. Stir in milk and 3 tablespoons melted margarine. Stir in mushrooms and remaining ingredients just until flour is moistened. Divide batter evenly among cups (cups will be almost full).

Bake about 30 minutes or until golden brown. Let stand 5 minutes; remove from pan. Serve warm. Refrigerate any remaining muffins.

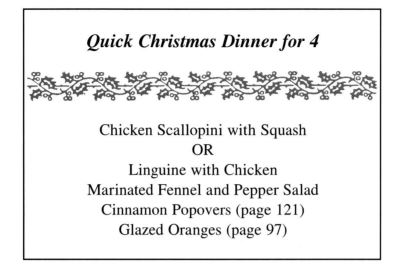

Quick Christmas Dinner for 4

Chicken Scallopini with Squash
OR
Linguine with Chicken
Marinated Fennel and Pepper Salad
Cinnamon Popovers (page 121)
Glazed Oranges (page 97)

Planning Guide

One or Two Days Before
- Prepare Glazed Oranges.

One Day Before
- Prepare Marinated Peppers and Fennel.

Several Hours Before
- Prepare ingredients for main dish.

- Grease pans for Cinnamon Popovers; measure ingredients.

About One Hour Before
- Heat oven; mix and bake popovers.
- Cook main dish.

Smoky Mushroom Spread

3 cups finely chopped mushrooms (about 8 ounces)

1 medium onion, finely chopped (about ¹/₂ cup)

1 clove garlic, finely chopped

1 tablespoon all-purpose flour

¹/₄ teaspoon salt

¹/₈ teaspoon salt

¹/₈ teaspoon pepper

1 teaspoon Worcestershire sauce

¹/₄ teaspoon liquid smoke

¹/₂ package (8-ounce size) cream cheese, cut into cubes

¹/₂ cup plain yogurt

1 slice bacon, crisply cooked and finely crumbled

Spray 10-inch nonstick skillet with nonstick cooking spray; heat over medium heat until hot. Cook mushrooms, onion and garlic in skillet about 2 minutes, stirring occasionally, until onion is tender. Stir in flour, salt and pepper thoroughly.

Stir in remaining ingredients except bacon. Heat until hot. Sprinkle with bacon. Serve hot or cold with melba toast rounds if desired. About 1¹/₂ cups spread.

Chicken Scallopini with Squash

A hearty dish to chase away winter blues, ready in a flash.

4 boneless, skinless chicken breast halves (about 1¹/₂ pounds)

1 cup thinly sliced zucchini

1 cup thinly sliced yellow summer squash

2 tablespoons olive or vegetable oil

¹/₃ cup dry white wine or chicken broth

¹/₄ cup whipping (heavy) cream

³/₄ teaspoon chopped fresh or ¹/₄ teaspoon dried thyme leaves

¹/₄ teaspoon salt

¹/₈ teaspoon pepper

Flatten each breast half to ¹/₄-inch thickness between plastic wrap or waxed paper, being careful not to tear chicken.

Cover and cook chicken, zucchini and yellow squash in oil in 10-inch skillet over medium heat 6 to 8 minutes, turning chicken once, until juices of chicken run clear and vegetables are crisp-tender.

Arrange chicken and vegetables on warm platter; keep warm.

Add remaining ingredients to skillet. Heat to boiling. Boil about 5 minutes or until thickened, stirring occasionally. Pour over chicken and vegetables.

Linguine with Chicken

2 tablespoons olive or vegetable oil

2 medium green bell peppers, chopped (about 2 cups)

2 cloves garlic, finely chopped

1 medium onion, chopped (about ¹/₂ cup)

2 boneless, skinless chicken breast halves

4 cups chopped roma (plum) tomatoes*

1 cup sliced or chopped ripe olives

1 tablespoon capers, drained

1 teaspoon salt

¹/₂ teaspoon pepper

2 flat fillets of anchovy in oil, drained

1 package (16 ounces) fresh or dried linguine

2 tablespoons chopped fresh parsley

¹/₂ cup grated Parmesan cheese

Heat oil in 10-inch skillet over medium-high heat. Cook bell peppers, garlic and onion in oil about 5 minutes, stirring frequently, until onion is tender. Add chicken breast halves. Cook uncovered 5 minutes, turning chicken once. Remove chicken; cut into ¹/₂-inch pieces. Stir chicken, tomatoes, olives, capers, salt, pepper and anchovy fillets into bell pepper mixture. Cover and cook over medium-low heat 30 minutes, stirring occasionally.

Cook linguine as directed on package; drain. Mix linguine and chicken mixture. Top with parsley and cheese.

* 2 cans (28 ounces each) Italian pear-shaped tomatoes, drained and chopped, can be substituted for the fresh tomatoes.

Marinated Fennel and Pepper Salad

Italian Dressing (below)

1 medium fennel bulb (about 5 ounces)

3 ounces mushrooms, sliced (about 1 cup)

1 small zucchini, cut into ¹/₂-inch slices (about 1 cup)

1 small red bell pepper, coarsely chopped (about ¹/₂ cup)

Prepare Italian Dressing. Cut fennel bulb lengthwise in half; cut halves crosswise into thin slices. Mix fennel, dressing and remaining ingredients in large glass or plastic bowl. Cover and refrigerate at least 4 hours, stirring occasionally.

ITALIAN DRESSING

3 tablespoons olive or vegetable oil

3 tablespoons red wine vinegar

3 tablespoons water

1 tablespoon finely chopped onion

1 teaspoon chopped fresh or ¹/₄ teaspoon dried basil leaves

1 teaspoon chopped fresh or ¹/₄ teaspoon dried oregano leaves

¹/₄ teaspoon salt

¹/₄ teaspoon sugar

¹/₄ teaspoon dry mustard

1 small clove garlic, finely chopped

Shake all ingredients in tightly covered container.

Leftovers Made Luscious

Sometimes we think of leftovers as a liability, when they actually are assets! Below you'll find inventive and creative ways to capitalize on your holiday leftovers.

Appetizers

❄ Serve small portions of leftover main dishes such as Quiche Lorraine or pasta dishes.

❄ Top a block of cream cheese with leftover salsa or bottled creamy salad dressing and chopped cooked shrimp. Serve with crackers or vegetable slices.

❄ Turn leftover breads and rolls into snacks. Split if thick, brush both sides lightly with melted margarine or butter. Sprinkle with Italian seasoning and Parmesan cheese and bake at 400° about 5 minutes or until light brown.

❄ Split leftover biscuits, popovers or croissants and top with shredded cheese and chopped green chilies. Broil or bake until cheese is melted for a quick Mexican snack.

❄ For a quick snack or appetizer, cut leftover baked potatoes into $1/2$-inch slices. Top with pizza sauce, your favorite pizza toppings and shredded cheese; broil or microwave until hot and cheese is melted.

Main Dishes and Meats

❄ Leftover hard-cooked eggs can be used for Italian Deviled Eggs, or chopped or sliced to top salads, casseroles or soups.

❄ Use leftover cheeses to make quick sandwich fillings, to add to salads or to stir into scrambled eggs.

❄ Finely chop or shred leftover cheeses into the same plastic freezer bag. Use for topping pizza, macaroni and cheese or when making quiche or cheese sauce.

❄ Use cut-up cooked poultry, meat and seafood in salads, casseroles, soups and stews. For an easy salad, combine cooked meat and equal parts mayonnaise or plain yogurt and your favorite bottled salad dressing.

❄ Make a simple chowder by adding leftover cooked vegetables and cooked fish, seafood or poultry to prepared cream-based soup.

❄ Stir any cut-up cooked poultry, fish or shellfish into your favorite spaghetti sauce or cream sauce and serve over cooked pasta or rice.

❄ Prepare a quick beef stroganoff by heating leftover beef mixed with equal amounts cream of mushroom soup and sour cream.

❄ Heat leftover sliced or cubed meat in prepared barbecue, pizza or taco sauce and serve in tortillas, pita breads or buns for quick hot sandwiches.

Side Dishes

❀ Use leftover muffins or popovers for dessert by filling with pudding or ice cream and topping with fresh fruit or your favorite dessert topping.

❀ Make French toast using leftover English muffins, bagels, challah bread, croissant halves, nut breads, whole grain or cinnamon-raisin bread instead of French or regular white bread.

❀ Thickly slice leftover nut breads, then cut into "fingers" or cubes for dipping into chocolate, fruit or other dessert sauces. Or, frost fingers or cubes with thinned leftover frosting and roll in chopped nuts or coconut for a sweet snack.

❀ Spread leftover pancakes with margarine or butter, softened cream cheese, peanut butter or fruit preserves. Top with sugar, chopped nuts, chocolate chips, sliced fruit or another favorite topping. Roll up and enjoy for a quick snack. Or, cut into 1-inch slices and place a toothpick in each—children will love them for a special snack.

❀ Mix chilled leftover cooked vegetables with bottled salad dressing for a last-minute salad.

❀ Freeze leftover cooked pasta and grains. Thaw and add to recipes calling for cooked pasta or grains.

Desserts

❀ Cube or coarsely crumble leftover cake. Layer with fresh fruit, pudding, ice cream and/or whipped cream.

❀ Mix crumbled cake with pudding and serve in ice-cream cones—great snacks for kids.

❀ Brush leftover pound cake or angel food cake slices with melted margarine or butter. Roll in coconut or chopped nuts and brown both sides under the broiler.

❀ Heat leftover frosting in the microwave for a fast glaze.

❀ Sandwich two leftover cookies around scoops of ice cream, with the scoop size dependent on the cookie size. Freeze for future snacks or desserts.

❀ Liven up leftover cookies or bars by adding a drizzle with melted chocolate or white chocolate.

❀ Crush Christmas cookies and use to make crumb pie shells.

❀ Crumble leftover cookies and layer alternately with softened ice cream and Hot Fudge Sauce (page 246) in a square pan; top with more cookie crumbs and drizzle the top with fudge sauce. Freeze at least 2 hours or until firm. To serve, cut into squares.

❀ Fold leftover crumbled cookies or cookie crumbs into sweetened whipped cream or yogurt and serve over fresh fruit. Or, blend leftover cookies with ice cream and milk for a quick cookies and cream shake.

❀ Make leftover brownies into brownie sundaes by topping with ice cream and hot fudge sauce.

❀ Stir leftover cooked rice into prepared packaged vanilla pudding mix for a quick rice pudding.

**Christmas Eve Feast
for 8**

Onion-Anchovy Tart
Holiday Stuffed Pasta
Lasagne
Or
Antipasto Toss
Italian Flatbread or Garlic Bread (page 141)
Stained Glass Tart (page 92)

Planning Guide

One or Two Days Before
- Prepare and bake Italian Flatbread.
- Prepare main dish for baking; cover and refrigerate.

Several Hours Before
- Prepare Antipasto Toss.
- Prepare Stained Glass Tart except—do not add whipped cream or jelly. Cover directly with plastic wrap and refrigerate.

About One Hour Before
- Bake main dish.
- Prepare Onion-Anchovy Tart for baking; cover and refrigerate.

About 15 Minutes Before
- Bake Onion-Anchovy Tart.
- Heat flatbread in 300° oven about 10 minutes.
- Toss salad.

At Dessert Time
- Complete Stained Glass Tart.

Antipasto Toss (page 231); Holiday Stuffed Pasta

Holiday Stuffed Pasta

24 uncooked jumbo pasta shells

2 cups spaghetti sauce

2 cups ricotta cheese

*1 cup shredded mozzarella cheese
(4 ounces)*

½ cup grated Parmesan cheese

*2 tablespoons chopped fresh
parsley*

½ teaspoon pepper

2 eggs

*1 cup Spinach Pesto (page 245) or
prepared pesto*

Heat oven to 350°. Cook pasta shells as directed on package; drain. Spread spaghetti sauce in rect-angular pan, 13 × 9 × 2 inches. Mix remaining ingredients except pasta shells and Spinach Pesto. Fill each pasta shell with about 2 tablespoons cheese mixture. Arrange filled shells on spaghetti sauce. Cover pan with aluminum foil and bake about 45 minutes or until hot. Serve with pesto. 8 servings.

Lasagne

1 pound bulk Italian sausage or ground beef

1 medium onion, chopped (about ½ cup)

2 cloves garlic, finely chopped

1 can (16 ounces) whole tomatoes, undrained

1 can (15 ounces) tomato sauce

2 tablespoons chopped fresh parsley

2 tablespoons chopped fresh or 2 teaspoons dried basil leaves

1 teaspoon sugar

½ teaspoon salt

9 uncooked lasagne noodles (about 8 ounces)

2 cups ricotta cheese or small curd creamed cottage cheese (about 16 ounces)

¼ cup grated Parmesan cheese

1 tablespoon chopped fresh parsley

2 tablespoons chopped fresh or 2 teaspoons dried oregano leaves

1½ teaspoons salt

2 cups shredded mozzarella cheese (8 ounces)

¼ cup grated Parmesan cheese

Cook Italian sausage, onion and garlic in 10-inch skillet, stirring frequently, until sausage is light brown; drain. Stir in tomatoes, tomato sauce, 2 tablespoons parsley, the basil, sugar and ½ teaspoon salt; break up tomatoes. Heat to boiling, stirring occasionally; reduce heat. Simmer uncovered about 1 hour or until thick.

Heat oven to 350°. Cook noodles as directed on package; drain. Reserve ½ cup of the sauce mixture. Mix ricotta cheese, ¼ cup Parmesan cheese, 1 tablespoon parsley, the oregano and 1½ teaspoons salt. Layer one-third each of the noodles, remaining sauce mixture, mozzarella cheese and ricotta cheese mixture in ungreased rectangular pan, 13 × 9 × 2 inches. Repeat 2 times. Spoon reserved sauce mixture over top. Sprinkle with ¼ cup Parmesan cheese. Bake uncovered 45 minutes. Let stand 15 minutes before cutting. 8 to 10 servings.

🔔 **You can make this lasagne ahead. After cooking, cover and freeze no longer than 3 weeks. To serve, cook uncovered in 375° oven until bubbly, about 1 hour.**

Antipasto Toss

1 can (15 ounces) garbanzo beans, drained

1 jar (6 ounces) marinated artichoke hearts,* undrained

¼ cup pitted ripe olives, drained and sliced

½ cup bottled herb-and-garlic or Italian dressing

2 bunches romaine, torn into bite-size pieces

1 bunch leaf lettuce, torn into bite-size pieces

2 hard-cooked eggs, sliced

½ cup sliced pepperoni cut into julienne strips

Freshly ground pepper

Toss beans, artichoke hearts, olives and dressing in large bowl. Top with romaine and leaf lettuce. Arrange eggs and pepperoni on salad greens. Sprinkle with pepper. Cover and refrigerate up to 4 hours. Toss just before serving.

* 1 can (14 ounces) artichoke hearts, drained, can be substituted for the marinated artichoke hearts. Increase dressing to ⅔ cup.

Onion-Anchovy Tart

3 tablespoons olive or vegetable oil

3 large onions, thinly sliced

1 tablespoon chopped fresh basil or thyme leaves

⅛ teaspoon white pepper

1 loaf (1 pound) frozen white or whole wheat bread dough, thawed

2 cans (2 ounces each) anchovy fillets, drained

10 oil-cured Greek olives, cut in half and pitted

Heat oil in 10-inch skillet until hot. Stir in onions; reduce heat. Cover and cook about 25 minutes, stirring occasionally, until onions are very tender. Stir in basil and white pepper.

Lightly grease cookie sheet. Shape bread dough into flattened rectangle on lightly floured surface. Roll dough with floured rolling pin into rectangle, 14 × 11 inches. Place on cookie sheet. Let stand 15 minutes.

Spoon onion mixture evenly over dough to within 1 inch of edge. Arrange anchovies in lattice pattern on onion mixture. Top with olives. Let stand 15 minutes. Heat oven to 425°. Bake 15 to 20 minutes or until crust is brown. Cut into 2-inch squares. About 35 appetizers.

*A New Year's Dinner
for 4*

Cheese Triangles
Shrimp Risotto
OR
Seafood Stew
Steamed Asparagus or Broccoli Spears*
Sweet-and-Sour Salad
Italian Flatbread (page 141)
Bûche de Noël (page 68)
Champagne or Sparkling Grape Juice

* Recipes not included.

Planning Guide

One or Two Days Before
- Prepare Bûche de Noël.
- One day before prepare Cheese Triangles; do not bake, cover and refrigerate.
- Prepare Italian Flatbread; cover tightly and store at room temperature.

Several Hours Before
- Prepare dressing and ingredients for Sweet and Sour Salad; do not toss.
- Prepare ingredients for main dish and vegetable.

About 2 Hours Before
- Prepare Seafood Stew.

About 1 Hour Before
- Prepare Shrimp Rissotto.

About 30 Minutes Before
- Cook vegetable.
- Bake Cheese Triangles.

About 15 Minutes Before
- Reheat Italian Flatbread in preheated 300° oven about 10 minutes, if desired.
- Toss Salad

Cheese Triangles

1 pound feta cheese*

2 eggs, slightly beaten

1/4 cup finely chopped chives

1/4 teaspoon white pepper

1 package (16 ounces) frozen phyllo sheets, thawed

1/4 cup (1/2 stick) margarine or butter, melted

Heat oven to 350°. Grease cookie sheet. Crumble cheese in small bowl; mash with fork. Stir in eggs, chives and white pepper until well mixed. Cut stack of phyllo sheets lengthwise into thirds. Cover with waxed paper, then with damp towel to prevent them from drying out. Use 2 sheets of phyllo for each strip. Place 1 heaping teaspoon cheese mixture on end of strip; fold phyllo strip end over end, in triangular shape, to opposite end. Place on cookie sheet. Repeat with remaining phyllo and cheese mixture. (Triangles can be covered and refrigerated up to 24 hours at this point.) Brush margarine over triangles. Bake about 20 minutes or until puffed and golden. About 36 appetizers.

* Finely shredded Monterey Jack cheese can be substituted for the mashed feta cheese.

Shrimp Risotto

1 pound medium raw shrimp in shells

2 tablespoons margarine or butter

1 medium onion, thinly sliced

1/2 cup dry white wine or chicken broth

1 1/2 cups uncooked Arborio rice

2 cups chicken broth

1 cup water

1/4 cup grated Parmesan cheese

Freshly ground pepper

Peel shrimp. Make a shallow cut lengthwise down back of each shrimp; wash out vein. Heat margarine in 12-inch skillet or Dutch oven over medium-high heat. Cook onion in margarine, stirring frequently, until tender. Reduce heat to medium. Add shrimp. Cook uncovered about 8 minutes, turning once, until shrimp are pink. Remove shrimp from skillet; keep warm.

Add wine to mixture in skillet; cook until liquid has evaporated. Stir in rice. Cook uncovered over medium heat, stirring frequently, until rice begins to brown. Mix broth and water; pour 1/2 cup mixture over rice. Cook uncovered, stirring occasionally, until liquid is absorbed.

Repeat with remaining broth mixture, 1/2 cup at a time. Stir in shrimp. Sprinkle with cheese and pepper.

Seafood Stew

6 fresh large mussels

6 large raw shrimp in shells

1/4 cup olive or vegetable oil

4 cloves garlic, finely chopped

1 small red chile, seeded and finely chopped

1 can (28 ounces) Italian pear-shaped tomatoes, drained and chopped

1/2 pound cod, halibut or sole fillets

4 small cleaned squid (calamari), if desired

1 salmon steak (5 to 6 ounces)

1 swordfish steak (5 to 6 ounces)

1 cup chopped fresh clams

8 cups chicken broth

1/2 cup dry white wine or chicken broth

1 tablespoon chopped fresh sage

Discard any broken-shell or open (dead) mussels. Scrub remaining mussels in cold water, removing any barnacles with a dull paring knife. Remove beards by tugging them away from shells. Place mussels in container. Cover with cool water. Agitate water with hand, then drain and discard water. Repeat several times until water runs clear; drain. Peel shrimp. Make a shallow cut lengthwise down back of each shrimp; wash out vein. Heat oil in 6-quart Dutch oven over medium-high heat. Cook garlic and chile in oil, stirring frequently, until garlic is golden; reduce heat to medium. Add mussels and tomatoes. Cover and cook 5 minutes.

Add shrimp and remaining ingredients to tomato mixture. Heat to boiling; reduce heat. Cover and simmer 1 hour, stirring occasionally. (Discard unopened mussels.)

Seafood Stew

Sweet-and-Sour Salad

1/3 cup coarsely chopped macadamia nuts or hazelnuts (filberts)

1 tablespoon sugar

Sweet-and-Sour Dressing (below)

3 cups bite-size pieces lettuce

3 cups bite-size pieces romaine

1 cup pineapple chunks*

2 medium stalks celery, sliced (about 1 cup)

2 green onions, thinly sliced

Cook nuts and sugar over low heat, stirring constantly, until sugar is melted and nuts are coated; remove from heat. Cool and break apart. Prepare Sweet-and-Sour Dressing. Toss nuts, dressing and remaining ingredients.

SWEET-AND-SOUR DRESSING

1/4 cup olive or vegetable oil

2 tablespoons sugar

2 tablespoons white vinegar

1 tablespoon chopped fresh parsley

1/2 teaspoon salt

Freshly ground pepper

Dash of red pepper sauce

Shake all ingredients in tightly covered container.

SWEET-AND-SOUR MANDARIN SALAD: Substitute sliced almonds for the macadamia nuts and 1 can (11 ounces) mandarin orange segments, drained, for the pineapple.

* 1 can (8 ounces) pineapple tidbits, drained, can be substituted for the fresh pineapple.

In the Spirit of Giving

Rosy Grape Jelly (page 249); Pear-Apricot Chutney (page 254); Nut-Flavored Oil (page 259); Herb Vinegar (page 259); Chocolate-Covered Candy Canes (page 266)

Fabulous Food Gifts

It's a lovely tradition to make gifts from your kitchen for friends and family, or your favorite Christmas bazaar. The recipes gathered here will surely delight you—and those who receive them! You'll find a selection of sauces, preserves, salsas and other enticing foods, along with wonderful ideas for packaging these warm and thoughtful gifts.

Savory Butters

These flavored butters are delicious with fresh bread, and they also are excellent on vegetables. Or use them to baste meat, poultry or fish when broiling or baking.

Beat 1 cup (2 sticks) margarine or butter, softened, and one of the following:

GARLIC: 2 teaspoons paprika, ½ teaspoon pepper and 8 cloves garlic, crushed.

HERB: ¼ to ½ cup chopped fresh or 1 to 2 tablespoons dried herb (basil, chives, oregano, savory, tarragon or thyme), 1 tablespoon lemon juice and ¼ teaspoon salt.

MUSTARD: ¼ cup chopped fresh parsley, ¼ cup Dijon or coarse-grained mustard and ¼ teaspoon salt.

SESAME: ¼ cup toasted sesame seed, 1 tablespoon Worcestershire sauce and 1 teaspoon garlic salt.

Store tightly covered in refrigerator up to 3 weeks or in freezer up to 2 weeks.

Sweet Butters

Pack about ½ cup of any of these wonderful butters in a pretty container and give with a loaf of homemade nut bread for a host or hostess gift. For easy slicing, shape butter into a log and wrap tightly in plastic wrap or waxed paper before storing.

Beat 1 cup (2 sticks) margarine or butter, softened, and one of the following:

ALMOND: 2 tablespoons finely chopped almonds and 1 teaspoon almond extract.

DATE: ½ cup finely chopped dates.

ORANGE: 2 teaspoons grated orange peel and 2 tablespoons orange juice.

RASPBERRY: 1 cup raspberries, crushed, and 2 tablespoons sugar or ½ cup raspberry jam.

Store tightly covered in refrigerator up to 3 weeks or in freezer up to 2 months.

Savory Butters; Sweet Butters; Individual Brioche (page 125)

Fruit-shaped Cheese Balls

4 ounces blue cheese, crumbled (about ⅔ cup)

2 jars (5 ounces each) process sharp American cheese spread

2 packages (3 ounces each) cream cheese, softened

1 teaspoon Worcestershire sauce

Paprika

About ⅓ cup grated Parmesan cheese

About 4 drops yellow food color, if desired

1 stick cinnamon

Lemon leaf

Brown paper

Vegetable oil

Crackers

Mix blue cheese, cheese spread, cream cheese and Worcestershire sauce in medium bowl with fork until blended. Cover and refrigerate at least 8 hours until chilled.

Divide cheese mixture in half. Shape one half into a ball on waxed paper. Sprinkle another piece of waxed paper with paprika. Roll cheese ball in paprika, coating thoroughly. Mold into apple shape.

Shape other half into a ball on waxed paper. Shake Parmesan cheese and food color in covered container until cheese is evenly colored. Sprinkle another piece of waxed paper with cheese. Roll cheese ball in Parmesan cheese, coating thoroughly. Mold into pear shape.

Make small depression in apple and pear for stem ends. Cut 2 small pieces from cinnamon stick. Insert cinnamon stick pieces for apple and pear stems. Insert lemon leaf in apple. Brush brown paper with vegetable oil; cut into leaf shape. Insert in pear. Serve with crackers. Store tightly covered in refrigerator up to 2 weeks or in freezer up to 4 weeks. 2 cheese balls (about 12 servings each).

🔔 **Make several batches at one time and freeze, so they will be on hand for impromptu entertaining as well as gifts.**

Frosty Smoked Salmon Spread

This delicious spread can be shaped into a ring, log, star, bell or other interesting shape to fit the occasion.

1 package (8 ounces) cream cheese, softened

1 pound smoked salmon, skinned and boned

¼ cup chopped green onions

¾ container (8-ounce size) cream cheese, softened (about ¾ cup)

¼ cup sunflower nuts, toasted, if desired

Crackers, tiny sliced bagels or vegetable slices

Mix 8-ounce package cream cheese, the salmon and onions thoroughly. Shape mixture into ring or ball. Frost with whipped cream cheese. Sprinkle with sunflower nuts. Cover and refrigerate at least 2 hours until chilled. Garnish with fresh herbs, if desired. Serve with crackers. Store tightly covered in refrigerator up to 2 weeks or in freezer up to 4 weeks. About 3 cups spread.

Frosty Smoked Salmon Spread

Creative Wrappings

Good news—those boxes, bags, cans, bottles and jars you've been saving can be recycled into unique personalized packaging for your special gifts. The ideas below should get you started, then let your imagination take over.

For Special Gift Tags and Decorations

❊ Make cookie gift tags by cutting out fun holiday shapes from rolled cookie dough before baking. Cut a hole in the top to attach, using the end of a plastic straw. Wrap in clear plastic wrap, then attach to presents with cord or ribbon. If cookies are left unwrapped, be sure wrapping paper is foil or plastic-coated.

❊ Glue unshelled nuts, cranberries, bits of evergreens and pieces of lace and ribbon to bundles of cinnamon sticks. Glue or tie to presents.

❊ Make the Raffia Herb Cluster (page 296) and attach it to a package wrapped in plain brown paper with raffia strands used as "ribbon" for a Southwest look.

❊ Tie a disposable flash camera to the top of a package with a sign that says "Open Me First" so Christmas festivities and traditions can be recorded on film.

For Boxes and Bags

❊ Give sturdy old boxes a new look by covering them with holiday giftwrap.

❊ Cut a design in the lid of a box, then wrap with paper, trimming flush with the cutout. Tape plastic wrap on the inside and your gift will show through.

❊ Large plastic garbage bags are perfect for large irregular-shaped gifts. Place holiday stickers randomly on the bag before filling and tie the opening with a bow with long streamers and add large jingle bells.

❊ Use lunch-sized or larger brown paper bags for gifts. Sponge-paint stencils on the outside (handmade or purchased). Then close the bag and fold down once or twice. Punch two or more holes across the top. Tie or weave ribbon or raffia through the holes. Add an ornament for a special touch.

❊ Cut out a design on one side of a bag and back the cutout with plastic wrap before filling so the contents show.

For Cans

❊ Cans with plastic lids work best. Cover the lid with paper or fabric or spraypaint.

❊ Cut giftwrap paper or fabric to fit, then paste to the can with glue or fabric adhesive.

❊ Spray the can with paint and individualize with stickers, glitter, paper or fabric cutouts.

❊ Use a glue gun to secure a large jingle bell, ornament or other "knob" to the lid.

❊ Tuck cellophane or tissue paper into the can before filling, cover your food gift with plastic wrap or place it in clear plastic bags.

For Jars and Bottles

At times it's more fun to have gifts on view rather than completely wrapped up, and glass jars and bottles are perfect for gifts on display. You can creatively embellish the lids by trying the suggestions below.

❄ Cover the jar lid of homemade or purchased jams, jellies or pickles. Use fabric scraps cut into a circle. Muslin is fun when stenciled or fabric paints are used with your original designs.

❄ Use acrylic paint for complete coverage when painting jar lids. Glue grosgrain or other festive ribbon in the appropriate width around the edge of the lid.

❄ Cover a lid with old or new buttons using a glue gun.

❄ Glue a small holiday toy to the top of a bottle and add a ribbon for a festive touch.

❄ Tie raffia in a bow around the neck of a vinaigrette bottle and glue on fresh or dried chiles, bay leaves and a bulb of garlic.

For Plates and Trays

❄ Colorful paper and plastic plates are perfect for baked foods. A *coated* paper plate won't absorb any grease from rich foods.

❄ Purchase a variety of attractive glass and pottery plates in different sizes all year long when they're on sale. Or, frequent yard sales, garage sales and estate sales. Give the plate as a gift mounded with bountiful cookies, candies or cakes, prettily covered in see-through wrap.

❄ Trays are harder to come by. Make your own in any shape and size with sturdy cardboard, then cover with foil giftwrap paper or aluminum foil. Or visit a paper warehouse store for their latest designs at reasonable prices.

For Other Containers

❄ Line a basket with a fun fabric napkin or kitchen cloth and fill with cookies or muffins. Overwrap all with clear plastic wrap and tie with a glittery bow.

❄ Give a food container such as a casserole as a gift, filling it with uncooked ingredients or the finished product. Be sure to include the recipe and storage instructions.

❄ Give a pasta bowl filled with different sizes and shapes of uncooked pasta. Leave it unwrapped, tying with a large ribbon and attaching spaghetti servers to the bow.

❄ A beautiful cookie jar filled with your favorite cookies along with the recipe.

❄ A stockpot with Calico Bean Soup Mix (page 271) topped with a bow and ornament.

Pumpkin Seed Sauce

1 cup shelled pumpkin seeds

1 small onion, chopped (about ¼ cup)

1 slice white bread, torn into small pieces

1 clove garlic, crushed

2 tablespoons vegetable oil

*2 tablespoons canned chopped green
    chilies*

1 cup chicken broth

½ cup whipping (heavy) cream

Dash of salt

Cook pumpkin seeds, onion, bread and garlic in oil, stirring frequently, until bread is golden brown. Stir in chilies.

Place pumpkin seed mixture in food processor. Cover and process until smooth. Stir in broth, whipping cream and salt. (Or place pumpkin seed mixture and about half of the broth in blender. Cover and blend until smooth. Stir in remaining broth, the whipping cream and salt.) Serve warm or cold with tacos, burritos, chicken or pork. Store tightly covered in refrigerator up to 2 weeks. About 3 cups sauce.

Pumpkin Seed Sauce; Spinach Pesto (page 245)

Fruited Cream Cheese Spread

1 package (8 ounces) cream cheese, softened

1/4 cup apricot, peach or other flavor preserves

Beat ingredients in small bowl on medium speed until fluffy. Store covered in refrigerator. About 1 1/4 cups spread.

Plum Barbecue Sauce

1 small onion, finely chopped (about 1/4 cup)

1/4 cup (1/2 stick) margarine or butter

1/4 cup chile sauce

2 teaspoons Dijon mustard

1 can (16 ounces) purple plums, drained, pitted and finely chopped

1 can (6 ounces) frozen lemonade concentrate, thawed

Cook onion in margarine in 2-quart saucepan about 2 minutes, stirring occasionally, until tender. Stir in remaining ingredients. Heat to boiling; reduce heat to low. Simmer uncovered 15 minutes, stirring occasionally; cool. Store tightly covered in refrigerator up to 2 weeks. About 2 cups sauce.

Spinach Pesto

For your favorite pasta lover, try packaging this pesto in 1-cup jars or other attractive containers, and give along with bags of pasta. Have fun personalizing your gift, and remember to include the directions for cooking!

4 cups firmly packed spinach (10 to 12 ounces)

1 cup firmly packed fresh or 1/2 cup dried basil leaves

1 cup grated Parmesan cheese

1 cup olive oil

1/2 cup chopped pine nuts or walnuts

1/2 teaspoon salt

1/4 teaspoon pepper

8 cloves garlic

Place 2 cups of spinach and remaining ingredients in food processor. Cover and process 1 minute. Add remaining spinach and process about 2 minutes, stopping processor occasionally to scrape sides, until finely chopped and smooth. (Or place all ingredients except spinach in blender. Cover and blend on high speed about 1 minute, stopping blender occasionally to scrape sides. Add spinach, 1 cup at a time, blending until smooth after each addition.) Serve over hot cooked pasta or spoon on top of a block of cream cheese for a quick appetizer spread if desired. Store covered in refrigerator up to 3 days or in freezer up to 3 months. About 3 cups pesto.

Hot Fudge Sauce

1 can (12 ounces) evaporated milk

1 package (12 ounces) semisweet
chocolate chips (2 cups)

½ cup sugar

1 tablespoon margarine or butter

1 teaspoon vanilla

Heat milk, chocolate chips and sugar to boiling in 2-quart saucepan over medium heat, stirring constantly; remove from heat. Stir in margarine and vanilla. Serve warm over ice cream. Store tightly covered in refrigerator up to 4 weeks. About 3 cups sauce.

TO MICROWAVE: Mix milk, chocolate chips and sugar in 8-cup microwavable measure. Microwave uncovered on high 6 to 8 minutes, stirring every 2 minutes, until thickened and smooth. Stir in margarine and vanilla until mixture is smooth and creamy.

ORANGE FUDGE SAUCE: Substitute 2 teaspoons orange-flavored liqueur for the 1 teaspoon vanilla.

Divine Caramel Sauce

2 cups sugar

1 cup light corn syrup

¾ cup (1½ sticks) margarine or butter

2 cups whipping (heavy) cream

Pinch of salt

1 teaspoon vanilla

Heat all ingredients except vanilla to boiling in heavy Dutch oven over medium heat, stirring constantly. Reduce heat slightly. Boil 30 minutes, stirring frequently, until sugar is dissolved and mixture is caramel colored. Stir in vanilla. Serve hot or warm. Store in refrigerator up to 2 months. About 4 cups sauce.

White Chocolate–Almond Sauce

Toasting the almonds is the key to keeping crispness in this rich, velvety sauce. Serve it over pound cake or chocolate ice cream.

2 tablespoons margarine or butter

1 cup slivered almonds

1 cup whipping (heavy) cream

1 package (12 ounces) vanilla milk chips

1 tablespoon almond-flavored liqueur or
¼ teaspoon almond extract

Pinch of salt

Heat margarine and almonds in 3-quart saucepan over medium heat 6 to 8 minutes, stirring frequently, until almonds are golden brown. Remove from heat. Stir in cream until well blended (mixture will spatter). Stir in chips. Heat over low heat, stirring frequently, until chips are melted. Stir in liqueur and salt. Store tightly covered in refrigerator up to 4 weeks. Stir before serving. About 2¾ cups sauce.

MICROWAVE DIRECTIONS: Place margarine and almonds in microwavable 8-cup measure. Microwave uncovered on high 3 to 4 minutes, stirring every minute, until almonds are golden brown. Stir in cream until well blended. Stir in chips. Microwave uncovered about 1 minute or until chips can be stirred smooth. Stir in liqueur and salt.

Hot Fudge Sauce; Divine Caramel Sauce; White Chocolate-Almond Sauce

Lemon Curd

1 cup sugar

2 teaspoons finely grated lemon peel

1 cup lemon juice (about 5 large lemons)

3 tablespoons firm margarine or butter, cut up

3 eggs, slightly beaten

Mix sugar, lemon peel and lemon juice in heavy nonaluminum 1¹/₂-quart saucepan. Stir in margarine and eggs. Cook over medium heat about 8 minutes, stirring constantly, until mixture thickens and coats back of spoon (do not boil). Immediately pour into one 1-pint container or two 1-cup containers. Store covered in refrigerator up to 2 months. About 2 cups curd.

🔔 **If using refrigerated lemons, microwave them on high about 30 seconds to bring to room temperature—they'll be easier to juice. Try an electric citrus juicer for a quick, thorough job.**

Prune-Almond Sauce

1¹/₂ cups apple juice

1 package (8 ounces) pitted prunes

2 tablespoons apple brandy, brandy or water

1 teaspoon grated lemon peel

¹/₂ cup slivered almonds

Heat apple juice and prunes to boiling; reduce heat. Cover and cook about 20 minutes or until prunes are soft. Drain prunes, reserving ¹/₂ cup liquid. Place prunes, reserved liquid, apple brandy and lemon peel in blender or food processor. Cover and blend on high speed, or process, until mixture is smooth. Stir in almonds.

Serve with ham or pork, use as a filling or topping for cakes and coffee cakes, or as a spread for bread. Store tightly covered in refrigerator up to 4 weeks. About 2 cups sauce.

TO MICROWAVE: Decrease apple juice to ³/₄ cup. Place apple juice and prunes in 1¹/₂-quart microwavable casserole. Cover tightly and microwave on high 6 to 8 minutes, stirring after 4 minutes, until prunes are soft. Continue as directed.

Apricot Sauce

1 package (6 ounces) dried apricots (about 1 cup)

2 cups water

2 to 3 tablespoons sugar

¹/₂ teaspoon ground cinnamon

1 teaspoon lemon juice

Heat apricots, water, sugar and cinnamon to boiling in 2-saucepan; reduce heat. Cover and simmer about 15 minutes or until apricots are tender.

Place apricot mixture and lemon juice in blender. Cover and blend on medium-high speed or process about 15 seconds or until smooth. Stir in 1 to 2 tablespoons water, if necessary, until desired consistency. Store tightly covered in refrigerator up to 2 months. About 3 cups sauce.

Rosy Grape Jelly

From champagne glasses to baby food jars this glowing, rosy jelly can be poured into any size container. Use glass or dishwasher-safe plastic and check the sizes of the containers so you have enough on hand for all the jelly.

2 cups cranberry juice cocktail

³/₄ cup grape juice

1 package (1³/₄ ounces) powdered fruit pectin

3¹/₄ cups sugar

Mix cranberry juice cocktail, grape juice and pectin in 3-quart saucepan until smooth. Heat to boiling over high heat, stirring constantly. Stir in sugar all at once. Heat to boiling, stirring constantly. Boil and stir 1 minute; remove from heat. Quickly skim off foam. Immediately pour into hot, sterilized jars, leaving ¹/₂-inch headspace. Let jars stand 1 hour. Wipe rims of jars. Cover with lids. Store in refrigerator up to 3 weeks or in freezer up to 6 months. Thaw before serving. About 5 half-pints jelly.

Pineapple-Apricot Jam

1 jar (6 ounces) maraschino cherries, drained and ¹/₃ cup syrup reserved

1 can (20 ounces) crushed pineapple in heavy syrup, undrained

6 ounces dried apricots, cut into fourths (about 1 cup)

¹/₄ cup water

3¹/₂ cups sugar

2 tablespoons lemon juice

1 pouch (3 ounces) liquid fruit pectin

Chop cherries; reserve. Heat pineapple, reserved cherry syrup, the apricots and water to boiling in Dutch oven, stirring occasionally; reduce heat. Cover and simmer about 10 minutes, sitrring occasionally, until apricots are tender. Stir in sugar, lemon juice and cherries. Heat to rolling boil over high heat, stirring occasionally. Boil and stir 1 minute; remove from heat. Stir in pectin. Immediately pour into hot, sterilized jars or glasses or freezer containers, leaving ¹/₂-inch headspace. Wipe rims of jars.

Golden Raspberry Jam

2 cups crushed golden or red raspberries (about 2 pints whole berries)

4 cups sugar

¹/₂ teaspoon grated lemon peel

1 tablespoon lemon juice

1 pouch (3 ounces) liquid fruit pectin

Mix raspberries and sugar. Let stand at room temperature about 10 minutes, stirring occasionally, until sugar is dissolved. Stir in lemon peel, lemon juice and pectin; continue stirring 3 to 5 minutes or until slightly thickened. Spoon into freezer containers, leaving ¹/₂-inch headspace. Wipe rims of containers; seal. Let stand at room temperature 24 hours. Store in refrigerator up to 3 weeks or in freezer up to 1 year. Thaw before serving. About 5 half-pints jam.

TO MICROWAVE: Decrease sugar to 3 cups. Mix all ingredients except pectin in 3-quart microwavable casserole. Microwave uncovered on high 11 to 13 minutes, stirring after 5 minutes, until boiling. Stir until sugar is dissolved. Stir in pectin. Continue as directed.

MIXED BERRY JAM: Substitute 1 cup crushed strawberries (about 1 pint whole berries) for 1 cup of the raspberries.

Herbed Tangerine Jelly

2 tablespoons dried marjoram leaves or whole cloves

2 cups boiling water

¹/₂ can (12-ounce size) frozen tangerine juice concentrate, thawed

1 package (1³/₄ ounces) powdered fruit pectin

3³/₄ cups sugar

Wrap marjoram tightly in cheesecloth. Place in 4-cup measure with 2 cups boiling water. Cover and let stand 10 minutes. To extract flavor, squeeze liquid from cheesecloth into water and discard cheesecloth. Add enough water to herb water to measure 2 cups.

Mix herb water, tangerine juice concentrate and pectin in 3-quart saucepan until pectin is dissolved. Heat to boiling, stirring constantly. Stir in sugar. Heat to rolling boil, stirring constantly; remove from heat. Immediately pour into hot, sterilized jars or glasses or freezer containers, leaving ¹/₂-inch headspace. Wipe rims of jars. Cover tightly; cool. Store in refrigerator up to 1 month or in freezer up to 2 months. About 4 half-pints jelly.

APPLE-PEPPER JELLY: Omit marjoram and first step. Substitute 1 can (6 ounces) frozen apple juice concentrate for the tangerine juice concentrate; the 2 cups water do not need to be boiling. Stir in 1 to 2 tablespoons crushed red pepper with the sugar. Strain before filling jars if desired.

Herbed Tangerine Jelly; Apple-Pepper Jelly; Lemon Curd (page 248)

Orange-Strawberry Jam

2 packages (10 ounces each) frozen sweetened strawberries, thawed

1 package (1³/₄ ounces) powdered fruit pectin

1 tablespoon grated orange peel

¹/₂ cup orange juice

3¹/₂ cups sugar

Mix strawberries, pectin, orange peel and orange juice in 3-quart saucepan until pectin is dissolved. Heat to rolling boil over high heat, stirring constantly. Stir in sugar. Heat to rolling boil, stirring constantly; remove from heat. Quickly skim off foam. Immediately pour into hot, sterilized jars or glasses or freezer containers, leaving ¹/₂-inch headspace. Wipe rims of jars. Seal immediately; cool. Refrigerate or freeze up to 3 months. Thaw before serving. About 4 half-pints jam.

Plum Preserves

4 cups sliced plums (about 1¹/₂ pounds)

2 cups sugar

¹/₂ cup water

1 stick cinnamon

1 small lemon, cut lengthwise into fourths, then into paper-thin slices

Mix all ingredients in 3-quart saucepan. Heat to boiling over medium heat, stirring frequently, until sugar is dissolved. Boil uncovered about 35 minutes, stirring frequently, until mixture begins to thicken; remove cinnamon. Immediately pour into hot, sterilized jars, leaving ¹/₄-inch headspace. Wipe rims of jars; seal. Cool on rack 1 hour. Store in refrigerator up to 2 months. About 3 half-pints preserves.

Spirited Apple Butter

Cranberry Conserve

2 cups packed brown sugar

2 cups water

2 packages (12 ounces each) cranberries

2 tablespoons grated orange peel

4 oranges, peeled and chopped

2 apples, peeled and chopped

1 cup chopped nuts

Mix brown sugar and water in Dutch oven. Heat to boiling; boil 1 minute. Stir in remaining ingredients except nuts. Heat to boiling; boil rapidly about 20 minutes or until cranberries pop and mixture thickens. Stir in nuts. Immediately pour into hot, sterilized jars or glasses or freezer containers, leaving ¹/₂-inch headspace. Wipe rims of jars. Cover tightly; cool. Store in refrigerator or freezer up to 3 months. Thaw before serving. About 5 half-pints conserve.

Pear Conserve

3 pounds pears, peels and sliced (about 8 cups)

4 cups sugar

³/₄ cup raisins

¹/₄ cup lemon juice

1 tablespoon grated orange peel

2 teaspoons grated lemon peel

1 cup broken walnuts

Mix all ingredients except walnuts in Dutch oven. Heat to boiling, stirring frequently. Boil uncovered 25 to 30 minutes, stirring occasionally, until mixture thickens slightly. Stir in walnuts. Immediately pour into hot, sterilized jars or glasses or freezer containers, leaving ¹/₄-inch headspace. Wipe rims of jars. Seal immediately; cool. Re-

Cranberry Conserve; Spirited Apple Butter

frigerate or freeze up to 3 months. Thaw before serving. About 4 to 5 half-pints conserves.

Seal immediately; cool. Refrigerate or freeze up to 3 months. Thaw before serving. About 5 half-pints conserve.

Spirited Apple Butter

When making the thicker pumpkin variation, cover the mixture with a splatter screen, a handy kitchen tool most often used for frying.

1 can (12 ounces) frozen apple juice concentrate

¹/₂ cup sweet red wine or apple juice

3 quarts quartered, pared and cored cooking apples (about 4 pounds)

1 cup apple brandy or apple cider

³/₄ cup packed brown sugar

1 teaspoon ground cinnamon

1 teaspoon ground ginger

¹/₄ teaspoon ground cloves

Heat apple juice, wine and apples to boiling in 4-quart Dutch oven; reduce heat. Simmer uncovered about 1 hour, stirring occasionally, until apples are very soft. Mash with potato masher if necessary to remove all lumps. Stir in remaining ingredients. Heat to boiling; reduce heat. Simmer uncovered about 2 hours, stirring occasionally, until no liquid separates from pulp. Immediately pour mixture into hot, sterilized jars, leaving ¹/₄-inch headspace. Wipe rims of jars; seal. Cool on rack 1 hour. Store in refrigerator up to 2 months. About 5 half-pints.

SPIRITED PUMPKIN BUTTER: Omit wine, substitute 3 cans (16 ounces each) cooked pumpkin for the apples, increase brown sugar to 1 cup and ground cinnamon to 1¹/₂ teaspoons. Mix all ingredients in 4-quart Dutch oven. Heat to boiling, stirring frequently; reduce heat. Simmer uncovered about 1 hour, stirring frequently. About 6 half-pints.

Pear-Apricot Chutney

**5 cups coarsely chopped peeled pears
    (about 2 pounds)**

3 cups sugar

$1/2$ cup chopped dried apricots

3 tablespoons lemon juice

**1 teaspoon finely chopped gingerroot or
    $1/2$ teaspoon ground ginger**

1 teaspoon grated lemon peel

Mix all ingredients in 3-quart saucepan. Heat to boiling over medium heat, stirring frequently. Boil 25 to 30 minutes, stirring occasionally, until mixture thickens. Immediately pour into hot, sterilized jars, leaving $1/4$-inch headspace. Wipe rims of jars; seal. Cool on rack 1 hour. Store in refrigerator up to 2 months. About 4 half-pints chutney.

Papaya Chutney

1 medium ripe papaya (about 1 pound)

$1/4$ cup white vinegar

$1/4$ cup lemon juice

1 tablespoon chopped fresh cilantro

1 tablespoon vegetable oil

1 tablespoon honey

**2 teaspoons grated gingerroot or $3/4$
    teaspoon ground ginger**

$1/4$ teaspoon chile powder

$1/8$ teaspoon ground cinnamon

Peel papaya. Cut papaya in half and scoop out centers. Chop papaya finely. Heat papaya and remaining ingredients to boiling in 10-inch skillet; reduce heat. Cover and simmer 40 minutes, stirring occasionally. Serve warm or cold. Store tightly covered in refrigerator up to 2 months. About $1 1/4$ cups chutney.

Corn Salsa

$1/4$ cup chopped green bell pepper

$1/4$ cup sliced green onions

2 tablespoons white wine vinegar

1 tablespoon vegetable oil

$1/4$ teaspoon salt

**1 jalapeño chile, seeded and finely
    chopped**

**1 can (16 ounces) whole kernel corn,
    drained**

**1 can (4 ounces) chopped green chiles,
    undrained**

Mix all ingredients. Cover and refrigerate about 1 hour or until chilled. Store tightly covered in refrigerator up to 3 weeks. $2 1/3$ cups salsa.

Cucumber Salsa

1 cup sour cream

1 cup plain yogurt

$1/4$ cup chopped fresh parsley

$1/4$ cup chopped fresh cilantro

1 teaspoon ground cumin

$1/2$ teaspoon salt

**2 medium cucumbers, peeled, seeded and
    coarsely shredded (about 2 cups)**

Mix all ingredients. Cover and refrigerate about 2 hours or until chilled. Store tightly covered in refrigerator up to 1 week. 3 cups salsa.

Corn Salsa; Black Bean Relish (page 256)

Black Bean Relish

1/4 cup finely chopped red onion

2 tablespoons white wine vinegar

1 tablespoon vegetable oil

1/4 teaspoon salt

1 medium tomato, finely chopped (about 3/4 cup)

1 small red bell pepper, chopped (about 1/2 cup)

1 serrano chile, seeded and finely chopped

1 can (15 ounces) black beans, rinsed and drained

Mix all ingredients. Cover and refrigerate about 1 hour or until chilled. Store tightly covered in refrigerator up to 2 weeks. About 2 1/2 cups relish.

Zucchini Relish

A refreshing relish to add to pocket bread sandwiches, especially chicken sandwiches.

1/4 cup chopped fresh cilantro

2 tablespoons lime juice

2 tablespoons olive or vegetable oil

1 teaspoon salt

1/4 teaspoon sugar

1/4 teaspoon pepper

2 medium zucchini, shredded (about 2 cups)

Mix all ingredients in glass or plastic bowl. Cover and refrigerate at least 1 hour. Store covered in refrigerator up to 1 week. About 1 1/4 cups relish.

Carrot-Pepper Relish

This is a bright addition to any relish tray. For a more novel approach, cut half or all the carrot slices into holiday shapes using small canape cutters.

3 pounds carrots, cut into 1/2-inch slices

2 medium green bell peppers, chopped (about 2 cups)

2 medium onions, sliced

2/3 cup sugar

2/3 cup white vinegar

1/2 cup vegetable oil

1 teaspoon salt

1 teaspoon Worcestershire sauce

1/2 teaspoon pepper

1/2 teaspoon dry mustard

1/2 teaspoon dried dill weed

1 can (10 3/4 ounces) condensed tomato soup

Cook carrots in 1 inch water (salted if desired) 8 to 10 minutes or until crisp-tender; drain. Mix carrots, bell peppers and onions in large glass or plastic bowl. Heat remaining ingredients to boiling, stirring occasionally; remove from heat. Cool 5 minutes; pour over vegetables. Store covered in refrigerator up to 3 weeks. About 10 cups relish.

🎄 **Use three 16-ounce bags of frozen, sliced carrots (thawed) instead of fresh carrots. You'll find the carrot slices to be slightly smaller.**

Carrot-Pepper Relish; Candied Dill Pickles (page 259)

Marinated Peppers

6 large red or green bell peppers

¼ cup olive or vegetable oil

2 tablespoons chopped fresh parsley

2 tablespoons lemon juice

2 tablespoons lime juice

1 teaspoon chopped fresh or ¼ teaspoon dried oregano leaves

1 teaspoon chopped fresh or ¼ teaspoon dried basil leaves

½ teaspoon chopped fresh or ⅛ teaspoon dried sage leaves

⅛ teaspoon pepper

½ teaspoon salt

2 large cloves garlic, finely chopped

Set oven control to broil. Broil bell peppers with tops about 5 inches from heat, turning occasionally, until skin is blistered and evenly browned. Place peppers in a plastic bag and close tightly. Let stand 20 minutes.

Remove skin, stems, seeds and membranes from peppers. Cut peppers into ¼-inch strips. Place in glass or plastic bowl. Shake remaining ingredients in tightly covered container. Pour over peppers. Cover and refrigerate at least 4 hours, stirring occasionally. Store tightly covered in refrigerator up to 2 weeks. About 4 cups.

MARINATED PEPPERS AND OLIVES: Prepare as directed—except cut peppers into fourths. Stir in 1 cup Greek or ripe olives, drained, and 4 ounces feta or mozzarella cheese, cubed, with the peppers. About 5 cups peppers.

Pickled Beets and Onions

2 cans (16 ounces each) sliced beets,
*   drained and liquid reserved*

1 medium onion, thinly sliced

1 cup packed brown sugar

1/2 cup granulated sugar

3/4 cup cider vinegar or white vinegar

2 sticks cinnamon

6 whole cloves

Mix beets and onion in large heatproof glass or plastic bowl. Measure 1 cup beet liquid. Heat beet liquid, sugars, vinegar, cinnamon and cloves to boiling. Pour over beets and onion. Cover and refrigerate at least 12 hours. Store covered in refrigerator up to 5 days. About 4 cups pickles.

Candied Dill Pickles

1 quart whole sour or dill pickles,
*   drained**

2 1/2 cups sugar

1/4 cup coarsely chopped pickled sweet
*   cherry peppers*

1 tablespoon finely chopped onion

1 teaspoon celery seed

1 teaspoon mustard seed

1 jalapeño chile (with seeds), finely
*   chopped*

Cut large pickles lengthwise into fourths, small pickles lengthwise into halves; drain. Mix all ingredients in large glass or plastic bowl. Cover and refrigerate at least 24 hours, stirring several times to dissolve sugar. Pack pickles in pickle jar or several small jars. Store covered in refrigerator up to 1 month. 1 quart pickles.

* Do not use kosher-type dill pickles.

Herb Vinegar; Nut-flavored Oil

Herb Vinegar

2 cups white wine vinegar

1/2 cup firmly packed fresh herb (basil,
*   chives, dill weed, mint, oregano,*
*   rosemary or tarragon)*

Shake vinegar and herb in tightly covered glass jar or bottle. Let stand in cool, dry place 10 days. Strain vinegar. Place 1 sprig of fresh herb in jar to identify if desired. 2 cups vinegar.

BERRY VINEGAR: Substitute 2 cups berries, crushed, for the herb.

GARLIC VINEGAR: Substitute 6 cloves garlic, cut in half, for the herb.

GINGER VINEGAR: Substitute 1/2 cup chopped peeled gingerroot for the herb.

LEMON VINEGAR: Substitute peel from 2 lemons for the herb.

Nut-flavored Oil

1 cup walnuts, almonds or hazelnuts
*   (filberts)*

2 cups vegetable oil

Place nuts and 1/2 cup of the oil in blender or food processor. Cover and blend, or process, until nuts are finely chopped. Place nut mixture and remaining oil in glass jar or bottle. Cover tightly and let stand in cool, dry place 10 days. Strain oil. Store tightly covered in refrigerator up to 3 months. 2 cups oil.

Fresh Herb Vinaigrette

Herbs add a welcome touch of summer to a winter gift.

½ cup olive or vegetable oil

½ cup white vinegar

1 tablespoon finely chopped green onion

1 tablespoon chopped fresh parsley

1 tablespoon chopped fresh herb (basil, marjoram, oregano, rosemary, tarragon or thyme)

Shake all ingredients in tightly covered container. Store tightly covered in refrigerator up to 3 weeks. About 1 cup vinaigrette.

NUTTY HERB VINAIGRETTE: Substitute walnut, hazelnut or almond oil for the olive oil.

LOW-CALORIE VINAIGRETTE: Substitute apple juice for the olive oil and decrease vinegar to ⅓ cup.

Oriental Dressing

⅓ cup rice wine vinegar or white vinegar

¼ cup vegetable oil

1 tablespoon sesame seed, toasted if desired

3 tablespoons soy sauce

2 tablespoons dry sherry

1 teaspoon grated gingerroot or ¼ teaspoon ground ginger

2 drops dark sesame oil, if desired

Shake all ingredients in tightly covered container. Store tightly covered in refrigerator up to 4 weeks. About 1 cup dressing.

Green Goddess Dressing

1 cup mayonnaise or salad dressing

½ cup sour cream

⅓ cup chopped fresh parsley

3 tablespoons chopped fresh chives

3 tablespoons anchovy paste or finely chopped anchovy fillets

3 tablespoons tarragon vinegar or wine vinegar

1 tablespoon lemon juice

⅛ teaspoon freshly ground pepper

Mix all ingredients. Store tightly covered in refrigerator up to 3 weeks. About 2 cups dressing.

Ruby French Dressing

1 cup olive or vegetable oil

⅔ cup ketchup

½ cup sugar

½ cup white vinegar

2 tablespoons finely chopped onion

1 tablespoon lemon juice

1 teaspoon salt

1 teaspoon pepper

1 teaspoon dry mustard

1 teaspoon paprika

Shake all ingredients in tightly covered container. Refrigerate at least 3 hours. Store tightly covered in refrigerator up to 4 weeks. Shake well before using. Serve on fruit or tossed salads. About 2⅔ cups dressing.

Oriental Dressing; Green Goddess Dressing

Festive Peppermint Marshmallows

These marshmallows are a sure-fire hit, especially when packaged as a gift with Hot Cocoa Mix (page 272). Have fun with the marshmallows by cutting them into your favorite shapes, using small, deep canapé cutters. Dip canapé cutters in cold water to keep them from sticking to the marshmallows.

¼ cup cornstarch

¼ cup powdered sugar

2 envelopes unflavored gelatin

½ cup cold water

1 cup granulated sugar

¾ cup light corn syrup

½ cup water

1 egg white

⅛ teaspoon cream of tartar

¾ teaspoon peppermint extract

Few drops red food color, if desired

Mix cornstarch and powdered sugar. Line rectangular pan, $13 \times 9 \times 2$ inches, with aluminum foil. Grease foil; coat with cornstarch mixture. Shake excess cornstarch mixture from pan and reserve.

Sprinkle gelatin on ½ cup cold water in small bowl to soften. Heat granulated sugar, corn syrup and ½ cup water to boiling in 2-quart saucepan, stirring constantly, just until sugar is dissolved. Cook, without stirring, to 250° on candy thermometer or until small amount of mixture dropped into very cold water forms a ball that holds its shape but is pliable; remove from heat. Stir in gelatin mixture until gelatin is dissolved.

Beat egg white and cream of tartar in medium bowl until stiff peaks form. Continue beating on high speed while pouring hot syrup in a thin stream into egg white. Add peppermint extract and food color. Beat on high speed until soft peaks form. Pour into pan and spread evenly.

Let stand uncovered at room temperature about 1½ hours or until top is dry. Turn out onto flat surface generously dusted with reserved cornstarch mixture and remove foil. Cut into about 1-inch squares with long knife dipped into cold water. Roll squares in cornstarch mixture to coat all sides. Drizzle with melted vanilla candy coating tinted with paste food color, if desired. Let stand uncovered on wire rack about 1 hour or until dry. Store in airtight container at room temperature up to 3 weeks. About 8 dozen marshmallows.

Festive Peppermint Marshmallows; Hot Cocoa Mix (page 272)

Fast and Fabulous Food Gifts

Candyland

❄ Tie candy canes together with ribbons and place them in a vase or holiday mug. The quick-to-fix Chocolate-covered Candy Canes (page 266) are an extra-special touch.

❄ Make ornaments or table favors using wrapped candy and a glue gun. Make a train engine by gluing a roll of ring-shaped candy to the flattest side of a package of gum. Glue 4 round peppermint candies to the gum for wheels. Glue a loop of narrow ribbon to one end of the top of the candy roll; glue a caramel on top of the ribbon ends for the engineer's cab. Glue a chocolate kiss to the other end of the candy roll for the smoke-stack and one to the same end of the gum for a snowplow. Add a tiny bow or touch of holly for decoration. Teddy bears, airplanes and Christmas trees can all be made with wrapped candy, de-pending on your imagination and the kind, shapes and sizes of wrapped candy purchased.

❄ Repackage purchased peanut brittle, fudge or other candy in attractive jars or other holiday containers. Add a touch of sparkling ribbon or foil-covered wire stars.

❄ Dip pretzel twists in melted vanilla or choco-late candy coating. Sprinkle with colored sugar if you like. Pretzels may be partially or totally coated. Or, dip into one color and drizzle with another. Make a wreath by arranging and over-lapping pretzels in a circle before they are dry.

❄ Dip pretzel rods (about 8-inch length) in melted candy coating. Let excess coating drip off. Dip pretzels into finely crushed peppermint can-dies. Let dry on waxed paper until set. Partially or totally coat pretzels. About 6 ounces candy coat-ing and 25 peppermint candies will coat 12 pretzel rods completely. Package pretzel rods in a small brown paper lunch bag. Turn the top down to show the pretzels and tie with a ribbon and an ornament to look like Santa's gift bag.

Sensational Sippers

❄ Place 3 or 4 individual packets of flavored hot chocolate or specialty coffees or teas in a mug. Tie a ribbon to the handle and give as a host or hostess gift.

❄ Fill a basket or paper bucket with shredded metallic paper and add 3 or 4 interesting flavors of bottled water, unusual fruit juices, small bottles of wines, beers or liqueurs.

❄ Give a package of chocolate-covered coffee beans along with the Mocha Mix, page 272.

❄ Package a coffee grinder with assorted kinds of coffee beans; an espresso/cappuccino cof-fee pot; individual packets of flavored coffees; flavored coffee creamers; coffee mugs; or chocolate-covered coffee beans.

❄ Give a unique teapot with one or more of the following: tea cozy; tea towels; assortment of imported teas; teacup and saucer; packaged scone mix with Sweet Butters (page 238); special honey; small jars of assorted jams and jellies.

Chocolate Spoons

❄ Melt 2 ounces semisweet chocolate. Dip fancy gold, silver or colored plastic spoons in melted chocolate, coating only the bowl of the spoon. Place spoons on waxed paper until chocolate is set. Refrigerate spoons until ready to use. Serve spoons with hot coffee, hot cappuccino or hot cocoa. Chocolate will melt as guests stir their beverages. Spoons can also be given as gifts. Wrap each in small square of plastic wrap or cellophane and tie with ribbon where the spoon bowl meets the handle. Makes about 8 spoons.

Gifts for the Cook and the Baker

❄ **For meat lovers:** A gift certificate for meat from their favorite meat market or grocery store; a broiling or roasting pan; a carving set; knife sharpener; a plastic cutting board; an electric knife; an assortment of meat and poultry seasonings.

❄ **For pasta lovers:** A large pot for cooking pasta; large colander or strainer; an assortment of dried pasta shapes; jarred pasta sauces; spaghetti server; Parmesan cheese shaker; cheese grater; pasta bowl; pepper grinder; pasta sauce mixes; pesto sauce (try the Spinach Pesto, page 236); checkered tablecloth and napkins; a bottle of wine; a gift certificate to your favorite Italian restaurant.

❄ **For the vegetarian:** Assortment of dried beans, peas, lentils and whole grains; assorted cans of beans, peas and grains; favorite recipes without meat.

❄ **For the pizza lover:** Regular or deep-dish pizza pans, 12 or 14 inches in diameter; packaged pizza crust mix; assorted tomato sauces; grated Parmesan or Romano cheeses; cheese shaker; pizza wheel.

❄ **For the salad lover:** Large salad bowl; salad tongs or servers; salad spinner; cheese grater; pepper grinder; a set of cruets; a plastic cutting board and good knives; an assortment of flavored croutons; assorted interesting bottled salad dressings; flavored oils or vinegars.

❄ **For the cookie baker:** An assortment of cookie cutters in different sizes; cookie molds; cookie stamps; cookie press; ingredients measured out for your favorite cookie recipe; cookie sheets; decorating bag and tips; assorted sprinkles; Christmas cookie plate or tray for serving.

❄ **For the bread baker:** Large bread mixing bowl; large wooden or plastic spoons; large rubber scrapers; large wire whisks; pastry brushes; bread pans, two $9 \times 5 \times 3$ inches, two $8^{1}/_{2} \times 4^{1}/_{2} \times 2^{1}/_{2}$ inches, three $7^{1}/_{2} \times 3^{3}/_{4} \times 2^{1}/_{4}$ inches, or six $4^{1}/_{2} \times 2^{3}/_{4} \times 1^{1}/_{4}$ inches; popover pans, muffin pans of various sizes; French bread pans; cookie sheets.

❄ **For the all-around baker:** Oven thermometer; minute timer; potholders; sturdy cooling racks; set of mixing bowls; set of measuring spoons; set of dry measuring cups; liquid measuring cups; turner; cookie sheets; springform pan (9-inch or a set); jelly roll pan (be sure it has 1-inch sides), $15^{1}/_{2} \times 10^{1}/_{2} \times 1$ inch; cake pan; tart pan (11-inch) along with a copy of the Macadamia-Pineapple Tart recipe (page 95).

Chocolate-covered Candy Canes

We think adding chocolate to candy canes is a great holiday touch! And it's a snap, especially when you use the microwave.

½ cup semisweet chocolate chips

2 teaspoons shortening

16 peppermint candy canes or sticks

Crushed hard peppermint candy or miniature chocolate chips, if desired

Line jelly roll pan, 15½ × 10½ × 1 inch, with waxed paper. Heat chocolate chips and shortening in 1-quart saucepan over low heat until melted. Tip saucepan so chocolate runs to one side. Dip 1 candy cane at a time into chocolate, coating about three-fourths of each stick with chocolate. Place in pan. Let stand about 2 minutes or until chocolate is almost dry. Roll chocolate-dipped ends in crushed peppermint candy. Let stand about 10 minutes or until chocolate is dry. Store loosely covered at room temperature up to 2 weeks. 16 candy canes.

TO MICROWAVE: Mix chocolate chips and shortening in 2-cup microwavable measure. Microwave on medium (50%) about 3 minutes or until chocolate chips are softened; stir until smooth. Continue as directed.

Deluxe Caramel Apples

Choose crisp eating apples, such as Granny Smith or Delicious, for the most satisfying crunch. For an even more "deluxe" apple, drizzle melted white chocolate over the dark chocolate. When set, wrap these apple treats in plastic wrap and tie a ribbon—and even a bell if you are so inspired—on each stick.

6 wooden skewers or ice-cream sticks

6 medium apples

1 cup coarsely chopped mixed nuts

2 tablespoons water

1 package (14 ounces) vanilla caramels

½ cup semisweet chocolate chips

1 tablespoon shortening

Insert skewer in stem end of each apple. Divide nuts into 6 mounds on waxed paper. Heat water and caramels over low heat, stirring occasionally, until caramels are melted and mixture is smooth. Keep mixture over very low heat. Dip each apple into caramel mixture, spooning mixture over apple until completely coated. (If caramel mixture hardens while coating apples, heat over low heat.) Roll side and bottom of each apple in nuts. Let stand on waxed paper. Heat chocolate chips and shortening over low heat until melted; spoon over top of each apple, allowing some to drizzle down sides. Let stand until coating is firm. Store loosely covered at room temperature or in refrigerator up to 1 week. 6 apples.

TO MICROWAVE: Prepare apples and nuts as directed. Place water and caramels in 4-cup microwavable measure. Microwave uncovered on high 3 to 4 minutes, stirring after 2 minutes, until caramels can be stirred smooth. Continue as directed. (If caramel mixture thickens, microwave about 30 seconds.) Place chocolate chips and shortening in 1-cup microwavable measure. Microwave uncovered on medium (50%) 2 to 3 minutes or until smooth.

Deluxe Caramel Apples

Gingerbread Popcorn Snack

A fun snack to serve any time during the holidays.

> *12 cups unsalted popped popcorn*
> *¹/₂ cup (1 stick) margarine or butter*
> *2 tablespoons molasses*
> *2 teaspoons ground ginger*
> *1 teaspoon ground cinnamon*
> *¹/₄ teaspoon salt*

Heat oven to 350°. Divide popcorn between 2 ungreased rectangular pans, 13 × 9 × 2 inches. Heat remaining ingredients until margarine is melted; pour over popcorn. Toss until well coated. Bake 8 to 10 minutes, stirring after 5 minutes, until crisp. Store tightly covered at room temperature up to 3 weeks. About 12 cups snack.

TO MICROWAVE: Place all ingredients except popcorn in 2-cup microwavable measure. Microwave uncovered on high 45 to 60 seconds or until margarine is melted; stir. Pour over popcorn. Toss until well coated. Pour half of the mixture in large microwavable bowl. Microwave uncovered on high 3 minutes, stirring every minute. (Popcorn will become crisp as it cools.) Repeat with remaining popcorn.

Buy already popped popcorn to speed up this recipe. If you use salted popcorn, omit the salt in the molasses mixture.

Sweet Mexi-Snacks

¹/₄ cup sugar

¹/₄ teaspoon cinnamon

4 flour tortillas (8 inches in diameter)

Margarine or butter, melted

¹/₄ cup semisweet chocolate chips

1 tablespoon milk

6 vanilla caramels

Heat oven to 400°. Mix sugar and cinnamon. Brush tortillas lightly on one side with margarine. Sprinkle with cinnamon-sugar mixture. Using scissors or pizza cutter, cut tortillas into 12 wedges. Arrange wedges in single layer in ungreased jelly roll pan, 15¹/₂ × 10¹/₂ × 1 inch. Bake uncovered until tortillas are crisp and light brown, 5 to 8 minutes. Cool. (Chips will become crisper as they cool.) Melt chocolate chips, milk and caramels until smooth; drizzle over chips. Let stand uncovered about 2 hours or until chocolate mixture is firm. 48 snacks.

Teddy Bear Snack Toss

2 cups teddy bear-shaped graham snacks

2 cups honey-nut toasted oat cereal

1 cup honey-roasted peanuts or 2 cups chocolate-covered peanuts

¹/₂ cup raisins

Toss all ingredients in large bowl. Store tightly covered at room temperature up to 2 weeks. About 6 cups snack.

Reindeer Snack

When you set out cookies for Santa, don't forget his hard-working reindeer! Of course, this crunchy mix is also very popular with hard-working humans.

3 cups popped unsalted popcorn

3 cups horn-shaped nacho cheese corn snacks

1 can (4 ounces) shoestring potatoes

2 cups pretzel chips or pretzel sticks

¹/₃ cup margarine or butter, melted

¹/₂ teaspoon chili powder

1 clove garlic, very finely chopped, or ¹/₄ teaspoon garlic powder

Heat oven to 300°. Mix popcorn, corn snacks, shoestring potatoes and pretzels in large bowl. Mix remaining ingredients; drizzle over popcorn mixture while tossing until evenly coated. Spread in ungreased jelly roll pan, 15¹/₂ × 10¹/₂ × 1 inch. Bake uncovered 15 minutes, stirring twice; cool. Store loosely covered at room temperature up to 2 weeks. About 9 cups snack.

TO MICROWAVE: Place margarine, chili powder and garlic in 3-quart microwavable casserole or bowl. Microwave uncovered on high about 1 minute or until margarine is melted; stir. Stir in popcorn, corn snacks, shoestring potatoes and pretzels. Toss until well coated. Microwave uncovered 6 to 8 minutes, stirring every 2 minutes, until toasted; cool.

Sweet Mexi-Snacks; Gingerbread Popcorn Snack (page 267)

Brown Rice–Barley Mix

When you buy the brown rice and barley for this mix, look for varieties that cook in ten minutes.

½ cup uncooked quick-cooking brown rice

½ cup uncooked quick-cooking barley

⅓ cup chopped smoked almonds, toasted

1 tablespoon instant minced onion

1 tablespoon parsley flakes

1 teaspoon chicken bouillon granules

1 teaspoon dried basil leaves

½ teaspoon dried chopped garlic

Mix all ingredients. Store tightly covered at room temperature up to 2 months.

BROWN RICE AND BARLEY

2 cups water

1 tablespoon margarine or butter

Brown Rice–Barley Mix

Heat water to boiling in 2-quart saucepan. Stir in margarine and Brown Rice-Barley Mix; reduce heat. Cover and simmer 10 to 12 minutes or until water is absorbed and barley is tender; remove from heat. Let stand covered 5 minutes. Fluff with fork before serving. Sprinkle with grated Parmesan cheese if desired. 6 servings.

🔔 **Make several batches of this mix at the same time. Set up your own "assembly line" by placing the number of plastic bags you need (1 per recipe) on a flat surface, or in large mugs, then measure ingredients separately into each bag.**

Brown Rice and Barley; Calico Bean Soup Mix (right)

Calico Bean Soup Mix

2 cups mixed dried beans (¹/₃ cup each of yellow split peas, green split peas, lima beans, pinto beans, kidney beans and great northern beans)

¹/₄ cup instant minced onion

2 teaspoons chicken bouillon granules

¹/₄ teaspoon ground cumin

¹/₄ teaspoon garlic powder

Mix all ingredients. Store tightly covered at room temperature up to 2 months.

CALICO BEAN SOUP

8 cups water

Calico Bean Soup Mix (above)

2 medium carrots, chopped (about 1 cup)

2 medium stalks celery, chopped (about 1 cup)

2 pounds smoked ham shanks or ham hocks or 1 ham bone

Heat water and Calico Bean Soup Mix to boiling in Dutch oven. Boil 2 minutes; remove from heat. Cover and let stand 1 hour.

Stir carrots and celery into bean mixture. Add ham shanks. Heat to boiling; reduce heat. Cover and simmer about 2 hours or until beans are tender. Skim fat if necessary. Remove ham shanks; remove ham from bone. Trim excess fat from ham. Cut ham into ¹/₂-inch pieces. Stir ham into soup. Heat until hot. 6 servings.

Spiced Tea Mix

¹/₂ cup orange flavor instant breakfast drink (dry)

¹/₂ cup instant tea

¹/₄ cup sugar

¹/₄ cup lemonade flavor drink mix (dry)

¹/₄ teaspoon ground cinnamon

¹/₈ teaspoon ground cloves

Mix all ingredients. Store in tightly covered container at room temperature up to 6 months. About 1 cup mix (24 servings).

For each serving, place 2 to 3 teaspoons mix in cup or mug and add ³/₄ cup boiling water. For 6 servings, place ¹/₃ cup mix in heatproof container and add 4¹/₂ cups boiling water.

TO MICROWAVE: For each serving, stir 2 to 3 teaspoons mix into ³/₄ cup water in microwavable cup or mug. Microwave uncovered on high for times shown in Timetable or until hot; stir.

Timetable

Servings	1	2	4*	6*
Minutes	1 to 2	2 to 3	4 to 5	6 to 8

* Arrange cups in circle on 12-inch microwavable plate; rotate ¹/₂ turn after half the time.

Raspberry Tea Mix

6 tablespoons instant tea (dry)

2 envelopes (5 ounces each) raspberry sugar-sweetened soft drink mix

Mix tea and drink mix (dry). Store in tightly covered container at room temperature up to 6 months. About 1 1/2 cups mix (24 servings).

For each serving, place 3 teaspoons mix in cup or mug for hot tea or glass for cold tea. Fill cup with 3/4 cup boiling water or glass with cold water; stir. For 6 servings, place 1/3 cup mix in container (use heatproof container for hot tea). Add 4 cups boiling water for hot tea or 4 cups cold water for cold tea.

To Microwave: For each serving, stir 3 teaspoons mix into 3/4 cup water in microwavable cup or mug. Microwave uncovered on high for times shown in Timetable for Spiced Tea Mix (page 266) or until hot; stir.

Hot Cocoa Mix

2 2/3 cups nonfat dry milk (dry)

1 1/2 cups cocoa

1 cup sugar

1/4 teaspoon salt

Mix all ingredients. Store in tightly covered container at room temperature up to 6 months. About 4 1/2 cups mix (72 servings).

For each serving, place 2 heaping teaspoons mix in cup or mug and stir in 2 tablespoons cold milk or water until smooth. Stir in 1 cup hot milk or water. Top with marshmallows if desired.

Spicy Mocha Mix

This has a wonderful aroma when heated! For extra excitement, try garnishing with white chocolate curls.

1/2 cup sugar

1/4 cup powdered or freeze-dried instant coffee (dry)

1/4 cup cocoa

1 teaspoon ground nutmeg

1/2 teaspoon ground cinnamon

Place all ingredients in blender. Cover and blend on high speed 15 seconds; stir. Cover and blend about 15 seconds longer or until completely mixed. Store in tightly covered container at room temperature up to 6 months. About 1 cup mix (24 servings).

For each serving, place 2 to 3 teaspoons mix in cup or mug and fill with 2/3 cup boiling water; stir. Top with whipped cream if desired. For 6 servings, place 1/4 to 1/3 cup mix in heatproof container and add 4 cups boiling water.

To Microwave: For each serving, stir 2 to 3 teaspoons mix into 2/3 cup water in microwavable cup or mug. Microwave uncovered on high for times shown in Timetable for Spiced Tea Mix (page 271) or until hot; stir.

Mocha Mix: Decrease cocoa to 2 tablespoons and omit spices.

Raspberry Tea Mix; Spicy Mocha Mix

Orange Cappuccino Mix

½ cup powdered nondairy creamer

½ cup sugar

¼ cup powdered or freeze-dried instant coffee (dry)

1 teaspoon dried orange peel

¼ teaspoon ground cinnamon

Place all ingredients in blender or food processor. Cover and blend on high speed 30 seconds, stopping blender after 15 seconds to stir, or process 5 to 10 seconds, until well mixed. Store in tightly covered container at room temperature up to 6 months. About 1 cup mix (24 servings).

For each serving, place 2 teaspoons mix in cup or mug and add ⅔ cup boiling water. For 6 servings, place ¼ cup mix in heatproof container and add 4 cups boiling water.

TO MICROWAVE: For each serving, stir 2 teaspoons mix into ⅔ cup water in microwavable cup or mug. Microwave uncovered on high for times shown in Timetable for Spiced Tea Mix (page 266) or until hot; stir.

Coffee Liqueur

3 cups vodka

2 cups water

2 cups granulated sugar

2 cups packed brown sugar

⅔ cup freeze-dried instant coffee (dry)

1 vanilla bean or 1 teaspoon vanilla

Mix all ingredients in 2-quart jar. Cover tightly and let stand at room temperature 2 weeks. Remove vanilla bean. Pour liqueur into bottles and seal. About 7½ cups liqueur.

Apricot-Cherry Cordial

The reserved fruit from the cordial can become a luscious topping for ice cream or cake. Mix fruit, ½ cup coconut, ½ cup slivered almonds and ½ cup maple syrup or honey. Cover and refrigerate for no longer than one week.

1½ packages (6 ounces each) dried apricots, each cut into fourths

1 package (6 ounces) dried pears or peaches, cut into small pieces

1 jar (10 ounces) maraschino cherries, drained and cherries cut in half

1½ cups sugar

1½ cups brandy

1½ cups vodka

Mix all ingredients in 2-quart jar. Cover tightly and let stand at room temperature 2 weeks, stirring mixture or inverting jar every day. Drain well, reserving fruit for another use. Pour cordial into bottles and seal. Serve well chilled or over cracked ice. About 2½ cups cordial.

Cranberry Cordial

After straining the cordial, the cranberries can be frozen with water to make a pretty ice ring for punch.

2 packages (12 ounces each) cranberries (6 cups), chopped

4 cups sugar

3 cups vodka

Mix all ingredients in 2-quart jar. Cover tightly and let stand at room temperature 2 weeks, stirring mixture or inverting jar every day. Strain; pour cordial into bottles and seal. Serve well chilled or over cracked ice. About 5 cups cordial.

Special Decorations

You can make an array of delightful Christmas decorations in your own kitchen! Try our delectable Gingerbread Village, or elegant Pastry Cornucopia. Children will love to help prepare the Holiday Cookie Train or Poppy the Penguin. Whatever you choose to create, enjoy placing your own unique stamp on holiday celebrations.

Santa Cookie Wreath

This wreath makes a fun centerpiece, especially when glowing red candles fill the center of the wreath.

> *1 package (14.5 ounces) gingerbread cake and cookie mix**
>
> *1/4 cup hot water*
>
> *2 tablespoons all-purpose flour*
>
> *2 tablespoons margarine or butter, melted*
>
> *6 ounces vanilla-flavored candy coating*
>
> *6 peanut-shaped peanut butter sandwich cookies*
>
> *Red sugar*
>
> *About 2 miniature marshmallows, cut into fourths*
>
> *12 miniature chocolate chips*
>
> *Red cinnamon candies*

Heat oven to 375°. Mix gingerbread mix (dry), hot water, flour and margarine in medium bowl with spoon until dough forms. Reserve one-fourth of the dough. Roll remaining three-fourths of the dough into 9½-inch circle, ¼ inch thick. Cut 4-inch circle out of center of 9½-inch circle to form wreath shape. (Add 4-inch circle of dough to reserved one-fourth dough.) Place 9½-inch wreath on ungreased cookie sheet. Bake about 15 minutes or until edges are firm. (Do not overbake.) Cool 1 minute before removing from cookie sheet.

Roll reserved one-fourth dough until ¼ inch thick. Cut with 2-inch holly leaf–shaped cookie cutter. Bake about 9 minutes or until edges are firm. (Do not overbake.) Cool 1 minute before removing from cookie sheet.

Heat candy coating over low heat until melted. To make six Santa cookies, dip one end of each peanut butter cookie into coating to resemble Santa's beard. Let dry on cookie sheet lined with waxed paper. When coating is dry, dip other end of cookie into coating (leaving middle of cookie plain to decorate for Santa's face). Immediately sprinkle red sugar over wet coating for Santa's hat, leaving ¼ inch of coating near cookie center plain to resemble trim of hat. Place a marshmallow fourth on the side of the hat to resemble a pom-pom.

Attach 2 chocolate chips to cookie, using coating, for the eyes. Attach 1 cinnamon candy to cookie, using coating, for the nose. Use remaining candies to decorate holly leaves. Attach Santas and holly leaves to wreath, using coating. 1 wreath (12 servings).

* Substitute half the dough recipe for the Gingerbread Village, page 277, for the mix, water, and flour in this recipe.

Gingerbread Village

It's fun to populate your village with ginger-bread people—trees or other accessory pieces. If using cutters less than 2 inches—check cookies a few minutes before minimum time.

1/2 cup packed brown sugar

1/4 cup shortening

3/4 cup dark molasses

1/3 cup cold water

3 1/2 cups all-purpose flour

1 teaspoon baking soda

1 teaspoon ground ginger

1/2 teaspoon salt

1/2 teaspoon ground allspice

1/2 teaspoon ground cloves

1/2 teaspoon ground cinnamon

Cardboard, about 28 × 10 inches

Aluminum foil or nonabsorbent gift wrap

Frosting (right)

Assorted candies, cookies, nuts and chewy fruit snack in 3-foot rolls

Heat oven to 350°. Grease square pan, 9 × 9 × 2 inches, and jelly roll pan, 15 1/2 × 10 1/2 × 1 inch. Mix brown sugar, shortening and molasses in large bowl. Stir in cold water. Stir in flour, baking soda, ginger, salt, allspice, cloves and cinnamon.

Press one-third of dough into square pan. Press remaining dough into jelly roll pan. Bake 1 pan at a time about 15 minutes or until no indentation remains when touched in center. Cool 5 minutes. Invert onto large cutting surface. Immediately cut jelly roll into fourths and then into buildings as shown in diagram. Cut square into braces as shown. Cool completely.

Gingerbread Village

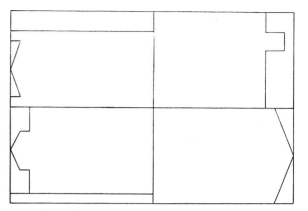

Cut jelly roll into fourths and then into buildings.

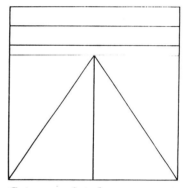

Cut square into braces.

Cover cardboard with aluminum foil. Decorate fronts of buildings as desired, using Frosting and assorted candies. Use Frosting to attach braces to backs of buildings, buildings to cardboard and sidewalk to cardboard. Complete by decorating as desired. One 4-building village.

FROSTING

2 cups powdered sugar

1/3 cup shortening

2 tablespoons light corn syrup

5 to 6 teaspoons milk

Few drops food color, if desired

Beat all ingredients until smooth and of spreading consistency.

Cinnamon "Apple" Rolls

It's amazing how real these "apples" look! They add a brightness to a brunch bread basket.

*1 package regular or quick-acting active
    dry yeast*

*1 cup warm unsweetened apple juice
    (105° to 115°)*

3¹/₂ to 4 cups all-purpose flour

¹/₃ cup sugar

1 teaspoon salt

*¹/₄ cup shortening or ¹/₄ cup (¹/₂ stick)
    margarine or butter, softened*

1 egg

³/₄ cup red sugar

1¹/₂ teaspoons ground cinnamon

40 raisins (about ¹/₄ cup)

¹/₃ cup margarine or butter, melted

5 sticks cinnamon

20 fresh mint leaves, frosted*

Dissolve yeast in apple juice in large bowl; let stand 1 minute. Mix in 2 cups of the flour, ¹/₃ cup sugar, the salt, shortening and egg; beat vigorously with wire whisk until well blended. Stir in enough remaining flour to make dough easy to handle. Turn dough onto lightly floured surface; gently roll in flour to coat. Knead about 3 minutes or until smooth and elastic. Place in greased bowl; turn greased side up. (Dough can be refrigerated at this point 3 to 4 days.) Cover and let rise in warm place 60 to 70 minutes or until almost double. (Dough is ready if indentation remains when touched.)

Grease 12 medium muffin cups, 2¹/₂ × 1¹/₄ inches. Mix red sugar and cinnamon. Punch down dough. Divide into 20 equal pieces; cover and refrigerate 8 pieces. Flatten each of the remaining 12 pieces into 2-inch round. Place 2 raisins in center for apple seeds. Bring sides of dough up over raisins; pinch edges to seal. Dip dough in melted margarine to coat completely; coat with sugar-cinnamon mixture. Place pinched sides down in muffin cups. Insert handle end of wooden spoon about ³/₄ inch in top of each, and rotate handle slightly to make indentation for stem. Cover and let rise in warm place 35 minutes.

Heat oven to 375°. Bake 14 to 16 minutes or until rolls just begin to brown under coating. Immediately remove from pan to wire rack. Repeat steps with refrigerated pieces. Cool rolls 30 minutes. Break each cinnamon stick into fourths. Insert in indentations in apples for stems. Place mint leaf next to stem. 20 rolls.

* To frost mint leaves, dip leaves into water and sprinkle with granulated sugar. Place on waxed paper until dry.

*Cinnamon "Apple" Rolls and Pastry Cornucopia
(page 280)*

Pastry Cornucopia

4 cups all-purpose flour

2 teaspoons salt

1½ cups shortening

2 eggs

⅓ cup cold water

aluminum foil

1 egg

2 teaspoons cold water

Milk

1 to 2 tablespoons sugar

Cinnamon "Apple" Rolls (page 278)

Mix flour and salt thoroughly in large bowl. Cut in shortening with pastry blender. Beat 2 eggs and ⅓ cup cold water; add to flour mixture. Mix with fork until flour is moistened (1 to 2 tablespoons water can be added if necessary). Gather pastry into a ball; divide into fourths. Keep pastry wrapped until ready to use.

To make mold for cornucopia, loosely crumple ten to twelve 12-inch squares of aluminum foil into balls. Stack balls in center of 20-inch sheet of foil; bring ends up and over balls, wrapping tightly. Press into shape of cornucopia, about 10 inches long and 5 inches high at opening. Spray mold generously with nonstick cooking spray.

To make base of cornucopia, roll one-fourth of pastry on floured cloth-covered surface into triangle shape about 1 inch larger than base of foil mold. Transfer to ungreased cookie sheet. Place foil mold on pastry base.

To make cornucopia, roll one-fourth of pastry into an oval, about 15 × 10 inches. Cut pastry oval lengthwise into 1-inch strips, using scalloped pastry cutter. Mix 1 egg and 2 teaspoons cold water. Brush 1 short strip with egg mixture; place strip, egg mixture side out, around tip of mold, forming a point. Starting with shorter

strips, brush one at a time with egg mixture and carefully drape over mold, egg mixture side out, overlapping preceding strip ¼ inch and allowing excess pastry to lie on pastry base.

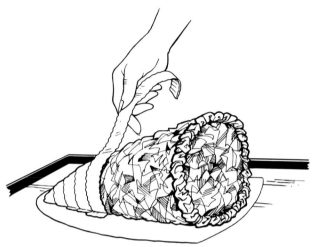

Roll and cut additional one-fourth of pastry into oval, 15 × 10 inches. Using longer strips, continue until mold is completely covered (do not trim any excess pastry at this point). Do not cover opening with pastry. Be sure all strips are pressed securely onto preceding strips and that there are no gaps.

Divide remaining one-fourth pastry into three parts. Divide one part in half; roll one half into rope, about 24 inches long and ¼ inch thick. Flatten rope with rolling pin to about ½-inch-wide strip. Cut strip lengthwise in half, using

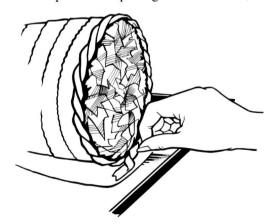

sharp knife. Twist halves together gently and loosely. Brush outer edge of opening of cornucopia with egg mixture. Place twist around opening; pinch ends to secure. Brush twist with egg mixture. Make additional twist with remaining half of one part dough. Brush egg mixture around base of cornucopia over the overhanging strips. Place twist around base, pinching ends to secure. Trim any excess pastry showing under twist; discard trimmings. Brush braid with egg mixture.

To decorate cornucopia, shape one part of remaining pastry into vines and grapes; roll and cut remaining one part pastry into leaves. Attach to cornucopia, using egg mixture. Brush entire cornucopia with egg mixture. Cornucopia can be covered and refrigerated at this point up to 24 hours, or wrapped carefully and tightly and frozen up to 1 month.

Heat oven to 425°. Bake 10 minutes or until set; remove from oven. Brush with milk; sprinkle generously with sugar. Reduce oven temperature to 350°. Bake 20 to 25 minutes longer or until golden brown. (If necessary, cover tip and front edge with aluminum foil to prevent excessive browning.) Cool on cookie sheet 5 minutes; loosen with large metal spatula and carefully slide onto wire rack. Cool at least 40 minutes. Carefully remove foil from cornucopia. Cover loosely and store in cool, dry place (do not refrigerate). Fill with Cinnamon ''Apple'' Rolls or as desired with cookies, rolls or candy for centerpiece. 12 servings.

Festive Cookie Place Cards

24 rectangular shortbread or butter-type cookies (about 3 × 2 inches)

1 cup Chocolate Frosting (page 26)

½ cup Creamy Decorator's Frosting (page 2)

Candies, animal-shaped cookies and candy decorations, if desired

24 sugar wafer cookies (about 2½ × 1 inch) or 12 square cookies

Frost tops of 3 × 2-inch cookies with Chocolate Frosting. Write names or initials on chocolate-frosted cookies, using Creamy Decorator's Frosting. Decorate with candies. Frost one long, narrow edge of each wafer cookie or cut square cookies diagonally to form triangle, and frost long edge. Press frosted edge on back of chocolate-frosted cookie, just below center, so frosted cookie will stand upright as place card, using wafer cookie as a brace. 24 cookie place cards.

Attach triangles to back of place cards with frosting.
Decorate as desired.

Holiday Cookie Train

Holiday Cookie Train

This train's destination is diversity! You'll love it as Santa's train, using traditional green and red frosting for its cheery messages. Make the train for any holiday—just change your color scheme and the messages to fit the holiday. Melted candy coating can be placed in a decorating tube with a No. 5 or No. 6 writing tip for printing your messages. Use the coating immediately, as it hardens quickly. If it should harden, just reheat until melted.

¹/₃ package (16-ounce size) graham crackers (one 5¹/₂ × 2¹/₂-inch packet)

6 ounces vanilla-flavored candy coating, melted

2 round cookies, such as chocolate or vanilla wafers

68 round hard peppermint candies (about 12 ounces)

Red, green and yellow paste food color

Assorted candies and decorations (colored sugar, peppermint candies, chocolate twigs or pretzels, licorice laces)

Reserve 1 graham cracker rectangle for train engine. Carefully break or cut remaining graham cracker rectangles in half into squares for train cars. Arrange crackers as shown in diagram or make shorter train as shown in photograph. Divide melted candy coating into 3 equal parts; reserve 3 parts.

To make engine, place 1 cracker square along top right of long side of reserved cracker rectangle. Break or cut another square in half into 2 small rectangles. Spread back of 1 small rectangle with some of remaining melted coating; attach to cracker square and reserved cracker rectangle to hold them together and resemble window (see diagram). Attach round cookie to bottom of reserved cracker rectangle under window for wheel, using melted coating. Let dry about 10 minutes. Turn over and attach window and cookie wheel to other side.

To make caboose, attach 1 small square of graham cracker to center of regular cracker square for window and 1 smaller rectangle on top of caboose, using melted coating (see diagram). Let dry about 10 minutes. Turn over and attach window to other side.

Tint 1 part of reserved melted coating with red food color. Or, if making small train, brush or spread over center of each square and immediately sprinkle with colored sugar. Print the letters for MERRY CHRISTMAS on one side of crackers, one letter on each cracker, with red coating; let dry. Turn each cracker over side to side except the engine and caboose.

Tint remaining part of reserved melted coating with green food color. Print HAPPY NEW YEAR! backward on other side of crackers, one letter on each cracker, with green coating; let dry. (See diagram below.) Decorate train as desired with remaining melted coating and assorted candies. For wheels, attach 2 peppermint candies to bottom of each cracker square, the caboose and the engine (attach candy to cookie wheel if desired), using melted coating; let dry. Turn crackers over. Attach peppermint candies to other sides; let dry. Stand up crackers on candy wheels so messages can be read from both sides.

Poppy the Penguin

If you like, you can divide the popcorn mixture in half and make two small penguins.

12 cups popped popcorn

¹/₄ cup (¹/₂ stick) margarine or butter

1 package (10¹/₂ ounces) miniature marshmallows

¹/₄ teaspoon peppermint extract

2 candy canes

6 ounces vanilla-flavored candy coating, melted

4 ounces chocolate-flavored candy coating, melted

Strawberry chewy fruit snack rolls or other strawberry fruit leather

Assorted candies

Discard unpopped kernels from popped popcorn. Heat margarine and marshmallows in Dutch oven over low heat, stirring constantly, until mixture is smooth; remove from heat. Stir in peppermint extract. Carefully fold in popcorn until evenly coated. Cool slightly.

To make penguin, shape popcorn mixture, using well-buttered hands, into a log about 9 inches long and 4 inches in diameter. Shape so one end is narrower, the middle is wider and the other end shaped to a point. Curve the pointed end to make a tail. Place candy canes on lightly buttered serving plate; set penguin upright on candy canes, turning the curved ends of the candy canes upright to resemble skis. Press popcorn mixture firmly onto candy canes.

Brush vanilla coating over penguin, coating completely. Refrigerate just until coating is set. Brush on chocolate coating for penguin's coat. Make stocking cap and scarf from fruit rolls; decorate with vanilla coating if desired. Complete penguin by decorating as desired with candies. One penguin.

TO MICROWAVE: Place marshmallows in 4-quart microwavable bowl or casserole. Cut margarine into 4 pieces; place on marshmallows. Microwave uncovered on high 1 minute; stir. Microwave uncovered 30 seconds to 1 minute 30 seconds longer or just until mixture can be stirred smooth. Stir in peppermint extract. Continue as directed.

Poppy the Penguin

Delicate Icing Snowflakes

4 cups powdered sugar

3 tablespoons meringue powder (available at craft and kitchen supply stores)

6 tablespoons warm water

Glitter, edible glitter or granulated sugar

Nylon thread, string or ribbon

Cover cookie sheet with waxed paper or cooking parchment paper. Enlarge patterns (see diagram) to 3 to 6 inches in size; slide patterns under waxed paper.

Beat powdered sugar, meringue powder and water in large bowl on low speed until sugar is moistened. Beat on high speed 5 to 7 minutes or until very glossy and stiff peaks form. Place icing in decorating bag with No. 10 tip. Or place icing in strong plastic bag; cut off a tiny tip from one corner of bag. Keep damp paper towel over tip when not in use to prevent frosting from hardening.

Trace patterns by piping on frosting, tracing longest lines of pattern first. Use a small paintbrush dipped into water to smooth any irregularities, working on each snowflake as it is piped. Lightly brush entire snowflake with water, and immediately sprinkle with glitter. Use only edible glitter or sugar if snowflakes are to be eaten. Let dry; remove from waxed paper. To hang as decorations, attach nylon thread to one end. About 1 dozen 5-inch snowflakes.

Delicate Icing Snowflakes

Mosaic Candleholders

Recycle smaller glass jars such as jam, jelly, pickle, spice and baby food jars into unique candlesticks. Smaller jars look attractive grouped together. You can also use glasses or shapely glass containers for your candlesticks. The amount of salt you need will vary, depending on the number and size of the jars you fill.

> *Table salt*
> *Red and green or assorted colors dry tempera paint**
> *Clear glass jars in assorted sizes*
> *Wooden skewer*
> *Candles in assorted sizes*
> *Ribbon, if desired*

Divide salt into 3 equal parts. Mix 2 tablespoons dry tempera paint per 26-ounce container of salt in heavy plastic bag or large jar. Seal bag or cover jar and shake to mix evenly. Using 2 or 3 colors of salt (including plain white), layer different colors in jar to within ¹/₂ inch of top. Push wooden skewer down inside edge of jar through layers of salt to create interesting design. Insert candle into salt, nestling it deep enough for support but being careful not to disturb salt design. Tie ribbon around neck of jar.

* Liquid food color also may be used. If salt gets too wet because of amount of liquid color added, let dry uncovered until moisture evaporates and salt runs smoothly.

Cinnamon-Apple Wreath

Rome or Rome beauty apples with their pretty red skin and white flesh are particularly nice in this wreath, though other types of apples are also attractive.

> *6 small apples, 2¹/₂ inches in diameter*
> *Lemon juice or lemon-lime carbonated beverage*
> *Wire racks*
> *Spray varnish, if desired*
> *6 sticks cinnamon, 10 inches long*
> *Straw wreath, 10 inches in diameter*
> *2 yards ³/₄-inch ribbon*
> *Hot-glue gun with glue sticks*
> *8 sticks cinnamon, 3¹/₂ inches long*
> *Silk leaves or bay leaves*

Heat oven to 200°. Cut apples lengthwise from stem end through core into ¹/₄-inch slices. Dip apples into lemon juice to prevent browning; place on wire racks. Carefully place wire racks on oven rack. Bake 3¹/₂ hours. Turn off oven. Let stand in oven six to eight hours or overnight.

Remove wire racks from oven and place on heat-proof surface. Let apples stand about 2 hours or until completely dry. Place dried apples on waxed paper. Coat each side with 2 light coats of spray varnish, following manufacturer's directions.

Tie 10-inch cinnamon sticks together. Attach to front of wreath with 6 inches of the ribbon. Glue dried apple slices and 3¹/₂-inch cinnamon sticks to front and side of wreath, using glue gun. Attach leaves to ribbon on 10-inch cinnamon sticks. Make a bow out of the remaining ribbon and attach to wreath. Attach wire hanger if desired. 1 wreath.

Cinnamon-Apple Wreath

Cookie Quilt Table Runner

Cookie Quilt Table Runner

Just like a quilter's fabric collection, your selection of colored dough adds individuality and charm to this "quilt." You'll find specific designs to follow, but feel free to create your own patterns as well. You can cut all the dough squares into triangles or rectangles to make whatever pattern you prefer.

> *1½ cups (3 sticks) margarine or butter, softened*
>
> *⅔ cup granulated sugar*
>
> *4 cups all-purpose flour*
>
> *Red or green paste food color**
>
> *Green or red sugar*
>
> *3 eight-inch squares cardboard*
>
> *Aluminum foil or nonabsorbent gift wrap*

Heat oven to 300°. Line square pan, 8 × 8 × 2 inches, with waxed paper, allowing ends of waxed paper to hang over opposite sides of pan for "handles." Beat margarine and sugar in large bowl on medium speed until fluffy. Beat in 2 cups of the flour on low speed until evenly mixed. Work in remaining flour with hands until dough holds together. If crumbly, work in 2 to 3 teaspoons margarine, softened.

Divide dough into 3 equal parts. Color 1 part dough by working in red or green food color with hands. (To prevent food color from staining hands, wear plastic gloves or insert hands into plastic bags.) Press dough evenly on waxed paper in pan, pressing edges firmly. Lift dough out of pan, using waxed paper handles, and invert onto ungreased cookie sheet. Remove waxed paper. If necessary, trim or reshape edges of dough so dough is square. Repeat with remaining 2 parts

Brush water over 1 square of plain dough; immediately sprinkle with green sugar. Leave remaining square of dough plain.

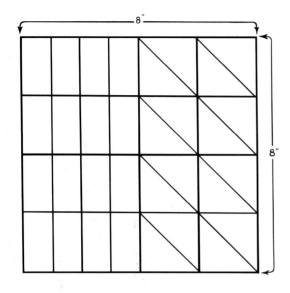

Cut each square as shown in diagram, using sharp knife. Half of each dough will be cut into rectangles and the other half into triangles. Accurate cutting is important for best appearance. Bake 20 to 25 minutes or just until edges begin to brown and dough is dry. Immediately recut the cut lines; let cookies stand on cookie sheet 5 minutes. Remove to wire rack; cool completely.

Cover cardboard squares with aluminum foil. Arrange cookies on cardboard as desired to make quilt squares (see designs right). If necessary, carefully trim ends of baked cookies, using sharp serrated knife in sawing motion. Three 8-inch quilt squares (32 cookies each).

* Egg Yolk Paint (page 2) can be substituted for the food color. Shape plain dough into 3 squares as directed. Brush Egg Yolk Paint evenly over 1 square of dough. Brush water over second square of dough; immediately sprinkle with green sugar. Leave remaining square of dough plain.

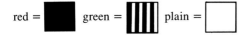

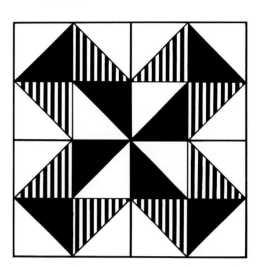

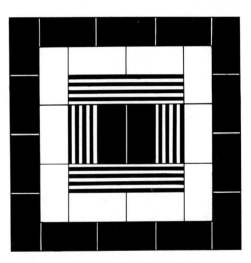

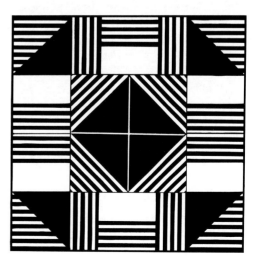

Spice-scented Ornaments

1 jar (about 1.9 ounces) ground cinnamon

1 tablespoon ground allspice or pumpkin pie spice

1/3 cup applesauce

2 tablespoons white glue or wood glue

Cookie cutters in assorted shapes

Straw or toothpick

Beads or buttons, if desired

Wire racks

Glue

Ribbon

Mix cinnamon and allspice in small bowl. Add applesauce and 2 tablespoons glue; mix until evenly moistened and dough forms. Knead dough on smooth surface until smooth and edges do not shred. Divide dough in half. Roll half of dough 1/4 inch thick between waxed paper. Cut into desired shapes with floured cookie cutters. Make a small hole in top of ornament with straw. To add texture and make designs on ornaments, use kitchen tools, such as sharp knife tip, can opener, skewers, cookie stamp, wire strainer or brush. If decorating with beads, make indentations in soft dough for gluing on beads when dough is dry. Repeat with remaining dough.

Place ornaments on wire racks. Let dry at room temperature 2 or 3 days, turning over once each day. Glue beads into indentations. To hang ornaments, insert ribbon through holes and tie. Do not eat ornaments. 12 to 15 ornaments (2 to 3 inches each).

Miniature Brownie Tree

You can achieve an astonishing number of looks by varying the element of this "tree." Experiment with different colors of frosting and ribbon, and try a variety of edible treats, such as doughnut holes, miniature muffins and cupcakes.

Chocolate Frosting (page 20) or White Frosting (page 64)

About 40 miniature brownies, muffins or cupcakes

8- or 10-inch foam cone

10-inch cardboard disk

Aluminum foil or nonabsorbent gift wrap

Glue

Toothpicks

8 yards 1/8-inch ribbon

Straight pins

Place Chocolate Frosting in decorating bag. Pipe holly leaves on center of each brownie with leaf tip; pipe on berries with round tip. Cover foam cone and cardboard disk with aluminum foil. Attack cone to disk, using glue, to use disk as base. Frost base with White Frosting for "snow" if desired; let dry.

Attach brownies to cone, using toothpicks, starting at base of cone. Cut ribbon into 8-inch lengths. Fold each piece of ribbon into thirds to make 2 loops, insert straight pin through center of ribbon and attach to cone between brownies. For a snowy effect, dust with powdered sugar if desired. 1 tree (about 40 brownies).

Frosted Candles

These candles are particularly fun when the decorations match your party theme, the decorated cookies being served, or the overall holiday decorations in your home. You can also continue the design onto the candleholder—frosting easily washes off glass and metal.

Vanilla Buttercream Frosting (page 68)

Food colors

Plain candles of any coordinating color, width and length

Glitter, tiny glitter shapes or candy sprinkles, if desired

Prepare Vanilla Buttercream Frosting; divide into desired number of parts for tinting with food color. Tint frosting with food color, mixing until well blended. Place frosting in decorating bag. Or place frosting in strong plastic bag; cut off a tip from one corner of bag. Lay candles on terry cloth towel or other nonskid surface that will not mar candle surface. Decorate candles by piping on frosting in shapes as directed below. Decorations toward bottoms of candles will remain intact longer. (Candles may be decorated while in candleholders, and decorations may be piped onto glass or metal holders. Be sure candle is securely seated in holder before decorating.)

HOLLY: Pipe on leaves using green frosting and leaf tip. When green frosting is set, pipe on berries using red frosting and small round tip.

SANTA: For Santa's face, spread frosting in a circle about one-third up from bottom of candle, using light pink, orange or beige frosting. Pipe on beard, mustache and a ring around the candle at the top of the face for the hat, using white frosting and small star tip. Add a red frosting dot for the nose and black frosting dots for the eyes.

SNOWFLAKES: Pipe on snowflakes of different sizes and shapes using white frosting and small round tip. Sprinkle with glitter.

TREE: Pipe on triangle shape using green frosting and small round tip; fill in triangle with frosting, moving back and forth. Pipe on tree trunk at base of triangle. Sprinkle with glitter, candy sprinkles or other tiny candies.

Shimmering Fruit Centerpiece

If you like, try a one-color metallic look, which will contrast dramatically with the greens. The color that you choose will be created by the paint, candles and ribbon that you select. You can also use plastic fruit if you wish.

Assorted fresh fruit, such as apples, oranges or grapes

Metallic spray paint (any color)

Glitter

Assorted ornamental greens (see Fruitful Bowl, page 294)

Base for centerpiece, such as covered cardboard, place mat or mirror)

3 short candleholders

3 yards metallic ribbon, 2 inches wide

3 yards metallic ribbon, 3/4 inch wide

Fine wire or hot-glue gun with glue sticks

3 ten-inch metallic taper candles (any color)

Spray fruit lightly with paint (natural fruit color can show through paint). Immediately sprinkle with glitter; let dry. Arrange greens on base. Nestle candleholders among greens. Arrange fruit on top of greens. Cut 2-inch ribbon crosswise in half. Make 2 bows, each with streamers in uneven lengths. Arrange on centerpiece as desired. Cut 3/4-inch ribbon into 18-inch lengths; loop into bows. Wire or glue bows to hold and nestle among fruits. Place candles securely in candleholders.

Fruitful Bowl

Soaking the wooden picks in bleach for five minutes before inserting into fruit will help the fruit last longer.

> *2 absorbent floral foam blocks (12 × 3 × 3 inches)*
>
> *Floral preservative, if desired*
>
> *Shallow waterproof container, 9 × 2 inches*
>
> *1/4-inch waterproof tape*
>
> *About 25 wooden picks or skewers (4 inches long)*
>
> *About 20 to 40 pieces assorted fresh fruit of similar size, such as apples, pears, lemons, oranges, limes, kumquats or grape clusters*
>
> *Assorted ornamental greens, such as princess pine sprigs, boxwood leaves, magnolia leaves, pittosporum leaves (available at florists' shops) or moss*
>
> *Fine wire*
>
> *Small flowers, such as statice or other dried flowers (statice dries nicely while retaining color), if desired*
>
> *Bows, colored flowers, small ornaments or garlands, if desired*

Soak foam blocks in water with floral preservative about 15 minutes, allowing foam to absorb water rather than pushing blocks to submerge them. Place foam blocks upright in container. Trim corners of foam at an angle to form tree shape, using knife, leaving top 3 to 4 inches in diameter. Fill container with extra foam pieces. Tape across foam and container several times with waterproof tape to anchor foam and container securely. (Stick end of tape on container, bring it up over foam and stick on opposite side of container.)

Insert wooden picks into fruit. Attach 3 pieces of fruit equally spaced around base of foam by inserting picks into foam. Attach remaining fruit to foam in a spiral pattern, starting above each of the 3 pieces of fruit and working from the base to the top. Wire clusters of greens onto wooden picks if necessary (some firm stems can be inserted directly into foam). Insert greens into open spaces. Attach flowers and bows. Store centerpiece uncovered in refrigerator up to 2 weeks (covering tightly causes fruit to spoil more quickly). Mist the leaves and add water to bowl occasionally.

Fruitful Bowl

Wheat and Herb Wall Decoration

Garlic-Herb Cluster

6 to 8 strands raffia, each about 40 inches long

Fine wire

2 or 3 large sprigs fresh rosemary or bay leaves

Hot-glue gun with glue sticks

1 bulb garlic

3 assorted small chilies of different colors (*jalapeño or serrano*)

Tie a bow in center of strands of raffia. (If one end of raffia is cut straight and other end is "natural," reverse half of the strands so all the cut ends won't be on one side.) Using a piece of wire about 12 inches long, wire the stem ends of the rosemary to the back of the bow, running the wire through the knot of the bow and twisting to secure. Glue the center of the bow, using glue gun. Glue the garlic bulb to the center of the bow, one loop and the rosemary. Using one end of same wire, wire the chilies to the cluster below the garlic. Twist other end of wire to make hanger for wall or to attach to package. Cluster will measure about 12 to 15 inches long. Chilies and rosemary will dry naturally.

Wheat and Herb Wall Decoration

25 to 30 stems of wheat, barley or oats

1 bunch of dried fresh herbs, such as tarragon or bay leaves

Hot-glue gun with glue sticks

3 yards 1½-inch ribbon

Berry or fruit spray

Silk leaves

Dried small white flowers

Glue the stems of grain and herbs together about 6 inches from the cut ends, using glue gun. Tie 6 inches of the ribbon tightly around the stems over the glued area. Make a Beautiful Bow (below) with the remaining ribbon and attach to stems, gluing to attach securely. Attach berry spray, leaves and dried flowers as desired, using glue.

BEAUTIFUL BOW

Leave a "tail" about 12 inches long (or longer). Hold ribbon at the 12-inch point and loop it back and forth with 4 loops on each side. Size of loops may be uneven but should be in proportion to the ribbon width, about 4 inches each. Leave a "tail" on the other end about 9 inches long.

Secure ribbon in center using twist-tie, ribbon, fine wire or string. (If using ribbon, fold lengthwise to make narrow.) Pull "tails" of ribbon down and work the loops upward, twisting and fluffing so the twist-tie doesn't show. Cut the ends of the tails at an angle or in a V shape.

Loop the ribbon back and forth with four loops on each side.

Starry Ice Beverage Cooler

Be sure to place the cooler on a dish with sides, so it won't leak as the ice melts. A quiche dish lined with greens would be a lovely choice.

½-gallon paperboard milk carton

1-liter clear plastic soft drink bottle

Ice cubes

Lemon peel, cut into star shapes

Cranberries

Fresh herb sprigs, such as thyme or rosemary

Water

Open milk carton completely at top; wash inside. Wash plastic bottle inside and out; remove any labels. Place plastic bottle in center of milk carton. Fill milk carton with ice cubes.

Arrange lemon peel, cranberries and herbs among ice cubes toward sides of milk carton. Tape top of bottle to milk carton to keep it from floating. Fill milk carton with water (do not fill bottle).

Freeze about 24 hours or until firm. Peel off milk carton. To use, place beverage cooler in deep tray. Fill bottle with beverage, using a funnel.

Globe Luminaria

The only limit to the number of these welcoming lights that you can make is your freezer space! If you'd like colored luminaria, add a few drops of food color to the water.

> *7-inch balloons*
> *Plastic containers, 6 or 7 inches in diameter*
> *Votive candles*

Fill each balloon with water until 6 inches in diameter; tie end. Place filled balloon in plastic container of similar size for support. Freeze at least 12 hours or until ice is about ½ inch thick around inside of balloon. (Balloon can be left outside for freezing if climate allows.) Remove balloon from container. Remove balloon from around ice ball. Chisel opening in top of ice ball; drain water. Place outside, insert candle and light candle.

Rock Candy Crystal Balls

These glowing crystal balls take on the color of the balloon that forms them. If you'd like an icier, crystal look, carefully pull out and remove the balloon when cutting away the neck.

> *4-inch balloons in desired colors*
> *Rock candy (about 8 ounces for each 4-inch ball)*
> *Hot-glue gun with glue sticks (five or six ¼ × 4-inch sticks; two or three ½ × 4-inch sticks)*
> *Assorted ornamental greens (see Fruitful Bowl, page 288)*
> *Base for centerpiece*
> *Miniature Christmas tree lights*
> *Ribbon or tinsel garlands, if desired*

Blow up each balloon until 2½ inches in diameter; tie end. Break or crush rock candy into ½-inch pieces. Glue a few candy pieces to each other, then glue the cluster to balloon. Continue gluing, working all around balloon, and gluing clusters to each other. Do not touch hot metal tip of glue gun to balloon. Leave ½- to 1-inch opening around the neck of the balloon. If keeping balloon inside after crystal ball is finished, glue top edge of candy firmly to balloon around opening. Let stand 30 minutes.

Cut away the neck of the balloon. If removing balloon, grasp balloon and gently pull away from inside of crystal ball (using tweezers will be helpful). Arrange assorted greens on base. Insert a Christmas tree light into the center of each crystal ball opening; arrange remaining lights among the greens. Decorate with ribbon.

Rock Candy Crystal Balls; Macadamia-Pineapple Tart

METRIC CONVERSION GUIDE

U.S. UNITS	CANADIAN METRIC	AUSTRALIAN METRIC
Volume		
1/4 teaspoon	1 mL	1 ml
1/2 teaspoon	2 mL	2 ml
1 teaspoon	5 mL	5 ml
1 tablespoon	15 mL	20 ml
1/4 cup	50 mL	60 ml
1/3 cup	75 mL	80 ml
1/2 cup	125 mL	125 ml
2/3 cup	150 mL	170 ml
3/4 cup	175 mL	190 ml
1 cup	250 mL	250 ml
1 quart	1 liter	1 liter
1 1/2 quarts	1.5 liter	1.5 liter
2 quarts	2 liters	2 liters
2 1/2 quarts	2.5 liters	2.5 liters
3 quarts	3 liters	3 liters
4 quarts	4 liters	4 liters
Weight		
1 ounce	30 grams	30 grams
2 ounces	55 grams	60 grams
3 ounces	85 grams	90 grams
4 ounces (1/4 pound)	115 grams	125 grams
8 ounces (1/2 pound)	225 grams	225 grams
16 ounces (1 pound)	455 grams	500 grams
1 pound	455 grams	1/2 kilogram

Measurements		**Temperatures**	
Inches	Centimeters	Fahrenheit	Celsius
1	2.5	32°	0°
2	5.0	212°	100°
3	7.5	250°	120°
4	10.0	275°	140°
5	12.5	300°	150°
6	15.0	325°	160°
7	17.5	350°	180°
8	20.5	375°	190°
9	23.0	400°	200°
10	25.5	425°	220°
11	28.0	450°	230°
12	30.5	475°	240°
13	33.0	500°	260°
14	35.5		
15	38.0		

NOTE
The recipes in this cookbook have not been developed or tested using metric measures. When converting recipes to metric, some variations in quality may be noted.

Index

Credits

GENERAL MILLS, INC.

Betty Crocker Food and Publications Center
    Director: Marcia Copeland
    Editor: Jean E. Kozar
    Recipe Development: Mary H. Johnson
    Food Stylists: Cindy Lund, Robin Krause, Lynn Lohmann
Photographic Services
    Photographer: Nanci Doonan Dixon

    Line Drawings by Tina Seemann